SOCIAL MOVEMENTS
AND NEW TECHNOLOGY

SOCIAL MOVEMENTS
AND NEW TECHNOLOGY

VICTORIA CARTY

Chapman University

**WESTVIEW
PRESS**

A Member of the Perseus Books Group

Westview Press was founded in 1975 in Boulder, Colorado, by notable publisher and intellectual Fred Praeger. Westview Press continues to publish scholarly titles and high-quality undergraduate- and graduate-level textbooks in core social science disciplines. With books developed, written, and edited with the needs of serious nonfiction readers, professors, and students in mind, Westview Press honors its long history of publishing books that matter.

Copyright © 2015 by Westview Press
Published by Westview Press,
A Member of the Perseus Books Group
2465 Central Avenue
Boulder, CO 80301
www.westviewpress.com

Westview Press books are available at special discounts for bulk purchases in the United States by corporations, institutions, and other organizations. For more information, please contact the Special Markets Department at the Perseus Books Group, 2300 Chestnut Street, Suite 200, Philadelphia, PA 19103, or call (800) 810-4145, ext. 5000, or e-mail special.markets@perseusbooks.com.

Designed by Jeff Williams

A CIP catalog record for this book is available from the Library of Congress.

LCCN: 2014950631
ISBN: 978-0-8133-4586-4 (paperback)
ISBN: 978-0-8133-4587-1 (e-book)

10 9 8 7 6 5 4 3 2 1

To those who struggle for social justice,
and especially our youth, God speed to you.

CONTENTS

Electronic technological innovations and applications have had a revolutionary impact on communication, the way social relationships are established and maintained, and how social movements emerge and develop. In *Social Movements and New Technology*, Victoria Carty provides a brilliant introduction to these topics, specifically on how new technologies are forcing modifications of social movement theories and how they have played crucial roles in recent major social movements.

The impact that individual access to the Internet and social media has had on social movements can be described in reference to Neil Smelser's classic framework for the development of collective behavior. First, movement participants' ability to bypass traditional media (which is often controlled by an anti-movement state or corporations) and overcome lack of physical proximity significantly expands the conduciveness of an environment for social movement development. Second, the individual's ability to video record experiences, conditions, and events and instantly communicate them to others in the digitally expanded public sphere increases the capacity to spread or intensify discontent with an existing regime or policy. Third, new electronic media enhances the ability to spread a shared belief regarding the cause of a problem, which Smelser noted is necessary to establish effective collective action to deal with that problem. The shared belief is an application of the sociological imagination that maintains that the problem people experience or are concerned about is due to social factors that are capable of being changed through collective action. Fourth, personal access to the Internet permits individuals to convey images of emotionally charged episodes of repression and injustice—what Smelser termed precipitating incidents—to a much wider population in a more convincing way than ever before possible. Being able to electronically witness these events further inflames people's discontent and reinforces the shared belief. These transmitted recordings act as sparks to ignite the powder keg of built-up frustration, motivating people to take action. Fifth, especially in the early phase of a social movement's development, the new personalized digital media lessens the need for clearly identifiable, charismatic, intellectual, and managerial social movement leaders. In the past, many of the functions in Smelser's analysis—such as initiating a movement and developing and communicating a shared belief—were carried out top down by social movement leadership. Now these functions are carried out horizontally among movement activists with little or no fixed leadership. And sixth, smart phones and other forms of digital communication allow movement participants to rapidly adjust to social control agencies' actions and develop new plans and tactics in response.

In *Social Movements and New Technology*, the author describes the effects of digital media on the most important recent social movements, including the MoveOn.org and Tea Party movements, the Arab Spring protests and revolutions, the Occupy Movement and its precursors, and the Occupy Student Debt and DREAMers movements. She explains how participants in these movements used the Internet and social media to get their messages out despite often unsympathetic traditional media and rapidly adjusted their tactics in response to the measures taken by hostile governments to stifle or repress them. Further, she describes how activists use the Internet to influence not only domestic opinion but also world opinion, with the goal of getting international support for their movements or at least making it more difficult for other governments to aid their adversaries.

The author notes that effective modern social movements combine the capabilities provided by digital media, the creation of "weak" Internet ties, and shared virtual identity with on-the-ground action that builds "strong" ties among mobilized participants and the resiliency to resist repression. Effective collective action may require the assistance or the formation of real world social movement organizations and leadership. But digital media provides a new means to constantly and effectively reinvigorate and re-democratize social movement organizations that may have become too authoritarian, bound by inertia, or collaborative with the status quo.

Digital media, the author notes, also provides whistle-blowers like Edward Snowden the ability to go global with their messages and revelations, undermining government and traditional media censorship and even stimulating movements in other nations.

The author does not ignore the fact that digital technology can also be used by established power holders to frustrate and disrupt social movements through tactics like blocking Internet or cell phone access, spreading false information, or setting up their own counter-movement websites. Governments also have the capability to use high-powered computers to spy on millions of individuals, recording and analyzing their telephone conversations, e-mails, text messages, and writings, as well as book, magazine, journal, and website preferences. Such information could be used to target and intimidate large numbers of actual or potential activists. The author also provides an excellent description of how the Islamic State in Iraq and Syria (ISIS) has demonstrated a sophisticated capacity to use digital media in attempts to influence public opinion and recruit new ISIS soldiers.

Throughout the book, the author integrates social movement theories and concepts, showing how these are useful in understanding the role of modern communication technology in social movements, while also noting how theoretical perspectives should be modified to reflect the impacts of digital devices and instantaneous global communication.

Social Movements and New Technology provides a comprehensive overview of how communication technology has been—and is being— used in recent and emerging movements and of the ways in which social movement development and organization are affected. It is a valuable resource for social movement scholars and courses on social movements and political sociology, and is an inspirational and instructive reading for contemporary and future movement activists.

James DeFronzo

My academic interest in social change and activism was first sparked while I was an undergraduate student taking a research methods class. I was having a hard time figuring out how to relate what we were learning to the real world, until one day the professor said something in the midst of her lecture that had a profound impact on me: "If you want to change the world, you have to understand how it works."

My interest at the time was to dedicate myself to service, perhaps even go abroad and do missionary work. I was also involved in some campus and community groups that were working on social issues, mainly because some of my friends were doing it and it seemed like a cool thing to do. Yet, even as a sociology major, I never thought about the structural sources of the social problems I was interested in. My professor's simple statement inspired me to think about what education is about, what our role is as citizens, and how a democracy should work.

My first involvement in major protest activity was against US involvement in the civil wars brewing throughout Central America in the 1980s and early 1990s. I then joined activists who organized against the impending Gulf War invasion of Iraq by the United States. Through nonviolent acts of civil disobedience, we blocked major freeway entrances to the university and held marches, demonstrations, "die-ins," and vigils. Though my commitment to these struggles was strong and I was very enthusiastic about spending time and energy on various causes, my professor's words stayed with me. I realized my knowledge of the historical and current US involvement in Central America was pretty shallow, and even more so when it came to matters in the Middle East. I also had no idea how the protests and meetings I began to attend were organized, who was doing the leg work, who was doing the recruiting, how they attained resources, why other people were spending time and energy to partici- pate in these causes—especially when it seemed our efforts were either ignored or, when noticed by the media, portrayed in a negative light. I would sometimes catch myself thinking, even as dedicated as I came to be, "Why am I even bothering with this? Why are all of these other busy people dedicating their time if nothing changes in the end?"

Over time, what I have learned as an activist-scholar reinforces my own professor's statement: if you want to effect social change, you have to be informed. This is what I hope to help the student become with this book. For each of the book's case studies, I outline the origins of these mobilizations, their fundamental grievances, and their context—in other words, the "why" of the social movement activity and protest. I also hope to explain what I struggled to understand as a young activist: the "how" of organized contentious politics. People always have grievances, but I would like us to contemplate how we can collectively make demands that can influence public opinion and create change. Last, and most important for the interests of this book, I hope to show how digital technologies have dramatically changed the way activists operate. Yes, activists still rely on civil disobedience and other traditional methods of protest politics, but their organizational structure and outreach are much different now.

You, as students, are the vanguards in the use of new digital technol- ogies, and it is the youth around the world who are at the forefront of both on-the-street protests and virtual forms of organizing. I hope this book helps students taking sociology, political science, media studies, or communication classes at the undergraduate or graduate level under- stand some aspects of the world around you—specifically, how and why protest activity has spiked recently and how new technology allows for new dynamics. This text, through the use of case studies from a global perspective, focuses on what is changing and what is staying the same in the struggle for social justice.

ACKNOWLEDGMENTS

My profound thanks go to the editors and staff at Perseus Book Group, including Amber Morris, Victoria Henson, Carrie Watterson, and especially Catherine Craddock, for her exceptional guidance, assistance, and availability. I am also incredibly grateful to the anonymous reviewers for their invaluable suggestions for revisions and insights. Those in my community and my colleagues at Chapman University inspire me; you are angels and I thank you for your wisdom and example.

The Digital Impact
on Social Movements

Digital natives, millennials, Gen Y, Gen 2.0: however you label them, the generation born roughly between 1980 and 2000 has been immersed in revolutionary digital technologies since birth. For those of you who fit into this age cohort, life was experienced very differently in the 1990s, and these technological novelties have had vast repercussions at the individual and societal level. The way people communicate has fundamentally changed with the advent of new information communication technologies (**ICTs**), from e-mail to Snapchat. Not only can messages, photos, and videos be sent instantly, they have the potential to be spread far and wide through social networks—and the ramifications have been felt in all areas of society.

On a personal level, new technology has resulted in a radical shift in the way individuals view themselves and their social ties. Students of previous generations, for example, interacted in a much more limited though intimate way. Friendships and ways of communicating consisted of conversations in the cafeteria at lunch, bonding through sports or other extracurricular activities, sitting next to someone in class and passing secret notes (on paper!), or having neighborhood playmates. The main vehicle of communication was physically going to friends' houses to see whether they were free to play or using the telephone—the one or two stationary phones inside the house that the whole family shared. In sum,

1

communication was initiated, shared, and sustained among people who knew each other personally, and it took effort on the part of the receiver and sender of information. This has changed in many ways as communication now, for many people, takes place to a great extent through digital venues, especially among youth. For example, in 2009 the average US teenager, on Twitter alone, was receiving or sending more than 3,000 messages a month (Parr 2010). In 2010 researchers at the University of Maryland conducted a study of two hundred students who were asked to abstain from using electronic media for twenty-four hours. Though everything else about their college experience was the same—they were surrounded by other students and their identity was intact—not being connected *virtually* to others horrified the participants. One student stated that he had never felt so "alone and secluded from my life." Another reported, "Although I go to a school with thousands of students, the fact that I was not able to communicate with anyone via technology was almost unbearable" (Ottalini 2010).

Many long-standing, profitable, and dominant businesses are now obsolete as digitized industries have replaced analog ones: Polaroid declared bankruptcy with the introduction of digital cameras in 2001, iTunes replaced Tower Records as the largest music retailer in United States, and the chain bookstore Borders, which at one point had more than one thousand stores throughout the United States, closed after the rise of e-reading technology such as Amazon's Kindle (Kansaku-Sarmiento 2011). These are just three examples, but the business world is littered with cases like these. Can anybody really be surprised that "Cyber Monday," the Monday after Thanksgiving, has overtaken Black Friday as the biggest sales day of the year (Carr 2011)?

Even religion has not escaped the technological revolution: the Catholic Church, one of the institutions that has traditionally been most resistant to change, has finally succumbed to the digital age. The electronic missal enables users to stream Mass online and has made the paper missalette (which contains prayers and Scripture readings) antiquated (Catholic PR Wire 2011). Instead of prayer cards, there is now a touch-screen "Saint a Day." The Vatican Observatory Foundation recently launched the Vatican-approved iPhone app "Daily Sermonettes with Father Mike Manning," and users can pray the rosary in their own "sacred space" through the "Rosary Miracle Prayer" app. Pope Benedict XVI used Twitter for

the first time in June of 2011, announcing the start of a news information portal that aggregates information from the Vatican's various print,
broadcast, and online media (Donadio 2012). The Vatican also now has
a YouTube channel and a Twitter feed (@pontifex) that has nearly 10
million followers in more than six languages. Pope Francis, the current
pope, has embraced new media as well. In a papal statement in 2014 he
praised the peer-to-peer sharing quality of new ICTs: "A culture of encounter demands that we be ready not only to give, but also to receive. . . .
The Internet, in particular, offers immense possibilities for encounter and
solidarity. . . . This is a gift from God" (Fung 2014).

Though the Vatican has not yet released an official response, in September of 2014 Pope Francis engaged with schoolchildren from Detroit
via Facebook when they pleaded with him, through a social media campaign, to visit Detroit during his upcoming tour of the United States slated
for 2015. They set up a Facebook page called "Let's Bring Pope Francis to
Detroit in 2015," which includes personalized letters to the pope and photos of students attending Catholic schools (Montemurri 2014a). At the all-
boys Loyola High School (a school that works in the tradition of the Jesuit
Order with an emphasis on service), students created a YouTube video
asking the pope to visit the area. One student is videotaped making a plea
aligned with social justice stating, "You are exactly what we stand for—
men for others" (Montemurri 2014b). Though students and the mayor of
Detroit (who has vocally supported the students' campaign) are awaiting
an official response from the Vatican, the fact that the students assumed
using ICTs was the best method to get the pope's attention reveals their
awareness that this is one of the key ways the pope connects to and inter-
acts with people.

NEW INFORMATION COMMUNICATION TECHNOLOGIES AND PROTEST POLITICS

Unsurprisingly, the rise of digital technology and social media also deeply
affects contentious politics as well as the organization of and participation
in social movements. Over the past several years, there has been an explosion of protest activity among young people around the globe as they
embrace a new vision of the future and demand radical changes in the

US HOUSEHOLD COMPUTER AND INTERNET USE, 1984–2011

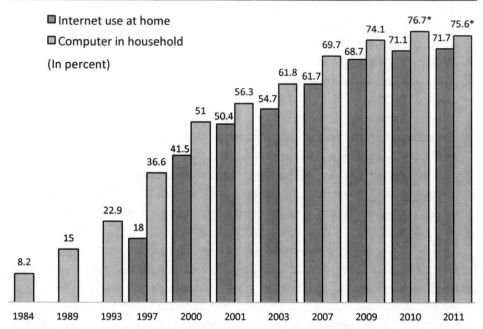

*Smaller changes between 2010 and 2011 were due partly to question wording and other instrument changes.

The dramatic and steady increase in computer and internet use over the last three decades has had vast repercussions at the individual and societal level.

Source: US Census Bureau, Current Population Survey, selected years.

existing economic and political systems. *Time* magazine, in fact, named the protester as its Person of the Year in 2011. We can only speculate as to the reasons for this upsurge in social movement activity, but scholar and cultural critic Henry Giroux emphasizes the influence of the communication field on the political environment:

> Alternative newspapers, progressive media, and a profound sense of the political constitute elements of a vibrant, critical formative culture within a wide range of public spheres that have helped nurture and sustain the possibility to think critically, engage in political dissent, organize collectively, and inhabit public spaces in which alternative and critical theories can be developed." (2012, 39)

In essence, the media ecology can either accelerate—or, conversely, impede—serious political discussion and debate, and ultimately facilitate displays of collective behavior. With new digital technology at their disposal, social movement actors have access to innovative media outlets that help nurture a new political terrain within which they can discuss grievances, disseminate information, and collectively make demands.

There are, of course, many factors to consider when examining recent forms of collective behavior—namely, the austere economic conditions around the globe, political disenfranchisement, and a lack of accountability among political elites. The focus of this book, however, is the use of digital technology in different social movements, communities, and campaigns—from the Indignados in Europe and Mexico, to women seeking social justice, to the Arab Spring in the Middle East and North Africa, to Occupy Wall Street and the DREAMers' quest for immigration reform, to the savvy digital organizing by political groups and communities in the United States. People are challenging political authorities, entrenched dictators, and political and economic systems once taken for granted. On a more micro and individual level, and particularly as it pertains to youth, individuals aided by digital technology are mobilizing to confront skyrocketing debt and current policies regarding immigration through contentious politics.

Indeed, the common thread that runs through all of these case studies in this book is the seminal use of ICTs (this includes the Internet, the World Wide Web, cell phones, texting, Instagram, social media, and social networks) to advance their respective causes. With the recent explosion of e-movements, e-protests, and e-activism, these organizational tools have become an essential component of social movement actors' repertoire. The emergence of social media networking sites is changing the nature of political struggle and social movement activism in the United States and around the world.

This book will explore how new Web 2.0 technologies enable, facilitate, and encourage social movement activity by allowing individual actors to share grievances, accelerate social movement activity, decentralize mobilization efforts, facilitate recruitment efforts through virtual forms of collective identity, and hold authorities accountable for their responses to protest activity with mobile devices.

It is important to remember while reading the case studies in this book that technology is a tool, and therefore it is neutral. It can be used for both progressive and reactionary social movements, and authorities can use ICTs against activists. For example, a government can track Internet use and e-mails and monitor cell phone activity to locate organizers of, and participants in, dissident politics. Corporations can block or limit service, and authorities can discredit protesters by engaging in disinformation or propaganda campaigns, taking advantage of the anonymity that digital media affords. Facebook can be used to build a community around a progressive cause, and it can just as easily be used to bully a classmate. Mobile video recording devices can keep police abuse in check, but they can also be used by terrorist groups to publicize their acts and recruit new members. The most recent example of this is the Islamic State of Iraq and Syria (ISIS), which will be discussed in Chapter 4. This book does not make the claim that digital technologies are all inherently good or progressive nor that they are the only resource to consider when trying to understand social movement activity. But the important role ICTs have played in recent social movement activity is undeniable, and the specific ways their use can translate into motivation, interest, and participation among social movement actors are worth examining.

As we will see throughout the text, social movement theory serves as a toolkit to unpack the conceptual ways in which ICTs influence the political landscape. This book analyzes the many ways that ICTs are changing the structure and tactics of social movements, and the case studies serve as illustrative (rather than conclusive) examples that can assist in updating social movement theories. What we will see is that by applying various theoretical frameworks in a comprehensive and holistic way and by updating them to include theories of new media, we can better make sense of contemporary forms of contentious politics. These are exciting times, both for those fighting for social change and those studying social movements!

WHAT ARE SOCIAL MOVEMENTS?

It is important to take a moment to clarify exactly what social movements are and how they are different from other forms of collective behavior. A social movement is neither a riot nor electoral politics. Rather, it is a sustained collective articulation of resistance to elite opponents by a plurality of actors with a common purpose (Tarrow 1998). According to Charles Tilly (2004), the three main elements of social movements are campaigns (long-term, organized public efforts that make collective claims on target authorities), repertoires (tactics that a group has at its disposal in a certain sociopolitical environment), and **WUNC** (worthiness, unity, numbers, and commitment). WUNC is an intentional effort by participants in a social movement to publicly present themselves and their supporters as worthy of support from other citizens, which Tilly (2004, 23) encapsulates this way: "Social movements' displays of worthiness may include sober demeanor and the presence of clergy and mothers with children; unity is signaled by matching banners, singing and chanting; numbers are broadcast via signatures on petitions and filling streets; and commitment is advertised by braving bad weather, ostentatious sacrifice, and/or visible participation by the old and handicapped. WUNC matters because it conveys crucial political messages to a social movement's targets and the relevant public."

Key to any social movement are mobilizing strategies—"those collective vehicles, informal as well as formal, through which people mobilize and engage in collective action" (McAdam, McCarthy, and Zald 1996, 3). More specifically, Tilly (2006) introduced the concept of a "**repertoire of contention**," which refers to the tactical forms from which social movement actors can choose at any given moment. Repertoires vary over time and across cultures, but some of the most widely used have included armed struggle, nonviolent civil disobedience, self-immolation, protests, rallies, demonstrations, teach-ins, global witnessing, and public vigils.

With the advent of the digital revolution, which began in 2004, social movement scholars and organizers have turned their attention to the new range of nuanced tools that activists have in their arsenal. As history reveals, every social movement is in part shaped by the technology available at the time and its influences on the tactics that social movement actors will pursue. Activists have always utilized the latest communication device to recruit, distribute information, and mobilize support, whether it be the pen, printing press, telegraph, radio, television, Internet, or high-speed digital technologies. Manuel Castells (2007, 239) summarizes the critical role of media in protest politics in the following way: "power relations . . . as well as the processes challenging institutionalized power relations are increasingly shaped and decided in the communication field."

TECHNOLOGY AS A SPARK FOR SOCIAL CHANGE

Technology has always played a critical role in shaping social movement pursuits, as far back as the printing press. In the 1700s, the proliferation of local newspapers, pamphlets, and independent printing presses proved critical to the American Revolution. US revolutionary Thomas Paine kindled the political environment with his widely read pamphlet *Common Sense* (advocating US independence from Britain). One of the key founding fathers of the United States, John Adams, stated, "Without the pen of the author of *Common Sense*, the sword of Washington would have been raised in vain" (Bernstein and Rice 1987). As Kaye (2011, 229) points out, the nation was founded as a nation by grassroots independent journalists: "Tom Paine was an unemployed or under-employed journalist, who wrote a pamphlet, *Common Sense*, and he said on the back of it, 'I think these are really important ideas but I can't go everywhere in America. If you like this pamphlet, the copyright is off. Copy it, print it up, and give it out to the next person.'" This radical movement toward free sharing of information is very common today with peer-to-peer sharing of digital information (a mechanism that will be discussed and analyzed throughout the ensuing chapters), yet we can see that it began hundreds of years ago via the printing press, the most innovative technology at the time.

More than a century and a half later, moving images became essential to political struggle. In 1930, as a part of his strategy to free India from British rule, Mohandas Gandhi invited reporters and newsreel teams to capture the footage of the 248-mile salt march he organized in 1930. Images of British soldiers beating peaceful marchers with clubs exposed to the world the repression of the Raj (Dalton 2012), swaying public opinion greatly in India's favor, which played a major role in India's independence. During the civil rights movement in the United States led by Reverend Martin Luther King, TV images of police violence, of fire hoses and police dogs set loose on activists engaged in civil disobedience across the South, even targeting children, with the most dramatic episodes occurring in Birmingham, Alabama, also garnered support for the demonstrators and energized the social movement.

Later, US public opinion regarding the Vietnam War changed drastically when footage of the carnage was brought into peoples' living rooms on the evening news, motivating the peace movement (Swerdlow 1992).

Similarly, the 1989 images of the peaceful students in Tiananmen Square overrun by tanks as they campaigned for democracy and freedom of speech significantly affected viewers' sentiments toward the Chinese government and military (James 2009).

New media platforms are changing the social movement terrain even more radically than previous technologies. Though communication and information systems have historically been fundamental sources of power and counterpower, and of domination and social change, this effect has been exacerbated by the explosion of digital technologies. As Marshall McLuhan declared decades ago with the introduction of television in the 1960s, "The medium is the message." The form of technology through which information is disseminated and received molds cultures; it introduces a new mind-set that alters the landscape of societies, as well as relationships and forms of interaction among individuals in those societies (McLuhan 1964). What is significant about new social media platforms and social networking sites is that, unlike television, they embody a radically individualistic and freelance format that encourages forms of self-expression.

WE ARE THE MESSAGE CREATORS

New media technologies allow users to become not merely receivers of the message but also the *creators* and *distributors* of messages. Indeed, the latest generation has an unprecedented degree of control over the production, distribution, and consumption of information and therefore over their cultural environment, which also has powerful implications for serious social and political change. The distribution of information is now immediate, worldwide, often free, and in the hands of ordinary citizens. New Internet media platforms and social networking sites, web publishing tools, and the proliferation of new mobile devices—there are currently more cellphones in the United States than there are humans (Kang 2011)—are all altering the political atmosphere.

In this new communication and media setting, almost anyone and anything can be recorded and disseminated without the permission of the elites (be they the professional mainstream press, corporate gatekeepers, the police, the military, or campaign managers). Through an emerging

New media technologies allow users to become not merely receivers of the message but also the creators and distributors of messages.

indigenous free press reliant on **"mojos"** (mobile journalists), citizens can broadcast unedited live footage from smart phones, flip cameras, and laptops that have digital audio- and video-recording capabilities. In terms of social movement activity, the ubiquity of camera-ready smart phones allows for authentic transparency, as live-streamers serve as journalist mediators between authorities and protesters. Individuals can also send video shots on mobile phones to international news services, which are then beamed via satellite all over the world, thus connecting mobile amateur journalists to the mainstream press. The images can also obviously be posted onto YouTube, Facebook, and other social networking sites where, if they go viral, can instantaneously capture national attention.

In fact, the very concept of journalism itself is being reconfigured. A perfect example of this happened during the 2011 re-election bid of former senator George Allen (R-VA) against Democratic nominee Jim Webb. As part of its strategy, the Webb campaign had a University of Virginia student follow Allen with a handheld video camera. At one of his rallies Allen introduced the tracker, S. R. Sidarth (who is of Indian American descent) to the crowd as Macaca (considered a racial slur). During the speech Allen interjected, "This fellow over here with the yellow shirt, Macaca, or whatever his name is. He's with my opponent. He's following us around everywhere. . . . Let's give a welcome to Macaca, here. Welcome to America and the real world of Virginia" (Sidarth is actually a US citizen, born in Virginia). The video of the "Macaca moment" was played more than 400,000 times on YouTube, and bloggers, especially at the *Daily Kos*, amplified the story (Shear 2011). The incident later appeared in an article in the *Washington Post*, illustrating how stories that originate in alternative media often filter into the mainstream media, thereby increasing the visibility and viewership of events. The taping and circulation of this incident helped to foil Senator Allen's re-election bid, with Webb winning by a narrow margin.

Mojos, as bearers of breaking news, oftentimes beat the mainstream press to highly relevant stories that can have a political impact. For example, amid the hunt for the mastermind behind the 9/11 attacks in the United States, a Twitter user in Pakistan, @ReallyVirtual, tweeted live as Osama bin Laden was being killed: "helicopter hovering above Abbottabad at 1AM (is a rare event)." The news of the assassination circulated on social media immediately and widely. This information was obtainable an hour before President Barack Obama's address from the White House announcing the killing on broadcast television (Patesky 2011). The proliferation of text messages and peer-to-peer sharing of this information via social networks facilitated ad hoc celebratory assemblies at Ground Zero, Times Square, and outside of the White House. This ability for strangers to organize quickly and in real time was facilitated through the several smart phone apps now available.

THE DIGITAL GRASSROOTING OF SOCIAL MOVEMENTS

New technologies are changing more than just the way individuals can share and disseminate information. The actual structure of digitally savvy social movement organizations (**SMOs**) is unique. Traditional movements tended to rely more on a hierarchical model of formal, well-established organizations with charismatic leaders and professional experts, which provided a clear set of grievances and demands as the cornerstone of the collective behavior. More recently, however, collective behavior manifests itself through a more horizontal infrastructure of connectivity. This broadens the public sphere, as citizens can now share grievances and express their opinions through peer-to-peer networks, contributing to the "electronic grassrooting of civil society." Castells (2001) coined this term to describe a new type of "informational politics" in which electronic media become the space of politics by framing processes, messages, and outcomes and results in a new kind of civil society.

These new types of communication flows change the organizational process, as collective behavior is now less dependent on professional leadership and expertise and operates at the grassroots level and in ad hoc settings. Unlike past forms of technology, which relied on the one-to-many flow of information, largely controlled by state or corporate interests (for example, heavy, though not exclusive, reliance on newspaper, television, or radio coverage during the civil rights struggle or the women's suffrage movement), the new media ecosystem is a bottom-up approach to communication. Ordinary citizens, equipped with their tech-savvy sense, now organize and hold politically oriented events to effect social change in both cyberspace and in local communities. Many contemporary social movements have an aversion to naming a specific leader or spokesperson, and some are conscientious about avoiding specific demands. Furthermore, social movement actors are often more flexible than activists who have participated in previous forms of mobilization, in that they demonstrate a proclivity to alter their demands and tactics as protest activities unfold. This approach is made possible by up-to-the-minute information sharing and organizing through new media.

This horizontal structure of social movements, made possible by digital technology, emerged in the early 1990s when the Internet was first utilized for protest activity. For example, the 1994 uprising by the Zapatistas (an indigenous and initially armed group in the southern state of Chiapas) against the Mexican federal government in an effort to protect their indigenous rights and access to land surprised the world, and the only way that the world knew about the revolution was because of the Internet. This new media resource disseminated firsthand accounts of developments in this remote region. The rebellion was not organized over the Internet (as access to computers was clearly lacking in this extremely poor and remote area of Mexico), but commentary, suggestions, debate, and reporting was shared in cyberspace on a peer-to-peer basis, which stirred interest and gained them international support (Cleaver 1998). The Zapatistas handwrote communiqués for distribution to the mass media and gave them to reporters or to friends of reporters, which were then typed or scanned and distributed through the Internet (Arquilla and Ronfeldt 2001).

Another early example is the successful attempt to shut down the World Trade Organization (WTO) ministerial meetings in Seattle in 1999. Despite a lack of face-to-interaction before the major demonstrations, organizations and individuals shared ideas and information as to how to best educate citizens about the WTO and its policies that were deemed harmful to both workers and the environment, as well as how to best plan and carry out the rallies. Demonstrators held protests in more than eighty locations in dozens of countries once the information sharing plateaued (Rheingold 2002). They organized these through the website seattle wto.org/N30 (now defunct), which put out action alerts in ten different languages letting those interested know how they could get involved.

GETTING THE MESSAGE OUT

New ICTs have made it easier and faster than ever before for activists to gain support for boycotts, garner signatures in petitions, or simply get the message out to people sympathetic to their cause. Effective online petitions and calls for boycotts abound, and this form of e-activism is now an integral part of most people's social media activity. There are websites, such as PetitionOnline.com, that host or link online actions as a free service through which visitors can create and maintain online petitions for any cause. Other sites feature action centers that allow citizens to choose from a menu of a variety of actions such as boycotts; online petitions; virtual sit-ins, rallies, and demonstrations; or e-mail or fax correspondence about a particular cause of concern (Earl et al. 2010).

In one particularly effective case, after a fourth-grade class in Brookline, Massachusetts, read *The Lorax*, by Dr. Seuss, they discovered on Universal Studio's website that the environmental themes, central to the story, were not going to be addressed in the upcoming film based on the book. The students started a petition on Change.org (host of the world's largest petition platform) demanding the movie company "let the Lorax speak for the trees" (Kristof 2012). The petition went viral and gathered more than 57,000 signatures. The studio, in response to the outcry, updated the movie site with the environmental message (Kristof 2012).

In another example, Molly Katchpople also used Change.org to pursue a cause. She petitioned Bank of America on the site to reconsider its plan to add a five-dollar-per-month fee on its customers' debit cards (Dias 2011). The petition drive was successful. Later, she put up another petition against Verizon, which also intended to raise its fees by five dollars a month. This also resulted in a victory when the corporation relented in less than forty-eight hours (Kim 2011). In both cases this online activism saved Americans billions of dollars.

After airline passengers were trapped on the tarmac for eight hours in Austin, Texas, on an American Airlines flight in 2009, one of the disgruntled passengers began an online petition, also using Change.org. The circumstances were horrid, as food and water supplies ran out, toilets overflowed, and patience wore thin. This individual effort snowballed into a national movement for reform across the entire airline industry. Individuals then collectively lobbied Congress to consider the Airline Passenger's Bill of Rights, which it did as the airlines voluntarily accepted the standards proposed by the petition. The bill, passed by the Senate on February 6, was entitled the FAA Reauthorization Bill (Shirky 2008).

A final example of online activism through the use of petitions is a group called Colorlines.com (a think tank that fights for racial justice). The group undertook a three-year campaign to convince mainstream news outlets to stop using the word "illegal" when referring to immigrants living in the United States without the proper documentation, on the basis that the term is racially charged and dehumanizing. They accomplished a major feat when the Associated Press, the largest news gathering organization, agreed to eliminate the use of the "I" word (Rosenfeld 2013). This is of particular significance because the Associated Press feeds hundreds of local television networks and newspapers and serves as a stylebook for all credentialed journalists.

Although large numbers truly make online campaigns effective, get the attention of those being targeted, and often translate into the perceived worthiness of the cause, it is important to keep in mind that these are more "flash campaigns" and not genuine social movements. They are not persistent mobilizations (an essential component for social movements according to Sidney Tarrow), and there is typically no clear sense of collective identity. Nevertheless, they give us insights into the tactics that those seeking social change can utilize, and online mobilization efforts do have the *potential* to transform into social movements. What the above examples also show is that it has never been easier, cheaper, and faster for activists to get their message out, quickly reach a critical mass, and mobilize into a formidable political campaign.

Because of the digital revolution, individuals now have an unparalleled degree of control over the production, dissemination, and consumption of information, which has a significant impact on their efforts to affect social change through displays of collective behavior. Indeed, the emergence of the Internet, social media networking sites, and e-activism are changing the nature of political struggle and social movement activism in the United States and around the world. As the case studies in this book will show, new ICTs are now an essential component of social movement actors' repertoire in their ability to facilitate and speed up the process of organizing, recruiting, sharing information, and galvanizing support among the public.

THE CASE STUDIES

Of course, not all social movements are impacted by ICTs. But the case studies in this book were chosen because of their timely, ongoing nature and because they have received substantial media attention in the mainstream press and on social networking sites. They are of particular interest to students because most are youth based and are related to issues that concern young people—a shaky economy, a dysfunctional political system, and perhaps most importantly skyrocketing student debt. Additionally, the text doesn't discuss only US- or North American-based social movement activity but looks at the global nature of social movements by examining outbreaks of contentious politics in various parts of the world. This provides students with an awareness of how some of the struggles that they may be familiar with in the United States compare and contrast to social movements in other parts of the world.

To understand contemporary displays of collective behavior, this book combines traditional and revised versions of social movement theory and complements them with theories that emphasize the role of digital technology in social movement activity. The case studies inform social movement theory by categorizing and evaluating the influence of new ICTs on the way social movements emerge and succeed, and each chapter outlines which theories are particularly useful given the particular case study.

By looking at the examples and case studies through this lens, we can best analyze and conceptualize the historical, political, and social context within which protest activity occurs, how activists mobilize (what strategies and tactics they employ and why they choose them), how new members are recruited and influenced to participate in often high-risk activities, how groups form alliances and use them to their advantage, the key role that these networks play in the sustenance of contentious politics, and how activists frame issues and use the mainstream and alternative media in addition to social networking sites to help sway public opinion in their favor. In sum, the theoretical frameworks serve as a toolkit that unlocks how a new generation of mobilized citizens is building new collectivities and representing a new type of digitally savvy activism.

STRUCTURE OF THE BOOK

Chapter 1 provides a summary of the history and trajectory of social movement theory as it has been developed and adjusted over the past few decades. It serves as a foundation for the analysis of recent social movements discussed throughout the rest of the book and lays the groundwork for the question, Are these digitally cutting-edge movements and uprisings forcing theorists to re-examine and refocus some of the more conventional explanations of collective behavior?

Chapter 2 explores ICTs as tools for social change outside of formal SMOs. We will see how ordinary citizens, with new powerful digital tools at their disposal, are organizing and mobilizing in ways that are distinct from previous mobilization efforts.

Chapters 3–6 examine specific contemporary social movements to highlight the relevance of new media in contentious politics and to explore how this use of ICTs and new media informs and updates social movement theories. These chapters examine the historical, cultural, social, and political context within which the movements occurred, how activists mobilized (their strategies and tactics), how they recruited and forged alliances with other groups, how they framed their issues and used the mainstream and alternative press to sway public opinion, and the outcomes or consequences of their mobilization efforts. They situate the movements in question within social movement theory and evaluate how well the various theories explain their emergence and evolution. Finally, the chapters will each ask the question, Does this case study give us reason to update or modify traditional social movement theories? At the end of each chapter a "Theory Toolkit" gives the reader a snapshot of the different theories that can be used to analyze the social movement.

DISCUSSION QUESTIONS

1. In what ways are social movements a distinctive form of collective behavior? Can you think of examples not provided in this book that might blur the line between social movements and other repertoires of contention? For example, in some cases, can we perceive armed struggle or war to be a social movement?

2. What does McLuhan mean by "the medium is the message"? How does the digital revolution fit into this schema? How has it played out in a recent social movement that this book does not cover? Are there flaws in his theory?

3. Mojos are important for mobilizing efforts and contentious politics. How can efforts of mojos potentially backfire? Create a scenario where this might be the case.

4. Think of ways in which "flash campaigns" might be considered social movements or turn into a sustainable campaign. Come up with some concrete examples from your own independent research.

CHAPTER ONE

Social Movement Theories

This chapter provides an overview of how the various theories of social movements have evolved over time. By learning about these different schools of thought, we will be well equipped to study the contemporary social movements highlighted in this book, putting them in context and analyzing how their use of ICTs have affected the repertoire of contention (Tilly 2006) they have at their disposal and the success of their endeavors. This chapter also lays the groundwork for a central question of this book: Do the case studies of contemporary social movements in this book give us reason to update or modify traditional social movement theories, and if so, how and why?

It is important to remember that social movement theories both challenge and complement each other. Different perspectives that attempt to interpret the dynamics of collective behavior are not mutually exclusive; by combining aspects of the various strands of social movement theories, we are better suited to understand more thoroughly how social movement actors navigate the social and political context in their organizing endeavors, recruitment efforts, and mobilizing strategies and tactics. What in the past were deemed as competing paradigms (micro or macro, rational or emotional, economically or culturally oriented) today can be recognized as mutually reinforcing (see for example the work of McAdam et al. 1996). Their conceptual and analytical insights, in conjunction with theories of new media, support recent research that suggests that wired activism does not replace but rather assists and promotes Castells's (2001) notion of the grassrooting of civil society—as organizing in cyberspace often facilitates contentious engagement on the streets.

A TRAJECTORY OF SOCIAL MOVEMENT THEORY

Through different theories, social movement scholars attempt to explain the emergence and timing of social movements, the social and political context in which they develop, recruitment efforts, the mobilization of resources, the way tactics and strategies change over time, and the outcomes and consequences of collective behavior. Early theories of collective behavior explained social movements through a micro-level lens rooted in social psychology. Sociologists during the first half of the twentieth century viewed them as random occurrences and emotionally charged responses among aggrieved individuals to unsatisfactory situations and conditions.

Structural strain and relative deprivation theories (the classical model) argued that social movements emerged among individuals who felt deprived of some goods or resources or experienced a sense of inequality in relation to others or to their expectations—in other words, people with grievances (Morrison 1978; Smelser 1962). Also underlying these theories was the "mass society" proposition, which suggested that movement participants consisted of those who were not fully integrated into society and suffered from anomie or **normlessness** (failure to abide by the rules) (Gusfield 1970; Kornhauser 1959).

However, the claim that social movements are a response to social strain or relative deprivation is problematic because it ignores the larger context in which movements arise (McAdam 1982). By identifying discontent as the most significant cause of social movements, early theories could not adequately explain how individual discontent translates into collective phenomena. Because most people feel deprived on some level at some point in time, these theories cannot explain why some individuals and groups mobilize and others don't—as well as when, where, and how. Therefore, scholars began to focus on the mobilization of external and internal resources, recruitment efforts, cultural explanations, and outcomes of collective behavior that were largely ignored by the traditional model.

Resource Mobilization and Political Process Theories

Beginning in the 1970s conceptualizations of social movement activists shifted. The resource mobilization theory argued that social movements are formed by rational social actors and SMOs undertake strategic political action (McCarthy and Zald 1973; Tilly 1978). Their resources include knowledge, money, media attention, labor, solidarity, organizational structure, legitimacy, and support from political elites. Theorists characterized protesters as purposeful and motivated on the basis of a calculation of the costs and benefits regarding participation, and SMOs as having organizational structures in place, both of which were considered prerequisites for action (Gamson 1975).

An important issue to consider when trying to understand social movement participation through a resource mobilization lens is the "free rider" problem. Olson (1965) hypothesizes that it was in fact rational for citizens to "ride free" on the actions of others. He argued that self-interest undermines the rationality of collective action and the possibility of movement emergence. Rationally, it makes sense for individuals to avoid time, energy, and financial costs, as well as possible retaliation from the authorities by leaving others to partake in social movement activities while hoping to reap the benefits of their efforts. Thus, it may be individually irrational for an individual to join an organization or participate in (especially risky) outbreaks of collective behavior if there are others already pursuing issues of concern. Therefore, scholars began to ask, under what circumstances do people decide to risk mobilizing for collective action? This in turn led to a more precise development of resource mobilization theory.

To address this cost-benefit trade-off, John McCarthy and Meyer Zald (1973) and Sidney Tarrow (1998) take a more structural or macro perspective, suggesting that it is not self-interested individuals who are responsible for social movement emergence but altruistic elites and professional organizations who contribute the resources. By contrast, more cultural or constructionist theories addressed the free-rider problem by focusing on how conscientious constituents, who may or may not benefit from a successful outcome, are oftentimes willing to contribute their individual resources to a particular cause for ethical or moral reasons. We will discuss culturally based theories below, but these scholars supplement resource mobilization theories with their contention that, in conjunction with the important contact of social networks, framing their issue to garner public sympathy will provide the motivation for people to contribute to a social cause.

A major point of focus among resource mobilization scholars is the role of leaders, or entrepreneurs. They serve as decision makers; provide sources of inspiration, charisma, and organizational strategies; often create new organizations; frame the major grievances and demands of the movement; create a sense of collective identity and draw in new recruits; and are critical to mobilizing resources and taking advantage of opportunities—for example, identifying potential for external support (Platt and Lilley 1994; Staggenborg 1988; McCarthy and Zald 1973). They are targeted by media outlets to articulate the movement's agenda (Gamson and Wolfsfeld 1993). Organizations that resist centralized leadership can have difficulty using the media to their advantage because the press cannot easily identify spokespeople to represent the cause (Gitlin 1980).

One of the drawbacks of the resource mobilization model is that it ignores the external political context at the macro level. It tends to emphasize instrumental action oriented toward political participation while paying little attention to the cultural and symbolic dimension of social life that often underpins such strategic action (Habermas 1989). The heavy focus on SMOs is further problematic in that many contemporary social movements do not have a traditional organizational structure and are better characterized as decentralized "social movement communities" that operate in an ad hoc fashion (Wollenberg et al. 2006).

The political process model, which emerged in response to these shortcomings, views social movements as greatly affected by resources *external* to social movement participants. It contends that agents evaluate the political environment and make calculations about the likely impact of their collective action. It is the political context that influences which claims they will pursue, which alliances they will seek, and which political strategies and tactics they will choose (McAdam 1982). Some groups may have an insurgent consciousness and resources to mobilize, but, because political opportunities are not open, they have little chance of success.

Political opportunities refer to the receptivity or vulnerability of the existing political system to challenge (Meyer 2005; Tarrow 2001). This vulnerability can be the result of one or a combination of any of the following conditions: a decline in repression (and thus increased tolerance for protest), fragmentation among political elites, electoral instability, broadening access to institutional participation, and support of organized opposition by elites (Tarrow 1996; C. Jenkins and Perrow 1977). The division among elites in particular allows social movement actors to manipulate the competition among powerful members of the polity, taking advantage of the openings that result from these struggles and potentially reducing the power discrepancy between insurgent groups and their opponents (Meyer and Minkoff 2004). These political opportunity structures are an intervening variable that increases or decreases the likelihood that social movement participants can activate resources, which helps explain why contentious events take place at some historical junctures and not at others.

Political Mediation

One drawback of the political process model is that it presupposes that all aspects of social movements—their emergence and dynamics, the cognition of participants and their susceptibility to join political protest, and their outcomes—are determined by macro structural relations. It also disregards the lenses through which activists perceive potential opportunities for their movements, that is, their subjective perceptions of reality and interpretive frameworks. To address these shortcomings, theorists of contentious politics introduced the political mediation model (Gamson 1990).

This paradigm examines the way that the social and political context in which participants are situated intersects with the strategic choices that social movement actors make. It also recognizes that opportunities are indeed situational, fluid, and volatile because they depend on the way actors *perceive* and *define* the situation before deciding what action should be taken (Meyer and Minkoff 2004). Another mediating variable, or "signal," that the political mediation model takes into consideration is public opinion and the ability of social movement actors to influence it in a way favorable to their cause (Soule and King 2006).

Cultural Theories: Collective Identity and Framing Analysis

Besides the availability of political opportunities and resources, there are other mitigating factors that can help explain the emergence of collective behavior, reasons for participation, and the strategic choices that social movement actors make. The "cultural turn" in social movement theory focuses mainly on the *why* (the meaning of collective action and subjective interests), rather than on the *how* (political conditions and resources available) of social movements. The understanding is that actors are not merely **utility maximizers** (acting primarily out of self-interest) but are often immersed in commitments to others, traditions, and broader ethical or moral sentiments, and an immaterial quality rooted in collective identity motivates individuals. Alberto Melucci (1996) defines collective identity as an interactive, shared process that links individuals or groups to a social movement through sustained interaction. It illuminates how individuals come to decide they share certain orientations and grievances and organize collectively. A concentration on collective identity therefore helps to bridge the gap between the structural foundations for action and the collective action itself. Francesca Polletta and James Jasper (2001) suggest that collective identity can be a *perception* of a shared status or relationship, which may be imagined rather than experienced directly. By appealing to identity, social movements motivate participants through intrinsic, nonstrategic rewards such as self-realization, personal satisfaction, and a sense of group belonging (Gamson 1992).

Key to forging collective identity and articulating shared meanings is the way organizers "frame" their issues to resonate with potential recruits and to build solidarity by linking participants' grievances to mainstream beliefs and values (Benford 1993). Scholars define a frame as an interpretive schema that an individual or group uses to interpret reality, on an ideological basis, by selectively omitting and emphasizing various aspects of the world (Snow et al. 1986). Frames are typically referred to as "**injustice frames**" that contain implicit or explicit appeals to moral principles (Ryan and Gamson 2006).

"Frame alignment" is a process through which activists articulate individual interests, values, and beliefs as congruent and complimentary with SMO activities, goals, and ideology. "Frame bridging" involves the ability of SMOs to reach people who already share their political orientation through consciousness-raising efforts and organizational outreach, thus enlarging the boundaries of an initial frame to include issues or social problems of importance to potential participants. And, finally, "frame amplification" appeals to deeply held values and beliefs in the general population and links those values and beliefs to movement issues (Snow et al. 1986).

For framing to be influential, organizers must persuade large numbers of people that the issues they care about are urgent, that alternatives are possible, that activists are worthy (or have moral standing), and that the constituencies they seek to mobilize can be invested with agency (Tarrow and Tilly 2006). David A. Snow et al. (1986) delineate that social movement actors must provide "prognostic," "diagnostic," and "motivational" frames. This means identifying problems (including attributions of blame or causality so that the movement has a target for its actions), posing solutions in a way that mobilizes participants and appeals to third parties, and stimulating a "call to arms" by encouraging people to take action to solve a given social problem.

New Social Movement Theory

There is no real agreement within the social movement literature as to what "new" social movements refer to. Nor is there consensus a new classification of collective behavior is needed. However, several theorists do argue that there is something distinct about a subset of contemporary social movements. Scholars introduced new social movement theory as an alternative to both the resource mobilization and political process models. Within this paradigm, these theorists emphasize different themes, have different approaches, and relate to traditional theories in a number of ways in an attempt to better analyze the shifts in contemporary forms of organizing that began in the 1980s. What they do have in common is a divergence from (at least to account for certain social movements) resource mobilization and political process theories and an increased emphasis on role framing and cultural processes (Gamson 1992; Hunt, Benford, and Snow 1994).

Anthony Giddens (1991), for example, argues that the age of late modernity has allowed the development of a "postscarcity economy" in which most people's basic survival needs are met, allowing them to focus on issues outside of class (the focus of most traditional/proletarian social movements). He contends that contemporary movements may be as much about changing people's understandings of themselves and the world around them as about changing laws and policies, with many acting on religious or moral claims, group loyalties, ideological conviction, and identities or in response to a perceived lack of meaningful access to decisions that affect their lives.

John Tomlinson (1999) describes new social movements as those based on **distantiated identity**, whereby individuals embrace a sense of what unites us as human beings: common risks and possibilities and mutual responsibility and shared morality. In other words, new social movements are indicative of an increased consciousness that embraces a global, compassionate perspective and involves grassroots activities across dispersed geographical locations and identity politics on a global scale.

For others, new social movements are viewed as a convergence of multiclass and multi-identity struggles in reaction to the colonizing intrusions of states and markets, and they are grounded in the resistance of the professional middle class to the rationalizing forces of modernity, social fragmentation, injustice, and the politicization of everyday life (Johnston 1994). The focus is more on resisting power in the social or cultural spheres, democratizing new and existing public arenas, and politicizing issues previously viewed as private to escape new and traditional forms of domination.

Therefore, civil society becomes the domain of struggle in that it combines political and public spaces. Although participants seek to bring about social change, they have no interest in claiming state power or economic gain; their focus is on control over the process of meaning, autonomy, creativity of relationships, and ways of defining and interpreting reality (Castells 2001; Melucci 1980). The slow food movement, with its emphasis on organic and locally produced food, or the downshifters social movement, which critiques excessive materialism and consumerism and calls for simple living, are good examples. By eschewing strategic questions and instrumental action in favor of symbolic expressions of resistance, the goal is often cultural and personal change. Actors are more concerned with retaining or re-creating endangered lifestyles and culture than with changes in the economic or public policy realm.

In terms of tactics, new social movement theorists emphasize the decentralized nature of power and resistance, and they assert that participants in contemporary social movements concentrate on everyday life and cultural and on symbolic forms of resistance. These can occur alongside or in place of more conventional political forms of contestation (J. Cohen 1985). Perhaps most significantly (and facilitated through emerging ICTs), new social movement theorists point out the distinctive organizational structure of new social movements. Melucci (1996) observes that the organizational features of many contemporary forms of collective behavior are constituted by loosely articulated, decentralized, egalitarian, and pluralistic networks. This structure permits multiple memberships and part-time participation, and there is little if any distinction between leaders and rank-and-file members, members and nonmembers, and private and public roles. This, in turn, magnifies the horizontal nature of social movement activity.

Michael Mann (2000, 57 [emphasis added]) describes these networks as "**interstitial locations** that consist of the nooks and crannies in and around the dominant institutions," where diverse groups of citizens can operate outside the formal political system and dominant institutions to raise new issues and promote new sets of values. He argues that groups that are marginal and blocked by the prevailing institutions can link together and cooperate in ways that transcend these institutions. The global peace movement, organizing the homeless to defend their rights through roundtables in Southern California, and efforts to stop deportation proceedings of undocumented individuals through forms of civil disobedience are some examples. In essence, new social movements refer to a diverse array of collective actors who are raising new issues, are the carriers of new values, operate in new terrains, employ new modes of action, and have presumably displaced the old social movements that focused more on specific issues such as class, race, or gender.

Most scholars now view the "new social movement" perspectives as a school of thought, varying in perspective, analysis, and approach, rather than as a "theory" per se (Klandermans, Kriesi, and Tarrow 1988). One limitation of this school as it has evolved is that scholars have mainly applied these theories to white, middle-class, progressive causes that cut across political and cultural spheres at the expense of paying attention to struggles that pertain to economic or racial issues. Another is a lack of continuity or commonality with historical predecessors, for example the labor, women's rights, or gay and lesbian rights movements that used many of the same tactics and shared similar ideologies (Johnston 1994).

SOCIAL MOVEMENT OUTCOMES

Research on social movement outcomes tries to address the crucial question of why social movements succeed or fail. In most cases it is difficult to categorically establish a direct causal relationship between attempts at collective behavior and successful results, but theorists point to a number of significant factors, including taking strategic advantage of existing political opportunities (Meyer and Minkoff 2004), employing particular tactics (Tilly 2006; McAdam 1982), expressing a clearly defined set of goals that movement supporters can relate to (Jasper 1997; Zald 1996), accessing resources and forming alliances that expand the movement's base of support (Gamson 1990; McCarthy and Zald 1977), and adopting specific organizational forms and practices (Ganz 2004; Piven and Cloward 1977).

Some scholars characterize successful outcomes as either challengers meeting their goals or the target of collective action recognizing the challengers as legitimate representatives of a constituency, thereby altering the relationship between the challengers and target (Marullo and Meyer 2007). Doug McAdam (1982) argues that *either* undermining the structural basis of the political system or enhancing the strategic position of insurgent challengers increases the political leverage exercised by challengers. Others note that outcomes do not just entail clear-cut victories or failures in the institutional political arena (C. Jenkins and Form 2006; Amenta and Young 1999). Rather, cultural variables such as changes in values and public opinion, the establishment of a collective identity or subcultures, and new cultural opportunities are significant elements of social movement outcomes (Polletta 2008; Earl 2004).

HOW TO THEORIZE SOCIAL MOVEMENTS IN THE DIGITAL AGE

There are different views regarding the influence of new media on social movements—what we will call theories of new media in this book—but what is clear is that the technology available at a particular time and within a given cultural setting affects mobilization efforts. Today, activists rely on digital and web-based tools in addition to material resources.

Some scholars view the digital revolution as having a positive effect on mobilizing endeavors. Castells (2001) argues that new ICTs invigorate an explosive type of informational politics, resulting in a new kind of civil society based on the electronic grassrooting of democracy. The diffusion of new technology prompts the development of horizontal networks of interactive communication through a many-to-many flow of communication. Theorists have long noted that social networks, relational ties, and friendships serve as an important channel for recruiting people to a cause, especially for high-risk protest movement actions (Snow et al. 1986; McAdam 1982). New ICTs greatly expand the potential of these networks to develop and mutate exponentially.

For example, Doug McAdam and Ronnelle Paulsen (1993) argue that, although the strength of social ties strongly influences recruitment on the individual level, weak social ties forged in the virtual sphere can effectively spread a social movement's message across diffuse networks. The virtual world now provides additional context to better determine the nature of individuals' interpersonal social ties (this could be friends, neighbors, coworkers, fellow students, church members, or other acquaintances) to a particular social movement. Many activists, particularly youth, receive information about mobilizations and contentious (as well as electoral) politics through digital channels from someone they trust that they may not receive otherwise, which Marco Giugni (1998) finds increases the likelihood of their participation.

Others note that new ICTs broaden the parameters of organization efforts because the obstacles to grassroots mobilization are lowered and are facilitated by what Bruce Bimber (2003) calls "**accelerated pluralism**." New technology allows organizers to reach a critical mass quickly and cheaply. In contrast to the one-to-many flow of information through mass communication media, with new ICTs and social media citizens can comment on and pass along information they receive (H. Jenkins 2006; Van Aelst and Walgrave 2003). They can therefore develop a sense of community in spite of physical distance in the form of "virtual public spheres" (Kahn and Kellner 2003). Additionally, these new types of information sharing are potentially resistant to state regulation, reducing a state's capacity to repress the distribution of political communication, thereby giving rise to a new type of civic engagement at the grassroots level (Bennett and Iyengar 2008). In sum, the soft power of new information technologies challenges the hard physical power of the state (Nie 2001).

Critical Perspectives of the Internet and New Media

Others are more skeptical of these utopian perspectives of the impact of digital media on collective behavior. Some theorists argue that discussion groups and listservs attract members with a particular predisposition to an issue, and they discourage challenges to the information they have and conclusions they have reached (Jordan 2001; Diani 2000b). This results in "cyber-balkanization" or the "echo chamber" effect. As Bruce Bimber and Richard Davis (2013) claim, the Internet is "par excellence" the medium for people to self-select interaction with like-minded people, which can lead to fragmentation and polarization.

Elite domination over cyberspace and control over listservs by list owners or gatekeepers—and problems regarding access to technology or the digital divide—are also important to address (DiMaggio et al. 2004). Skeptics contend that new media platforms, created through digital tools based on past e-mail communications and Internet use, can be manipulated by elites (Hindman 2007). State authorities can also use sophisticated monitoring software for surveillance and repression via social media, especially when material is deemed political or critical of the government.

Sometimes states or other authorities activate disinformation or propaganda campaigns in lieu of or in addition to blocking access to communication devices. These are called astroturf (the opposite of grassroots) operations, and some are indeed very sophisticated. Tobacco companies in the United States, for instance, have a long history of creating astroturf groups to fight attempts to regulate them. China trains thousands of commentators and pays them (thus, their name, the 50cent Party) to post progovernment comments on the web and steer online opinion away from criticism of the Communist Party (Monbiot 2011). As the *Daily Kos* blogging group describes the process: "Companies now use 'personal management software' which multiplies the efforts of the astroturfers working for them, creating the impression that there is major support for what a corporation or government is trying to do. The software creates all the online furniture of real people who possess them—a name, email account, web page and social media. It automatically generates what looks like authentic profiles" (Leyden 2008).

Working within a broader theoretical paradigm, critical theorist Jürgen Habermas has long argued (his argument was put forth before the emergence of new ICTs but is relevant to later discussions) that mainstream media has negatively impacted the public sphere, the areas of social life where citizens can freely discuss and debate societal concerns that are important to them outside of public authority. His ideas are important for us to consider because of the attention he pays to how the control of the media and information can undermine participatory democracy and communicative action.

Alberto Melucci elaborates on Habermas's concept of the public sphere, calling it an "intermediate public space" where citizens can politicize civil society by making their messages heard, thereby entering the process of political articulation (1996). The public sphere consists of information distributors such as print media as well as physical social spaces. Habermas also uses the concept of the "ideal speech situation" in which communication is not constrained by political or economic forces. Rather, all are free to participate in dialogue and debate and on equal terms.

Habermas fears that the realm of the "public space" has been colonized, as relationships are increasingly mediated by money and power, and that entrenched political parties and interest groups now substitute for participatory democracy (1993). In other words, public opinion, he argues, once based on the outcome of debate, discussion, and reflection (what he refers to as communicative action) is now constrained by media experts who shape, construct, and limit public discourse to those themes they validate and approve. The outcome is a decline in democracy, individuality, and freedom and an increase in social control.

Updating Habermas's concerns, some theorists claim that virtual social relations in cyberspace are not a substitute for more traditional forms of community and protest, because they lack the interpersonal ties that provide the basis for the consistency of collective identities and the ability to mobilize new members (Putnam 2000; Pickerill 2003). Underlying this concern is an ongoing discussion about whether new forms of media and technology are weakening standard forms of political and social engagement, inducing anomie and eroding social capital by enabling users to retreat into an artificial world (Nie and Erbring 2000; Kraut et al. 1998). The result is a reduction of social capital of the very networks that enable individuals and groups to work together to pursue common objectives as technology drives a wedge between individual and collective interests (Putnam 2000).

However, other research suggests that new ICTs do not necessarily decrease social movement participation. The data show that this participation is contingent on what people use digital platforms for. Those who use digital platforms for entertainment purposes have a lower level of participation in social movement activity than those who use it for information, sharing, learning, and political purposes (Bimber 2003). Boulainne's (2009) research found that in the United States informational content accessed through online services was positively associated with increased political participation.

There are also contradicting perspectives on whether social media enhances or decreases the ability to create and nurture collective identity among activists. Some studies highlight that the instantaneous peer-to-peer sharing that allows for the development of collective identity before protest activity on the street even begins is a critical asset for activists (Boulainne 2009). Though there are indeed certain limitations to engaging exclusively in cyberactivism—at times reducing participation to mere "**clicktivism**"—in generating and sustaining social movements, the analyses in the following chapters demonstrate that social movement actors indeed rely on ICTs as a key resource. In particular, they will show that mediated forms of communication have not necessarily replaced, but tend to accompany, those based on face-to-face interaction. H. Jenkins (2006) uses the term "civic media" to describe how new electronic media often fosters face-to-face civic engagement and a participatory culture, referred to as the "**spillover**" effect, that is, the symbiotic relationship between online and offline activism. Dutta-Bergman's (2006) research finds that individuals living in communities with Internet access are more likely to be involved in local community organizations than those living in communities without.

While this debate continues to fuel interesting theoretical and political discussions, scholars agree that ICTs have altered the communication field and that this has led to important repercussions for collective behavior as the contours within which groups and individuals can voice concerns are expanding. Although it is important to recognize the more critical perspectives of new media and its impact on contentious politics, the case

THEORY TOOLKIT

SUMMARY OF DIFFERENT THEORETICAL PERSPECTIVES

Relative Deprivation/Social Strain. Holds that individuals participate in collective behavior because they feel deprived of goods or resources, and therefore they experience social strain. These theories consider acts of collective action rooted in a sense of alienation.

Resource Mobilization. Views social movement actors as rational agents, and key resources for a campaign to emerge are organizations, knowledge, funding, key allies, support from political elites, and access to the media. This theory also focuses on the role of leadership in any given campaign and the free-rider problem.

Political Process. Examines the external and macro-level political and social context to explain the outbreak of social movements and revolutions. A particular focus is on the vulnerability of authorities to challenge and openings in the formal political system that challengers can exploit.

Political Mediation. Pays strong attention to public opinion and how this can serve as leverage to social movement actors, and to the role that a perception of a possible victory play in fueling and sustaining social movement activity.

Cultural Theories—Framing and Collective Identity. Focus is on micro-level dynamics and the "how" rather than the "why" of social movements. Constructionist use of framing, and most importantly an injustice frame, and establishing a strong sense of collective identity are key.

New Social Movement Theories. Now considered an eclectic school of thought rather than a theoretical framework. This school opposes Marxist interpretations of collective behavior rooted in class struggle. Its emphasis is more in alignment with cultural theories. It also pays attention to contemporary forms of organizational structure that are more decentralized.

Theories of New Media. Emphasize how new ICTs are impacting social movement organizing and mobilization efforts. Although some theorists emphasize how 2.0 technologies are an asset to forms of collective behavior (it is cheap, fast, does not rely on a lot of traditional resources or formal leaders or organizations), others warn of particular caveats (the downfalls of "clicktivism" and threats to collective identity, among others).

studies in this text provide some examples of the ways in which ICTs can be beneficial to organizing and sustaining social movement activity.

CONCLUSION

Tilly's notion of the repertoire of contention, which we discussed in the introduction, refers to the arsenal at the disposal of activists at a particular historical juncture to make demands on authorities. The changes that the digital revolution has brought urge us to incorporate the role of technology into a more comprehensive approach to theorizing social movements. As the following chapters will demonstrate, social media now serves as a key collective tool that helps to sustain connectivity in both the virtual and real world. Though formal SMOs are still an important resource in effecting social change and promoting certain agendas, they are now accompanied by nontangible resources and new kinds of organizational structures. Social media and ICTs also allow us to think about collective identity, as well as the ability of citizens to express public dissent and organize and to hold authorities accountable, in different ways.

DISCUSSION QUESTIONS

1. Social movement theory evolved over time and each theory emphasizes certain aspects of collective behavior that entail both strengths and weaknesses. Pick a contemporary social movement and apply one or more of the theories discussed in this chapter. Which ones fit best and why?

2. Write about a social movement currently in the news that can only have taken place because of the digital revolution. How does what you describe help to update traditional theories of social movements?

3. Find a cause where the use of ICTs has been detrimental. Explain how and why, and tie your results to the discussions in this chapter.

CHAPTER TWO

New Digital Capabilities and Social Change

Although the digital capabilities of the new technological age allow for creative new ways to share information that bypass the mainstream press, sometimes leading to spontaneous action in the streets, not all such events can be considered social movements. Many are not sustained activities, a qualification noted by Tarrow (2001), or fail to display all four aspects of Tilly's (2004) conceptualization of WUNC (worthiness, unity, numbers, and commitment). In other words, in some outbursts of collective behavior, there is no genuine commitment to a cause or campaign, which is what makes social movements a distinct form of contentious politics. It is important to recognize that not all that is public is collective action.

In this chapter we will explore recent cases of cyberactivism that, although technically "public," are not necessarily considered social movements or collective action. They nevertheless demonstrate how powerful online activism is in contemporary society and how it can affect social change. The examples in this chapter show the extent to which ICTs have facilitated the grassrooting of civil society—enhancing awareness about, and interest in, political and social issues—and also how they have been used as tools to challenge political and economic elites and bring public awareness and justice to cases of rape and oppression. And while a lot of activism these days happens only online, when movements do go the streets, wired activism does not replace, but rather complements and often increases, on-the-ground protests.

HACKTIVISM AND MEMES

Hacktivism typically refers to individuals breaking into information systems and compromising data. Cyberterrorism (the most destructive form of hacktivism) consists of illegal attacks or threats of sabotage against computers, networks, and stored data to intimidate or coerce a government, business, or individual to further a political or social objective (Denning 2010). It involves breaking into computer systems; stealing personal data; vandalizing or altering websites; e-mail spamming; disruption, denial or redirection of service (DDoS); sabotaging data and systems; launching computer viruses, worms, and Trojan horses; and conducting fraudulent transactions (Earl et al. 2010).

Many of these forms of hacktivism are facilitated by user-friendly software tools that are easily available online at no cost (Earl 2010). Electronic Disturbance Theater (EDT) is one of the leading online groups that organize these kinds of virtual sit-ins by publicly distributing an app called "FloodNet" that reloads requests to the targeted website every few seconds. By organizing specific times when certain websites will be hit by thousands of protesters, hackers hope to crash the site. A related tactic is e-mail bombing, sending large file attachments to the target's e-mail address to flood the server (Earl 2010). Other hacktivists create fake websites (or website parodies), copying the graphic design of the original but altering the content. Successful mock websites often employ a similar domain name to cause confusion among people trying to access the legitimate site (Bennett 2003).What makes these perpetrators hard to thwart or to prosecute is the use of zombie networks to hide their identity.

One of the most advanced among these types of hackers, a group called the Yes Men, creates parody websites that are particularly critical of corporations and governmental entities that they view as corrupt. Participants in the group have impersonated the US Chamber of Commerce, the leadership of the WTO, and dozens of other government and corporate officials (Britt 2010). They temporarily drove millions of dollars off Dow Chemical Company's stock value by posting a false news report on a faked BBC World News site that Dow was taking responsibility for the 1984 Bhopal disaster (a major gas leak at one of their Indian facilities, which was classified as one of the worst industrial catastrophes, killing over 15,000 people) and would compensate the families affected (CNN 2004).

Anonymous is typical of this new form of SMO ally because the group is an enigmatic, leaderless, decentralized global online entity energized by a host of causes. According to its website, it "is committed to freedom of information and the right of people to be informed about what the government is doing in their name." There are no real members. Rather, it is an amalgamation of people who are drawn together through a shared affinity for pranks (trolling) to affect social and political change. Any individual who tags him- or herself Anonymous can carry out an attack in its name (Sengputa 2012). Members often spread **memes**, which are ideas, actions, or styles that spread through a culture in a manner analogous to genes in a biological system. Individuals who spread memes are often called culture jammers, thriving on symbolic forms of protest and resistance. They typically consist of loosely organized networks of friendships or random groups of activists who operate alone. One of the underlying sentiments is a critique of commercial media and culture that feed into corporate interests, which they view as subjugating freedom, democracy, and creativity (Lasn 1999).

Anonymous first gained recognition in 2008 when it confronted the Church of Scientology. On January 14 of that year, a promotional video (produced by the church) featuring actor Tom Cruise was posted without church authorization on YouTube and other social networking sites and quickly became a popular meme. The church asked that the video be taken down from YouTube as well as the various other sites that reported it and threatened legal action for copyright infringement. This backfired as the video proliferated across many more sites with continuous repostings defended under the Fair Use Doctrine. The church claimed the video was posted through pirated means (Warner 2008). Subsequently, YouTube was forced to remove it under the threat of litigation, but the website Gawker.com, loosely associated with Anonymous, refused to give in to threats and further circulated the video.

This wired activism soon spilled over into the streets. Chanology (a subset of Anonymous committed to protesting Scientology) distributed other YouTube videos entitled "Call to Action" and "Declaration of War," which encouraged a global day of protest outside of the Church of Scientology on February 10. Another, labeled "Message from Chanology" accusing the church of Internet censorship and declaring Chanology's mission to "expel the Church from the Internet." Four days after the video was released, it had been viewed 800,000 times, and in less than two weeks it had been accessed more than 2 million times. A follow-up video, called "Code of Conduct," delineated more than twenty rules participants were asked to respect while demonstrating; at the heart of the code was to keep the protests peaceful. Upward of 7,000 protests were held in more than a hundred cities in twenty-six countries, and within a day supporters posted approximately 2,000 images on Flickr (Landers 2008). Chanology's website, projectchanology.com, also suggested numerous actions activists could engage in against the church and maintained a Facebook page in conjunction with Anonymous (Schliebs 2008).

This online group also used hacktivism as part of its repertoire by distributing DDoS attacks to try to bring down the church's website and succeeded in crashing the main web portal on and off for a week in January (Himmelein 2009). Most of the attacks originated from hot and zombie networks (computers or hosts connected to the Internet that are in some way compromised), and it was therefore impossible to find the perpetrators. Activists also used more traditional types of technology through an onslaught of blank faxes and prank phone calls. In return, the websites associated with Chanology, as well as sites that disseminated information regarding the protests received DDoSs of their own (Landers 2008). This exemplifies that technology is a *neutral* tool that can be utilized by both the challengers and the target of protest, a fact sometimes overlooked by theories that address how the digital revolution impacts social movements.

Memes as a Form of Cyberactivism

One of the earliest circulations of a popular meme to get the attention of both the alternative and mainstream press took place in 2001 during the peak of the United Students Against Sweatshops movement. Nike, Inc., was one of the main targets, under intense scrutiny for labor abuses in its offshore factories. That year MIT graduate student Jonah Peretti e-mailed Nike requesting the word "sweatshop" be stitched onto his shoe, through a personalizing service Nike had begun offering on its website. In its response the company declared that for a number of "technical" reasons (such as the word "sweatshop" being slang), it could not accommodate his request. Peretti replied by providing Nike with the *Webster's* dictionary entry. After several exchanges Nike admitted that the company reserved the right to reject anything "we consider inappropriate or simply do not want to place on our products." The final response from Peretti was, "Could you send a color snapshot of the ten-year old Vietnamese girl who makes my shoes?" (Peretti 2001).

Peretti e-mailed the electronic correspondence to twelve friends, and within a period of a few weeks it reached millions of people. At the height of circulation, he was receiving five hundred messages a day from all six continents. Articles about the correspondence began appearing in progressive and technology-oriented publications such as *Salon.com*, the *Village Voice*, and *In These Times*. This quickly filtered up from the micromedia to the mass media. *Time* magazine, the *Los Angeles Times*, the *Wall Street Journal*, *Business Week*, and NBC's *Today Show* all covered the story, and as a result the brand's reputation became increasingly endangered.

Nike eventually conceded to the activists' demands and improved labor conditions. Nike spokesperson Veda Manager acknowledged that the Internet played a role in the company's decision to accommodate student demands. She explained, "You make changes because it's the right thing to do. But obviously our actions have clearly been accelerated by the web" (Klein 2000, 393). Peretti's exchange is an example of how ordinary citizens can use forms of micromedia to reach others in the new networked environment with limited or no cost. It also gives insight into the relationship between alternative and mainstream media, and how they can reinforce each other.

Sometimes viral digital feeds originate in traditional, mainstream media. One example of this is the White House Correspondents Association dinner that took place in 2006 when comedian Stephen Colbert chastised President Bush, his cabinet, and the media (including the White House press corps, who hosted the event) regarding their handling of the 2003 invasion of Iraq, the disastrous response to Hurricane Katrina, and a host of other issues. The event ran on C-Span and then spread to YouTube, where it became the number-one download (Morford 2012). Despite the backlash against Colbert's speech in the mainstream media, the ratings for his television show, *The Colbert Report*, increased 37 percent the following week (N. Cohen 2006).

FIGHTING RAPE AND OPPRESSION THROUGH CYBERACTIVISM

In March of 2013 two high school football stars of the Big Red program (which is famous for winning several state championships) in Steubenville, a small town of about 18,000 in Ohio, were found guilty of gang-raping a sixteen-year-old girl. One will be serving at least two years in the state juvenile system and the other player will serve at least one year. Witnesses of the attack who were attending the party circulated dozens of text messages, videos, and cell-phone pictures of the incident, which played a major role in the initial prosecution of the suspects and later fed into the ensuing fury over the assault among citizens and groups across the United States (Oppel 2013). Anonymous's use of confrontational and threatening tactics led to the prosecution of two young men accused of rape. The tactics included tracing their electronic whereabouts during and after the attack and assisting in bringing widespread attention to the crimes.

Because the victim had passed out and therefore had no memory of the events, the young girl was unable to testify. The facts of the case were therefore put together through digital media. The parents of the young woman brought a flash drive to the authorities that was full of social media postings about the flagrant assault, and this initiated the investigation (Zirin 2013). One Instagram message, for instance, included a picture of the unconscious girl accompanied by tweets that read "rape" and "drunk girl" (Zirin 2013). The police then sought out the assailants and took their cell phones. They found more digital traces of the event and public sharing of the alarming attack, from which they were able to create a re-enactment of the crime. This quickly garnered not only national attention but international coverage of the case as well, which demonstrates that crime scenes can be investigated in the virtual world similar to the ways that they are in the real world.

Following a *New York Times* article that first brought the incident to national awareness, attention to the case soared exponentially when Anonymous released a video that one of the students (though never charged) involved in the assault recorded during and after one of the rapes. In December, Anonymous initially sent out a "partial dox," which is a list of names and addresses of those allegedly involved in the rape. This was accompanied by a threat of further leaks if the alleged perpetrators failed to apologize by January 1. When there was no apology, the

The Guy Fawkes mask has become a popular symbol for Anonymous.

group released the entire twelve-minute video (Welsh-Huggins 2013). This exposed the crime for all to witness with their own eyes and is an example of how, with the availability of digital technology, crimes that in the past may have had little chance of being investigated now come under more scrutiny, sometimes because of the perpetrators' demonstrating their own guilt in cyberspace.

The public became even more outraged when an attempted cover-up came to light because of evidence detected in the digital sphere. For example, quarterback Trent Mays (who was convicted) texted a friend about his coach saying, "I got Reno. He took care of it and shit ain't gonna happen, even if they did take it to court. Like he was joking about it I'm not worried" (Grieco and McCarty 2013). This put the football program under even more scrutiny. The alleged criminals finally realized the gravity of the situation, and later Mays sent a message to a friend asking him to stop the distribution of the video. He advised him, "Just say she came to our house and passed out" (Zirin 2013). However, this would prove to be a futile attempt at damage control as the story had gained much traction both in cyberspace and then in the mainstream media. In response to the growing accusations and outrage, town authorities launched a website of their own called "Steubenville Facts" in an attempt to defend themselves against the accusations of the cover-up. This countermeasure by using new technology once again emphasizes the fact that technology is a neutral tool that can be utilized by challengers as well as by those who are the target of dissent.

The fallout was significant and the bad publicity warranted action to be taken to protect the school authorities and coaching staff. It is likely that this was a strategy to draw attention away from the potential danger posed by critics of the football team and the school rather than a pretense of social justice, a tactic trying to portray themselves as victims. Anonymous was subject to similar criticism when it exposed the insensitive response by the school and football squad in addressing the issue, indeed an attempt to sweep it under the rug. The school superintendent requested that armed guards be posted on the premises of district schools in response to threats made by critics on Facebook. More than one thousand protesters congregated outside of the county courthouse calling for additional and more stringent charges against the alleged rapists. Following the trial many male advocates showed their support for combatting the extant rape culture. One man, Charles, in an act of online activism posted a popular Facebook text and photo that circulated widely with a sign read: "I stand with Jane Doe because when I became a victim of a sex crime, no one asked me if I was drunk or what I was wearing or what I had done to make it happen" (Welsh-Huggins 2013).

The Steubenville case received a great deal of attention in the mainstream press. Although the following examples may not have garnered as much media recognition, they nonetheless demonstrate the importance of ICTs in organizing for social justice. These cases primarily originated on, and were organized through, the Internet and other ICTs.

The upscale lingerie retail store Victoria's Secret is no stranger to protest as feminist groups have, over the years, aggressively decried the body image that the corporation promotes. Many claim that the unrealistic body types they use in their marketing strategies contribute to eating disorders, unnecessary plastic surgery, and low self-esteem among females. The company was recently the target of outrage among activists for introducing its new PINK line of underwear that is marketed under the tagline "Bright Young Things" (Walsh 2012). Some of the imprints on the undergarments read, "sure thing," "call me," and "feeling lucky." The main objection to the line is that the product trivializes rape and demeans women by insinuating that they are open to sex without being asked (Radley 2013). Another strongly held grievance is that this marketing campaign sexualizes young girls at too early an age and gives confusing messages (especially the panties that read "yes" "no" "maybe") to potential sexual partners.

A feminist group called FORCE: Upsetting Rape Culture electronically organized protests against the PINK line in conjunction with the national parent organization Mommy Lobby. They mobilized supporters to demonstrate outside of Victoria's Secret stores in an attempt to shame the corporation. Attendees wore underwear that read, "no means no" and "ask first" (Walsh 2012). This framed the message in a way that declares it is a woman's decision whether or not to have sex, and that it is not a given. They also held consent theme parties and marches to raise awareness about rape and framed their events in a way that sought to emphasize the distinction between rape and consensual sex. At one event FORCE "consent enthusiasts" hosted Operation Panty Drop to satirize the line of underwear by leaving consent-themed panties in more than a dozen Victoria's Secret stores across the United States (Arnowitz 2013). Similar "panty drops" were held in parts of Europe.

FORCE also created an antirape spoof website of Victoria's Secret called pinklove.com. This led viewers to believe that the company was releasing a new line of "flirty, sexy" underwear with "powerful statements" for its PINK lingerie line (Radley 2013). This was a hoax as there was no such product, but it went viral and spread rapidly over the Internet and social networking platforms.

Another form of electronic activism was propelled by a pastor in Houston, Texas, who posted an open letter on his blog regarding the "Bright Young Things" line. He stated, "I don't want my daughter to ever think that her self-worth and acceptance by others is based on the choice of her undergarments. I don't want my daughter to ever think that to be popular or even attractive she has to have emblazoned words on her bottom." In less than a week the blog was visited 3.5 million times (Radley 2013).

In an effort to stop the damage to its reputation, Victoria Secret's contacted some of the companies that were hosting FORCE's and Mommy Lobby's information online, such as Facebook and Pinterest, to try to convince them to deny service to the challenging groups. The corporation tried to defend itself from the growing criticism electronically in another way: on its website Victoria's Secret claimed that the line of underwear and the advertising campaign was aimed and eighteen- to twenty-two-year-olds. However, the CEO of the company, behind closed doors at a conference, was recorded admitting the truth behind the marketing strategy. He stated, "When somebody's fifteen or sixteen years old, what do they want to be? They want to be older, and they want to be cool like the girl in college, and that's part of the magic power of PINK" (Arnowitz 2013). Protesters used this remark to further shame the company.

SlutWalks is another online campaign that embrace contentious activities to combat rape. In January of 2011, a police officer in Toronto, while speaking to university students, made a callous comment that "women should avoid dressing like sluts in order to not be victimized by rape" (Sonakshi 2011). In response feminist activists organized protests in more than seventy-five cities across the world. The group's Facebook pages explains, "When we began SlutWalk, it was in our city as a response to a specific dynamic in Toronto and we had a very specific goal in mind: to demand better from protective services and institutions in our city of Toronto; we wanted to loudly and fiercely fight victim-blaming and slut-shaming mentalities and ideas that persistently circulate around sexual assault in our city" (Gilmore 2011).

The events were not exclusive to women. Some men marched in solidarity with female SlutWalkers carrying signs that said, "She shouldn't have to hang out with me just to feel safe" (Gilmore 2011). This is an excellent example of successful framing—projecting how collective identity is forged across gender lines based on a perceived shared status and potential risks. Framing the issue this way allowed the campaign to be translated into widespread grievances among the general public, not just women.

A protest sign reading, "I was wearing pants + a sweater, was it my fault too?" taken during SlutWalk 2012.

SlutWalks demonstrate that social movement actors often build on what other activists have done before them, and they sometimes borrow their tactics and strategies to further their own ends. As the lesbian, gay, bisexual, and transsexual movement did with the word "queer," for example, the SlutWalkers took ownership of a derogatory word and reappropriated it with an empowering connotation—one that makes the statement that they will dress as they see fit and should be able to do so without the fear of rape. And, more importantly, if an assault does occur, women cannot be blamed for the attack because of their attire. Whereas this appropriation took years for lesbian, gay, and transsexual activists to accomplish, with the facilitation of social media, feminists were able to reappropriate the world slut almost instantaneously (Gibson 2013).

On the other side of the world, demonstrations against rape in India drew international attention to the country's epidemic of violence against women, who historically have been viewed and treated as second-class citizens (Prasad and Nandakumar 2012). An even broader issue and a reflection of the devaluation of females in much of India is the high level of infanticide of girls. Currently in India there are 1,000 boys for every 927 girls, the most unbalanced rate since 1947 (Westcott 2014). Also demonstrative of a lack of respect for women, a female is raped every thirty minutes in the country, according to the Commonwealth Human Rights Initiative (Westcott 2014), and rape is the fourth-most reported crime against Indian women—though many rapes go unreported because of the shame that this brings not only to the individual victim but also to her family (Kumar 1993). The rape of young girls (minors under the age of eighteen) is particularly disturbing. For example, whereas in the United States minors comprise 17.4 percent of all rape victims, the rate is 33 percent in India (Troup-Leasure and Snyder 2005). Since the 1990s rape has increased by 240 percent, and there is speculation that rape is a backlash against women working outside the home and therefore becoming more economically and socially independent and also more visible (Shiva 2013).

In one recent event a twenty-three-year-old woman was gang-raped on a bus for hours and later died as a consequence. Thousands of demonstrators took to the streets a few days later outside the Parliament building and residence of the president. Authorities responded with aggression and violence by shutting down the capital, blockading roads, and using fire hoses, tear gas, and batons to disperse the crowds (Yardley 2012).

The demonstrators organized protests through social media that transformed into occupations of public spaces. On Twitter, "Rashtrapati Bhavan," which in English translates as "presidential palace," became a top-trending text in response to police brutality against the peaceful protesters. As later events unfolded, some of the most popular Google searches over the perusing weeks were "Delhi gang rape," "Rape in Delhi," and "gang-rape victim" (Prasad and Nandakumar 2012). Organizers of the resistance also started an online petition on Change.org called "President CJI: Stop Rape Now!" It called for President Pranab Mukherjee and Chief Justice Altmas Dabir, to intervene and take immediate action against the rapists, and it received more than 65,000 signatures (Lakshmi 2013). Additionally, activists created nearly a dozen Facebook pages in support of the cause. The "aurat Bandndh" page called on women to go on strike from any work- or family-related responsibilities for a day, thus dramatizing how women, though critical to the functioning of society, are still viewed as inferior in the eyes of many Indian citizens, consequently making them victims of intimidation and sexual violence (Prasad and Nandakumar 2012).

Protests and demonstrations continued to escalate because of the inept handling of the situation by the government—a government that was already alienated from youth culture and the media through which they dialogue (Lakshmi 2013). The damage to its reputation through shaming tactics filtered into the mainstream press and beyond through electronic formats. The news magazine *India Today*, for example, featured an article entitled "Clueless in Blunderland" that explained the debacle. It read, "While the young demonstrators were screaming their lungs out, old politicians were still wondering whether they should clear their throats" (Prasad and Nandakumar 2012). Hence, in India there was a digital divide, a generational divide, and a gender divide.

Another tragic rape-related event in India put the spotlight on the government even more brightly and critically: in April 2013 a five-year-old girl was tortured and raped. The Asian Center for Human Rights attests that between 2001 and 2011 there were 48,338 cases of child rape (Mahindra 2012). This case led to more massive protests that were organized online, and the demands and grievances were consistent with those discussed in the previous incident: more protection for women and more serious penalties for sex crimes. Hundreds stormed the police headquarters in New Delhi, demanding the resignation of the police commissioner because of a police response that was deemed too slow, dismissive, and far too inadequate. When the parents of the child tried to file a missing persons report, for example, the officers did not even register the case. Eventually, the government did respond to these protests and to the agitation related to the rape case of the twenty-three-year-old as well. It passed tougher laws that include the death penalty for repeat sex offenders or if the victim dies as a result of the attack (Gardner 2013).

In another gender-related issue that received significant media attention, in 2011 a young Saudi Arabian woman, Manal al-Sharif, called for a protest in June to oppose the restrictions on female drivers. Saudi Arabia is the only country in the world that does not allow women to drive. She put forth her call to action in April with a Facebook page. Prior to the protest, however, al-Sharif posted videos of herself driving through the town of Al Khobar and was subsequently arrested and jailed for nine days. Supporters posted more than 30,000 comments about her appeal

Social media was an extremely important tool for the young Saudi women who, in 2011, organized a protest against their country's restrictions on female drivers. It not only helped spread the message but created a virtual collective identity that would have been nearly impossible to create on the streets.

and arrest on Twitter within just a few days of her arrest. Social media was essential in not only spreading her message but also in gaining support for her cause and creating collective identity, if only virtually. This is because public gatherings are illegal in Saudi Arabia and women are strictly forbidden to publicly communicate with unrelated men or even to meet with individuals outside their family (Mahanta 2011).

The online distribution of the firsthand accounts quickly reached a critical mass and sparked furor and motivation among Saudis, as well as women in other countries, to agitate for the broadening of women's rights. The campaign drew international attention, and US citizens organized a petition drive on Change.org. More than 10,000 people signed an open letter to Secretary of State Hillary Clinton, encouraging her to publicly support giving Saudi women the right to drive, which she did (Mahanta 2011). The fact that Clinton, at the time, was holding a high-ranking position within the US government and that the United States is a close ally of

Saudi Arabia, gave supporters of the cause both legitimacy and leverage to sway public opinion in their favor.

DIGITAL WHISTLE-BLOWING AND THE EXPANSION
OF THE PUBLIC SPHERE

Digital capabilities have also redefined whistle-blowing, and whistle-blower groups are in fact helping to expand the public sphere. One such group is Lulz Security, or LulzSec, a global hacker collective that emerged as a spin-off of Anonymous. The entity has released many "data dumps" and, like Anonymous, goes beyond mere pranks to expose what members perceive to be fundamental flaws in economic, political, and legal systems (BBC 2011). In one instance it targeted Arizona for being a "racial-profiling, anti-immigrant police state." Participants released private intelligence bulletins, training manuals, personal e-mail correspondence, names, phone numbers, addresses, and passwords that belonged to members of Arizona state law enforcement (Estes 2011). On its Twitter account LulzSec posted this press statement regarding the leak of the Arizona documents: "We are releasing hundreds of private intelligence bulletins, training manuals, personal email correspondence, names, phone numbers, addresses, and passwords belonging to Arizona law enforcement. We are targeting AZDPS specifically because we are against SB1070 and the racial profiling anti-immigration police state that is Arizona" (Chapman 2011).The group has also attacked Sony Pictures Entertainment, the US Senate, and the Central Intelligence Agency (CIA). In June 2011 the group declared it was disbanding but would individually operate as hackers under a variety of other banners (Sengupta and Bilton 2011). LulzSec's online handbook includes tips on how hackers can safeguard their identity by avoiding websites that track online activity and how to disguise their Internet provider (Sengupta and Bilton 2011).

WikiLeaks is another leaderless and now well-known organization that was established in 2006 when a handful of anonymous individuals associated with the group published classified information and demanded more transparency regarding government policy. The website describes the organization this way: "WikiLeaks is a non-profit media organization dedicated to bringing important news and information to the public. . . . We publish material of ethical, political and historical significance while keeping the identity of our sources anonymous, thus providing a universal way for the revealing of suppressed and censored injustices." Embodying the grassroots and revolutionary mission of the group, and its disgust with mainstream media's coverage of events, founder (and spokesperson but not leader) Julian Assange asks, "How is it that a team of five people has managed to release to the public more suppressed information than the rest of the world combined? It is disgraceful" (*Christian Science Monitor* 2012).

WikiLeaks has ultimately redefined whistle-blowing by gathering secrets and then releasing them instantly and globally. It first distributed thousands of restricted US diplomatic cables first on its own website and then made them available in its archives for download through peer-to-peer sharing (Agence France Presse 2012). Its disclosure of thousands of US government documents showed hackers that they could use their skills to participate in a new way in the public sphere, serving as a driving force in the transformation of journalism in the digital age.

One of the most revealing reports was classified video depicting US troops shooting civilians (including two Reuters reporters) in Iraq from an Apache helicopter in July of 2007 and then celebrating the attack. The video, available at www.collateralmurder.com was published on April 5, 2010. Chelsea (formerly known as Bradley) Manning, the US officer who leaked the government documents, uploaded around 700,000 classified US military and diplomatic documents to WikiLeaks, which then made them available to a select few news outlets. She explained in court that she initially tried to deliver the documents to the *Washington Post* and the *New York Times* because she was disturbed about the "inhumane treatment of Iraqis and Afghanis at the hands of U.S. troops," but when they declined she sent the trove of material to WikiLeaks anonymously, thereby stepping into the role that print journalism declined to perform (Davis 2012).

Manning was arrested in May 2010 after confessing that she was responsible for the leak. Charges include aiding the enemy, stealing US government property, and computer crimes. Hundreds of supporters gathered on December 17, 2011, outside the US military base where evidence against her was presented before a military judge, and globally fifty protests took place in her support (Davis 2012). In early August 2013 she was found guilty of twenty of the charges, but not the most serious one of aiding the enemy, al Qaeda (Quelly 2013).

Manning's prosecution poses fundamental questions regarding the constitutional rights of US citizens to expose crimes committed by those holding office, and underlying this are concerns about free speech, dialogue, and debate (Hedges 2013). Following the verdict Julian Assange made the following statement: "This the first ever espionage case against a whistleblower. It is a dangerous precedent and an example of national security extremism. . . . It can never be that conveying true information to the public is 'espionage.' . . . In 2008 presidential candidate Barack Obama ran on a platform that praised whistleblowing as an act of courage and patriotism. That platform has been comprehensively betrayed. His campaign document described whistleblowers as watchdogs when government abuses its authority. It was removed from the Internet last week" (McGreal 2010).

The response to WikiLeaks from government officials and other political elites was sharp and targeted, calling for retaliation. Pentagon spokesperson Geoff Morell condemned the leaks, arguing that the release of classified material was a "gift to terrorist's organizations" (Assange 2012). Former Alaska governor Sarah Palin labeled WikiLeaks "an anti-American operative with blood on its hands whom we should pursue with the same urgency we pursue al Qaeda and Taliban leaders" (Corn 2010). Representative Peter King of New York called it a "terrorist organization," and former Connecticut senator Joe Lieberman stated that it "has violated the Espionage Act." In a similar vein, Secretary of State Hillary Clinton said that the leaked cables would "sabotage peaceful relations between countries" (Assange 2012).

The site was eventually forced to change its domain name and switch to various servers around the globe to avoid prosecution. Many financial institutions including Bank of America, Visa, MasterCard, and PayPal refused to process any transactions for WikiLeaks. As a reprisal for caving in to government pressure, Anonymous launched a DDoS, Operation Payback, which crippled all of them (Addley and Halliday 2010). This reaction underscores how powerful this new repertoire is given the perceived threat among the authorities of the expansion of the public sphere.

Another case that raises intriguing questions regarding digital whistle-blowing is that of Edward Snowden. He formerly worked for both the CIA and the National Security Agency, and in 2013 he released a series of classified documents to the mainstream media, which is now considered the most important leak in the history of whistle-blowing in the United States (Savage 2013). What he divulged was the extent of the National Security Agency's intrusive surveillance programs, which had the consent of the federal government. Similar to the Manning whistle-blowing situation, the perception of his actions has been polarized both nationally and internationally. Some are calling for amnesty under the First and Fourth Amendments. Others are rallying for him being convicted of treason.

He was charged with espionage in June of 2013 by the Department of Justice, and his passport has been revoked by the Department of State. He is currently in Russia and seeking asylum from a number of countries (Savage 2013). Those who support amnesty launched a "We the People" petition on the official White House website asking for him to be pardoned, securing 100,000 signatures in less than two weeks (Bimber and Davis 2013). As a follow-up event and to keep the case in the public eye, in October 2013 activists organized a demonstration in the Capitol with a rallying theme of "stop watching us" to protest surveillance by the federal government (Campbell 2014)

The polarization continues, and Snowden's fate is yet to be resolved. Interestingly, despite his ostracism from certain circles, Snowden was voted as the *Guardian*'s Person of the Year in 2013 and was named *Time* magazine's Person of the Year runner-up that same year. Additionally, a movie entitled *Classified: The Edward Snowden Story* is slated for release in the fall of 2014 (Campbell 2014).

CONCLUSION

ICTs are greatly affecting how people mobilize for political, social, and economic causes at the grassroots level. New forms of hacktivism, website parodies (or memes), cyberactivism, and digital whistle-blowing are all being used to challenge political and economic elites, and they serve as important political resources. Perhaps most importantly, the WikiLeaks and Snowden cases bring to light ways in which digital whistle-blowing is changing the face of journalism, disseminating information to the public that the mainstream press has failed to—or decided not to—cover.

DISCUSSION QUESTIONS

1. What are the different types of cyberactivism? In what ways are they similar to or distinct from social movements as defined in the introduction? How does digital whistle-blowing affect the legal and political landscape? Research other whistle-blowing endeavors that have taken place in cyberspace, and discuss the results.

2. Aside from the groups discussed in this chapter, research online groups that use various forms of hacktivism or memes. What causes do they support? In your assessment, have they been affective?

3. In the struggle for women's rights, how has new media served as an ally? Investigate other instances of gender- or rape-related cases that have implications for the way that we think about and use social media.

4. Look up ways that cyberbullying is now a prominent issue in our society. How do the themes in this chapter relate to what you discover?

CHAPTER THREE

MoveOn.org and the Tea Party

This chapter examines two SMOs, or, as we will see, what can more accurately be described as **social movement communities** (a term that Wollenberg et al. 2006 use). They are on opposite ends of the political spectrum: MoveOn.org, which is a left-wing organization that advocates for progressive causes, and the Tea Party, which is a conservative entity that is more reactionary in its agenda.

In a snapshot, MoveOn.org is known as one of the original and most successful digital public policy advocacy groups. It has been hailed for its pioneering tactics in support of progressive issues, and it raises large amounts of money to support Democratic candidates. MoveOn.org is made up of MoveOn.org Civic Action, which is a 501(c)(4) nonprofit corporation, and MoveOn Civic Action, which focuses on education and advocacy as they pertain to national issues. It also has a federal political action committee that contributes to the campaigns of many candidates across the country.

The Tea Party arrived later on the scene and in some ways, like MoveOn.org, resembles a social movement community more than a formal social movement in the typical sense, though its structure is more disparate and harder to classify. In essence, the Tea Party is an umbrella organization, an amalgam of somewhat loosely connected groups that consist mainly of libertarians, religious conservatives, independents, and some citizens new to politics who are frustrated with the contemporary political landscape. What unites the various groups is a shared, yet loosely held, set of beliefs. They are sometimes linked to national organizations such as the Tea Party Express and the Tea Party Nation, though they mostly operate independently (Williamson, Skocpol, and Coggin 2011). Other associated groups operate exclusively online, such as the National Tea Party Federation, whose goal is to enhance and facilitate communication among the various groups affiliated with the Tea Party.

These two very different organizations give us some important insights into contemporary forms of social movement organizing in the United States that cut across both contentious and institutional politics. Both groups rely on some traditional methods that have been used in previous social movements, while concomitantly adopting other more innovative tactics. They demonstrate that what is often perceived as a zero-sum game between new and old activism is a false dichotomy: online and offline activism often reinforce each other. There are strong similarities between the organizational structure of MoveOn and the Tea Party as well as the combination of online and offline strategies they employ—they are both hybrids of sorts when it comes to promoting social change. This chapter invites us to think theoretically and conceptually about what constitutes a social movement in the digital age, which subsequently raises questions as to how to best theorize the tactics and strategies of nuanced groups such as these.

Furthermore, a central concern of this chapter is how online sharing of information and e-activism lead to mobilization on the ground, or the spillover effect. We consider whether virtual activism replaces, complements, or has no effect on concrete forms of participation for social and political change.

A comparison of the two groups also raises the question of how to define grassroots organizations and their relationship to the public sphere, or communicative action, as posed by Habermas (1993, 1989). Chapter 1 noted his concerns about the shrinking role of the public sphere with the onset of television and the encroachment of professional experts (elites in the media and other major corporations) and contended that they have come to dominate public dialogue and debate, and civil society in general. However, the arrival of the Internet and digital technology prompts us to update his theory as the old top-down and hierarchal structures and modes of communication are being challenged, in some ways, by grassroots entities. MoveOn and some of the Tea Party groups are examples of

MoveOn's model for electronic recruitment shows how "weak" virtual ties can lead to activism in the streets.

Castells's (2001) informational politics that result in the electronic grass-rooting of democracy.

MOVEON.ORG

MoveOn emerged in the late 1990s in cyberspace via an online petition. In 1998, during the height of the Monica Lewinsky scandal, Silicon Valley computer entrepreneurs Wes Boyd and Joan Blades created an online petition that called on Congress to censure but not impeach President Clinton. Boyd e-mailed it to thirty friends, and within two weeks more than half a million people had signed the petition (Bennet and Fielding 1999). A few years later he heard from Eli Pariser, who had created an online petition urging moderation and restraint in responding to the September 11 terrorist acts. This petition also exploded in popularity, and at Boyd's suggestion the two merged their websites, and MoveOn.org was born (Markels 2003). The organization currently has more than 5 million members, and its running slogan is "Democracy in Action."

MoveOn's main strategy is to activate people on a few different issues at a time, often for short durations as legislative battles change, and this model allows it to play an important role as a campaign aggregator—inviting people in on a particular issue and then introducing them to additional issues (Markels 2003). According to Boyd, what unites MoveOn activists is support for progressive issues and a different type of politics, and the Internet is an essential tool for staying politically connected.

The organizational features of MoveOn are representative of contemporary social movements as theorized by new social movement theorists such as Melucci (1996): they are constituted by loosely articulated networks that permit multiple memberships and part-time participation, and there is little if any distinction between leaders and rank-and-file members, members and nonmembers, and private and public roles. MoveOn is often members' first step into political action, and what brings them to take that step is typically an e-mail message sent from one of the organizers or forwarded from a family member, friend, or colleague. This resonates with Castells's (2001) concept of informational politics and Giugni's (1998) research on the importance of electronic forms of communication among trusted sources that would-be participants in a social or political cause may not receive otherwise. For many members contributing money to a candidate or a political ad in response to an e-mail is the first time they participate in politics outside of voting (Boyd 2003).

MoveOn's success also highlights the importance of flexible and contingent forms of (wired) collective identity that developing theories of new media address, in particular Giugni's work noted above. Pariser explains:

> Every member comes to us with the personal endorsement of someone they trust. It is word-of-mouth organizing in electronic form. It has made mixing the personal and political more socially acceptable. Casually passing on a high-content message to a social acquaintance feels completely natural in a way handing someone a leaflet at a cocktail party never would. The "tell-a-friend" phenomenon is key to how organizing happens on the Net. A small gesture to a friend can contribute to a massive multiplier effect. It is a grassroots answer to the corporate consolidation of the media. (Boyd 2003)

As the statement shows, the way information is sent, received, and accessed represents a more pluralistic, fluid, and issue-oriented group politics among many contemporary activists that theories of new media, as well as theories of new social movements, recognize. Members and organizers of contemporary forms of collective behavior increasingly operate outside of state-regulated and corporate-dominated media and rely on innovative actions mainly mediated across electronic networks. These in turn enable new forms communicative action that assist in recruitment efforts and can result in concrete forms of mobilization. This exemplifies the grassrooting of civil society that Castells (2001) describes, and it is also illustrative of H. Jenkins's (2006) conceptualization of the importance of civic media in participatory democracy and the spillover effect. These new outlets for organizing can help update resource mobilization theory and illustrate how collective identity is established in new ways, thus calling for a modification of cultural theories to account for weak ties that lend to activism in the streets.

New Technology Campaigns

In terms of campaigns, from its inception, MoveOn's website has distributed e-mail action alerts that inform its members of important current events and has provided petitions and contact information of members' elected officials so that members can respond to those events. Its first campaign supported candidates running against impeachment backers. In 1999, in less than twelve weeks, it signed up over 500,000 supporters and received pledges of $13 million (Burress 2003). As a great example of e-activism, in June of that same year it set records for online fundraising by collecting more than $250,000 in five days, mostly in individual donations under $50 (Potter 2003).

Once the Clinton impeachment trial ended, MoveOn centered much of its energy on the peace movement in the wake of the 9–11 attacks. It hosted the online headquarters for the Virtual March on Washington—an act of online civil disobedience to protest the imminent invasion of Iraq. It was sponsored by the WinWithoutWar Coalition, which serves as an online umbrella organization for the peace movement. Using e-mail connections to coordinate and organize a protestor base, on February

26, 2003, more than 200,000 individuals signed up and made more than 400,000 phone calls and sent 100,000 faxes to every senate office in the United States with the message DON'T ATTACK IRAQ! (MoveOn 2004). Every member of the US Senate also received a stream of e-mails, clogging virtual mailboxes in Washington, DC.

Another tactic MoveOn has used repeatedly as part of its repertoire is candlelight vigils, organized completely online. The March 16 vigils against the pending invasion of Iraq involved more than one million people in more than 6,000 gatherings in 130 countries and were organized in six days by MoveOn over the Internet (Stewart 2003). The online resource Meetup made the event possible, speeding the flow of politics, what Bimber (2003) refers to as accelerated politics. MoveOn's fundraising ability also contributed to the antiwar effort. In less than one week, members raised $37,000 over the Internet to run an advertisement in the *New York Times* on December 11, 2002, thus using alternative media to infiltrate mainstream media in an effort to influence public opinion. In February 2003 MoveOn solicited donations to raise $75,000 in just two hours to place an antiwar advertisement on billboards in four major American cities with a similar message (Stewart 2003).

Although resource mobilization theory has always directed attention to the need for financial backing for political mobilizing efforts, typically the assumption was that most of this would consist of large sums of money from organizations or wealthy individuals. With new technology, however, organizers of a political campaign can instead, as this example shows, raise large sums of money through relatively small donations, and quickly, through word-of-mouth sharing of information online. This beckons us to modify resource mobilization theory to account for these new digital tactics for garnering resources.

After the invasion of Iraq began, MoveOn members petitioned their congressional representatives to continue the inspections for weapons of mass destruction. More than one million signatures were collected in less than five days and were delivered to the UN Security Council. Signatory names and comments were also sent to the petitioners' respective congressional representatives. Additionally, on a single day 200,000 people called their representatives, and, in the run-up to the Senate vote on the Iraq resolution in October of 2003, MoveOn volunteers met face to face with every US senator with "Let the Inspections Work" petitions (Utne

2003). The organization also started to more aggressively engage in political campaigns, urging its supporters to donate money to Democratic House and Senate members who had opposed the Iraq resolution.

In sum, during the above campaigns MoveOn excelled at garnering available resources, people, and computer skills to increase sociopolitical awareness, influence public opinion, mobilize citizens and network with other SMOs, and help elect progressive candidates. It did so by using new technology to tap into submerged networks that could participate in Internet-mediated forms of civic engagement. Therefore, theories of new media best explain the success of MoveOn. Resource mobilization theory also informs our understanding of new groups such as MoveOn.org with its attention to traditional resources that activists have at their disposal such as labor power, financial backing, and support of allies and influential elites.

Cultural and Symbolic Tactics: Combining New and Traditional Media

Cultural and symbolic forms of political expression, as advocated by cultural theorists of social movements and certain strands of the new social movement school of thought, are viewed as key variables to a social movement's success. These tactics played another central role in MoveOn's repertoire of contention.

For example, the group used celebrities for political purposes. One of the group's first interactions with Hollywood came when filmmaker and cofounder of Artists United to Win Without War Robert Greenwald organized celebrities to join the Virtual March on Washington (Brownstein 2004).

Over one hundred celebrities joined as members of this group, including Matt Damon, Martin Sheen, and Mike Farrell. One of the most direct and visible forms of protest occurred when filmmaker Michael Moore spoke out against the war at his acceptance speech at the 2003 Oscars only a few days after the invasion: "We live in a time where we have a man sending us to war for fictitious reasons. Whether it's the fictitious duct tape or the fictitious orange alerts, we are against this war. Mr. Bush. Shame on you. Mr. Bush, shame on you" (Zakarin 2013). That same night at the Oscars ceremony, Susan Sarandon and Tim Robbins flashed peace signs to photographers. Actor Sean Penn went even further in resisting the war by traveling to Iraq in 2002. On his return he commented, "I cannot conceive of any reason why the American people and the world would not have shared with the Iraqis the evidence of the claim to have weapons of mass destruction. I think that the more information we push for, the more information we are given, the better off we are all going to be, and the right thing will happen" (Zakarin 2013).

Other celebrities who traveled internationally also spoke out against the impending invasion. For example, actor Dustin Hoffman publicized his displeasure during an awards ceremony in London, claiming, "This war is about what most wars are about: hegemony, money, power and oil." In Berlin actor Richard Gere spoke out as well, saying, "We have to say 'stop,' there's no reason for a war. At the moment, Hussein is not threatening anybody" (Zakarin 2013). Perhaps the most radical departure from the US government's agenda was the country music trio the Dixie Chicks at a concert in London. Lead singer Natalie Maines opined that she was "ashamed" that President Bush was also from Texas, where she was born and raised. Upon return to the United States, several country stations refused to play the Dixie Chicks' music in retaliation for her remarks.

MoveOn also has given substantial financial support to a number of Greenwald's films and documentaries to promote more independent and critical voices outside of mainstream and corporate-dominated media. Its website offered his *Uncovered: The Next War on Iraq* DVD as a premium to members who pledged thirty dollars or more, and approximately 8,000 individuals made pledges within the first three hours. More than 2,600 members hosted screenings in their homes and at community venues, and the movie was ultimately distributed in theaters across the country (Deans 2004).

House parties are another innovative tactic MoveOn uses to broaden the public sphere and the realm of civil society by combining the private and public spheres. It also adds to the explanatory power of theories that focus on the importance of collective identity (for example Snow et al. 1986; Benford 1993) and of morally and ethically based reasons for participation in collective behavior that some of the new social movement theories recognize (Giddens 1991; Tomlinson 1999; Johnston 1994). A few years later MoveOn provided free copies of Greenwald's *Iraq for Sale* and *The Ground Truth* documentaries for members to show at house parties. After viewing the films attendees made phone calls and wrote letters to

House parties are an innovative tactic MoveOn uses that broadens the public sphere and the realm of civil society by combining the private and public spheres.

voters. MoveOn also helped Greenwald finance *Outfoxed: Rupert Murdoch's War on Journalism*. Taking advantage of the mainstream media, it also took out a full-page ad in the *New York Times* declaring, "The Communists had *Pravda*. Republicans have Fox" (Deans 2004).

In other cases various directors and film producers helped MoveOn construct homemade advertisements once sufficient funds were raised by its members. The "Real People" ads, for instance, were created by documentary filmmaker Errol Morris and featured ordinary members of the Republican Party explaining why they were crossing party lines to vote for Democratic nominee John Kerry (Deans 2004). This was the first time both the content and the funding for an ad campaign came from the grassroots membership of an organization, typical of social movement communities operating without an established vanguard (Wollenberg et al. 2006). The "Bush in 30 Seconds" ads challenging administration policies were shown during his State of the Union address. Grammy-nominated musician Moby helped to design them, held a competition for members to submit ads, and recruited a panel of celebrity judges that culminated in an awards show in New York City to raise funds for other anti-Bush television ads (Stevenson 2004).

This example shows us that the roles of leaders, spokespersons, formal SMOs, and elite allies—all of which played a prominent role in the development of the resource mobilization framework—are less relevant for many contemporary mobilizations. Theories of new media and some components of the new social movement school of thought are more useful because they highlight the decentralized and more egalitarian structure of today's contentious politics (Melucci 1996 most directly brings this to our attention). Also helpful is Mann's (2000) conception of the interstitial location, where activists promote their agendas outside the formal political system and traditional institutions.

The organization and its supporters also combatted infringement of corporate and elite domination of the cultural sphere in the fight against censorship when theaters across the United States were being pressured by right-wing groups to bar *Fahrenheit 9/11*, Michael Moore's controversial film. It asked members to pledge to see the film on opening night with other members to send a message to theater owners that the public supports Moore's message of peace (Moveon.org, e-mail to all members). Bridging the offline and online worlds and combining entertainment with serious political discussion, more than 4,600 parties were thrown across the United States, and at each Moore spoke to members over the Internet about his movie and his hope they would each bring at least five nonvoters to the polls for the upcoming November 2004 election (Brownstein 2004). This novelty bridges entertainment, activism, and institutional politics.

During the ten-week Don't Get Mad, Get Even! events preceding the 2004 election, MoveOn and America Coming Together held rallies and rock concerts that incorporated celebrity appearances by artists, authors, and actors. As part of the Rock the Vote tour, they jointly held a concert in New York City right before the Republican National Convention that featured rock stars such as Bruce Springsteen, the Dave Mathews Band, Pearl Jam, REM, the Dixie Chicks, Jackson Browne, and John Mellencamp. Some MoveOn members threw house parties to watch the concert, at which members wrote letters to swing-state voters. Additionally, relying on mainstream media platforms, "Don't Get Mad, Get Even!" television advertisements featured celebrity activists such as Matt Damon, Rob Reiner, Woody Harrelson, and Al Franken (Carty 2010).

Thus, MoveOn combines conventional forms of organizing with more nuanced tactics. Rock concerts that support their cause, pledging to view

Michael Moore's film, and throwing house parties each serve to open up the public sphere more broadly to ordinary citizens (which Habermas feared we are losing to corporate and elite control) and are also displays of symbolic forms of protest. With this in mind, we can modify some of Habermas's theory to account for new tactics, many of them aided by new technology (for example, the organization of house parties through web-based tools). Parts of new social movement theories help in our assessment of how MoveOn operates as these kinds of activities also serve to politicize new areas of social life.

Bridging Online and Offline Activism

MoveOn continued its grassroots mobilization during the 2006 midterm election. Recognizing the essential role of on-the-ground (public) efforts to complement e-activism, it trained and supported volunteers on the ground to organize rapid responses to events and to hold news conferences, editorial board meetings, and rallies to target vulnerable Republican incumbents. As both political-process and political-mediation scholars would suggest (for instance Meyer 2005; Tarrow 2001; Soule and King 2006), politicians are vulnerable during election years and swaying public opinion is key, and these two theories assist us in clarifying MoveOn's strategizing. According to a Yale University study, the emphasis on face-to-face voter mobilization through social networks increased turnout by seven percentage points (Middleton and Green 2007). Prior to the election MoveOn members held more than 6,000 actions in these districts and organized 7,500 house parties (MoveOn 2007 annual report).

Members also donated enough money to establish the Call for Change program that used web-based tools and a call-reporting system to reach voters. Once again circumventing professional pollsters (and once again Mann's [2000] interstitial locations is fitting here), the web-based "liquid phone bank" allowed MoveOn members to call from wherever they lived into wherever they were needed within a day or two. Middleton and Green (2007) found that the phone bank was the most effective volunteer calling program ever studied and that it increased voter turnout by almost 4 percent.

Also during the 2006 election, a successful framing approach allowed MoveOn to combine parody and serious political discourse. Cultural as well as new social movement theories (Gamson 1992) that evaluate the effectiveness of social movement activity by their framing of issues are applicable here. For example, activists deployed the metaphor of being caught red-handed by displaying giant foam red hands and signs as they followed their representatives to town hall meetings, appearances, and fundraisers, questioning their allegiance to special interests. In Virginia Beach, members attended every Coffee with Thelma event that Representative Thelma Drake held and asked questions about her allegiance to special interests. In Louisville, Kentucky, members rallied at a gas station to tell voters about Representative Ann Northup's ties to big oil with flyers describing war profiteering. Members in Fayetteville, North Carolina, attended a defense contractor tradeshow that Representative Robin Hayes sponsored. During this campaign alone local media wrote more than 2,000 stories about MoveOn's actions (MoveOn.org 2008 annual report), and, of the nine long-shot races members targeted, five won. As an overall tally, in 2006 Democrats supported by MoveOn lost four and won eighteen races, which helped build a Democratic majority in the Senate (Center for Responsive Politics 2006).

The red-handed campaign represents what MoveOn does best—framing issues in a way that resonates with voters and taps into their frustration, using humorous and innovative techniques by employing diagnostic and prognostic framing (Snow et al. 1986). Its success at harnessing popular entertainment to broadcast alternative voices, whether in the form of rock concerts, fundraisers, Bush-bashing ads, publicity stunts, or supporting alternative forms of media, and doing this jointly with representatives of the artistic community, is something MoveOn has excelled at.

The Importance of Social Media

As MoveOn evolves and relies on new resources and tactics, new media are becoming increasingly important to understanding how it now operates. The group still uses e-mail extensively but now also relies heavily on other forms of social media. In response to the negative ads against President Obama by Republican Super PACs that played out on television during the 2012 elections, for example, MoveOn stated in a March 1 e-mail,

Over the last year we've been quietly developing a groundbreaking plan to counter these lies through social media sites like Facebook and Twitter—where millions of people now get their news, bypassing the corporate media. The results so far have been amazing. There have been 65 million views in the last year. We increased our web traffic tenfold. And we tripled our audience of Facebook fans who can spread the word. But to counter Fox's lies this election we need to raise $200,000 to pay for the researchers, editors and developers necessary to ramp up.

A link was included at the end of the e-mail asking members to chip in fifteen dollars to help fund the efforts.

MoveOn's recent strategizing has some theoretical implications for our understanding of contentious politics. It illustrates that people are now receiving news through sources outside of corporate-dominated media, and the news that they are receiving through digital outlets such as Facebook and Twitter is being shared in a horizontal fashion, through peer-to-peer networks. Therefore, SMOs' direction of social movement activity and dispersion of information is being complemented by these informal and decentralized hubs of activity, informing us how we can update resource mobilization theory put forth by Tilly (1978) and McCarthy and Zald (1973). We can complement this work with recent analyses that incorporate theories that focus on new media. Most prominently, Castells's (2001) notion of an explosive informational politics and grass-rooting of democracy, McAdam and Paulsen's (1993) recognition of the importance of weak social ties forged in the virtual sphere that spread information about mobilization efforts in support of a cause, Bimber's (2003) reference to accelerated pluralism, and Kahn and Kellner's (2003) emphasis on the importance of virtual public spheres in initiating and sustaining momentum for social movement activity all come into play.

Another e-mail read, "This is the strategy. Every day, a team of 50 of MoveOn volunteer editors will collect the most timely and persuasive progressive news and opinion from around the web. Graphics debunking Republican lies about the economy. Live video coverage of the Occupy movement. . . . Then we'll push the most timely and persuasive stuff out to hundreds of thousands of people, who share it with millions more. We believe that people-powered media, funded by people like us, can be a secret weapon against the conservative noise machine" (March 9, 2012). This statement further indicates how reliant social movement actors are on web-based tools to share information, create a critical mass of support through peer-to-peer sharing, and create new sources of collective identity and community, thus broadening the public sphere on which much of Habermas's (1989, 1993) theorizing is based. It also supports Bennett and Iyengar's (2008) claims that new forms of grassroots civic engagement though online forms of communication can be resistant to state and corporate regulation.

MoveOn continued its distribution videos that spoof serious political challenges during the 2012 presidential election. It launched a video, "Mitt's Office," in which actor Justin Long played Mitt Romney—depicting him as caring only about the 1 percent. The e-mail that disseminated it asked members to share the video with friends and family on Facebook or via e-mail (December 26, 2012). That same month it asked members to protest laws that would restrict voter registration drives and early voting and require voters to present photo IDs at the polls, and it urged them to donate money to try to prevent the laws from passing (January 13, 2013). Supporters protested outside of federal courthouses to contest the ruling on *Citizens United* (which allowed corporations, as well as unions, to donate undisclosed and unlimited amounts of money to candidates running for office), and MoveOn sent a petition to call on President Obama to sign an executive order that would require corporations that do business with the government to disclose their political spending and declare support for a constitutional amendment to get big money out of politics permanently.

After President Obama announced a federal investigation into Wall Street in his January State of the Union address, an e-mail from MoveOn stated, "This is truly a huge victory for the 99% movement. Hundreds of thousands of us signed petitions, made calls, and held signs outside in the cold to make this issue something that President Obama couldn't ignore. Here's some of what MoveOn members and our allies did to bring about this victory" (January 26, 2012). It went on to note that members engaged in Facebook and Twitter activity, and it included a link where readers could post a message of thanks on the White House Facebook wall. It then stated, "And, we need to keep pushing for more wins for the 99%, including our campaigns to get big money out of politics and tax the rich fairly. . . . MoveOn doesn't get big checks from ban CEOs! So please click here to donate to keep the momentum going" (January 24, 2012).

MoveOn is not as grassroots as it may appear, however. For instance, it works in collaboration with powerful progressive groups such as the American Civil Liberties Union, America United for Change, and United for Peace and Change. Though it does not receive any funding from corporate donors, it has received substantial financial support from international financier George Soros, who spent millions of dollars opposing President George Bush's re-election in 2004 (Drehle 2008). One difference from those funding Tea Party organizations, as we shall see later in the chapter, is that his motivation, as a peace activist, is to support a cause rather than to influence a political party.

In conclusion, MoveOn perhaps can best be conceptualized as a hybrid in terms of its status (part insider/part outsider) and a chameleon in terms of tactics (disruptive yet also engaged in the institutionalized side of the continuum of contentious/institutional politics). Though the social movement organization, or community, emerged as a dissident organization, it eventually evolved into more of a political advocacy group that supports pinpointed candidates for office and operates in an ad hoc fashion without a traditional organizational structure. The case of MoveOn also illustrates that nuanced ICTs have not replaced traditional models of organizing nor replaced activism in the material world. Rather, they have altered the contours of mobilizing strategies and participatory democracy in important ways that vary along the spectrum of contentious and electoral politics. What makes this entity additionally intriguing is the way its online operations allow it to not only straddle the virtual and material spheres in terms of collective identity, organization, and mobilization, but to also engage in both protest and institutional politics.

The case of MoveOn.org leads to the logical question of whether this new type of SMO is an anomaly or can we expect other SMOs to adopt similar ways of organizing and mobilizing. To address this query the next section provides an analysis of the Tea Party, which many view as the conservative counterpart to MoveOn (though it has a more institutionalized structure and forms of financial and strategic backing). An examination of this group allows us to draw some comparisons to, and differences from, MoveOn in terms of agenda and organizational style, and it poses

The multiple groups that constitute the Tea Party have been able to take advantage of current political trends, in part by forming networks with other constituencies.

similar theoretical questions that can aid our understanding of contemporary forms of collective behavior.

THE TEA PARTY

The Tea Party has been compared to MoveOn.org in terms of its organizational structure and the tactics it employs (though as we will see some of these comparisons are not accurate). In fact, FreedomWorks and other groups behind the Tea Party have long declared their intention to create the equivalent to MoveOn. Broadly, TEA (taxed enough already) Partiers hope to spearhead a movement that aims to reduce government spending and taxes, through an umbrella organization made up of various politically conservative groups and factions. It is this ideological connection that fosters a sense of collective identity among the disparate groups and individuals.

The Tea Party is also flexible and at face value, at least, leaderless, as it is composed of unconnected collections of local chapters with varying agendas. This organizational structure clearly resembles that of a new social movement: an assembly of roughly affiliated groups consisting of supporters rather than members in the traditional sense. Wollenberg et al. (2006) refer to these types of organizational structures as "social movement communities" rather than SMOs, and these are also at the forefront of Khan and Kellner's (2003) research on virtual public spheres as well as Bimber's (2003) work on the accelerated pluralism that new ICTs allow for. Therefore, as with MoveOn, we are encouraged to revise and update resource mobilization theory in some ways to account for these new types of horizontal structures, and we should also update cultural theories to understand what constitutes collective identity and how it is created.

In addition to the Tea Party Nation and Tea Party Express affiliations mentioned earlier in this chapter, there are other core groups that represent the interests of Tea Partiers. For example, Tea Party Patriots is a for-profit organization that organizes national conferences. It was born out of resistance to the Wall Street bailouts and what members view as runaway government spending. At the center of its agenda is an endeavor to restore the founding policy of the constitution, limited government control, and a free market economy (Kroll 2012).

Tea Party Express is a political action committee that actively campaigns in support of specific candidates. It is extraordinarily successful in this capacity. According to the Federal Election Committee, it raised $6.6 million during the 2010 midterm elections, making it the single biggest independent supporter of Tea Party candidates (Williamson, Skocpol, and Coggin 2011). Similar to MoveOn's success in the 2006 and 2008 elections, the Tea Party's influence was undeniably decisive in the 2010 elections, as supporters propelled Republicans to huge gains in the House, helped secure Senate victories for some barely known candidates such as Rand Paul, and captured seven hundred seats in state legislatures (Tanenhaus 2012).

The Tea Party's Impact on Electoral Politics

Political process theory (Tarrow 1996; McAdam 1982; C. Jenkins and Perrow 1977) argues that social movement agents have an advantage when the existing political system appears to be vulnerable to challenges, and this is especially true during times of electoral instability. This advantage is further enhanced when opponents can manipulate competition between key figures in the polity. The multiple groups that constitute the Tea Party have been able to take advantage of current political trends, in part by forming networks with other constituencies, and therefore resource mobilization theory is particularly relevant to grasping and assessing the success of the Tea Party.

For example, joining forces with the Campaign to Defeat Barack Obama (a Tea Party–linked political action committee), the Tea Party entered Governor Scott Walker of Wisconsin's recall fight in the wake of his attempt to curtail collective bargaining rights for public workers. Copying MoveOn's example, Tea Party groups used both digital and mainstream media to pursue the cause. Through e-activism it blasted several e-mails to supporters and launched a $100,000 money bomb fundraiser to help defend Walker, and it ran television ads defending his policies (Kroll 2012). In the summer of 2011 Tea Party Nation, together with Tea Party Express, launched a four-day bus tour across Wisconsin defending six Republicans facing recall elections for their roles in the collective bargaining battle (the Walker recall election will be discussed in more detail in a later chapter). Just like MoveOn, the Tea Party groups' use of new information and media technologies is often complemented by contentious politics in the material world.

One of the Tea Party's first successes was when barely known Republican Scott Brown ran a grassroots campaign in the Massachusetts special election to win the seat vacated by Ted Kennedy, which had been held by Democrats since 1978. Resource mobilization theory contributes to our understanding of this victory given the financial backing provided by wealthy Tea Party advocates who used digital means to fundraise. They emulated some of MoveOn's tactics by organizing an online money bomb (raising more than $1 million online in twenty-four hours) and orchestrated an "on the ground" get-out-the-vote campaign (Stauber 2010). This again combined online and offline activism, and it forged institutional and extrainstitutional political activity. In another simulation of MoveOn's approach, through its Take America Back website it offered a web-based call center through which members could talk to voters from anywhere.

Allies as a Key Resource

One of the distinctions between the Tea Party and MoveOn is the Tea Party's reliance on powerful allies (as already noted, the Campaign to

Protesters rally against government taxation and spending policies at the US Capitol on September 12, 2009.

Defeat Barack Obama was key to the struggle in saving Walker's job)—though this is not to deny that MoveOn also has some wealthy financial backers. One of the major groups funding and organizing the Tea Party is FreedomWorks (formerly chaired by Dick Armey, former Republican Speaker of the House). This SMO provides abundant resources in terms of money, advice, knowledge, and personnel to invigorate and sustain the movement. It helped to organize the first Tea Party March on Washington on September 12, 2009, in conjunction with Glenn Beck's 912 projects and the Tax Day Tea Party campaign (such as Fox News) for the event (Bai 2012). It also utilized mainstream media to try to influence public opinion and promote civic engagement. On May 13 Beck launched this project on his Fox News program. He also mobilized it through a social networking site built by his production company, Mercury Entertainment Group (Rose 2010). The 912 demonstrations were planned over the Internet, with local chapters coordinating activities through digital tools such as Meetup.com and Ning.com. The occasion was designed to build national unity around his stated nine principles and twelve values rooted in commitment to the United States and good morals and ethics (labeled the "Take America Back" convention).

Americans for Prosperity, another core group behind the Tea Party, together with FreedomWorks provided funding for the ensuing eight hundred Tea Party protests held across the United States during the Tea Party Express bus tour (Bai 2012). Fox News gave extended coverage of the cross-country caravans that appealed to the media through the use of historical costumes, props, and catchy slogans (Rose 2010). The unpredictable protests, accompanied by symbolic displays of rebellion and disruptions of town hall meetings, as part of the Tea Partiers' repertoire, were also media friendly in their spontaneity and entertainment value. These symbolic forms of political protest parallel some of the tactics that MoveOn uses, and new social movement theories and constructionist theories can help us make sense of them. The use of symbolic displays of grievances and demands, and framing issues in a clear way that resonates with disgruntled citizens is something that both groups have mastered. They also open up the public sphere for more discussion and innovative forms of communicative action (using Habermas's 1993 terms).

The events that the Tea Party hosted and the rhetoric they engaged in are good examples of both frame alignment and frame amplification as promoted by social movement theories that focus on cultural aspects of social movements at the micro level (Snow et al. 1986 in particular). This is a tactic that activists can use to tap into deeply held morals, values, and beliefs that are congruent with other SMOs and that are embedded in the general population. Participants also used frame bridging to resonate with other organizations calling for resistance to the federal government. They also situated diagnostic framing in a way that promoted a critique of what they perceived to be the radical socialist agenda of the Obama administration. Other prognostic and motivational frames were embedded in a call to arms, with slogans such as "take your country back" and "what we need is revival and revolt!" (Rose 2010).

How to Define the Tea Party: Astroturf or Grassroots?

Some of the organizations that are affiliated with and support the Tea Party are corporate, while others are more grassroots in nature, and this led to some criticism of the Tea Party. Critics argue that its attempts to frame itself as a grassroots and ad hoc popular uprising are contrary to the reality of how the Tea party is structured and funded. For example, the supposed spontaneous interruptions and heckling of both Democrats and moderate Republicans during the 2009 town hall meetings were not entirely unrehearsed. Much of this was orchestrated and funded by well-established insider groups such as FreedomWorks and Americans for Prosperity. It is the Koch brothers (David and Charles) who provide most of the funding for both of these groups. They own 84 percent of Koch Industries, which is the second-largest privately held US company, and they financially back a number of libertarian and conservative organizations and think tanks, such as the Cato Institute, as well Tea Party candidates, through their political action committee (Fisher 2012).

The Tea Party groups that participated in the caravans also received advice and encouragement from Beck's (no longer available) national website (912project.com), and other conservative leaning websites such as ResistNet.com (also no longer in service) provided talking points. FreedomWorks suggested particular questions Tea Party representatives should ask at the town halls and maintained a link detailing how members could infiltrate the meetings, spread inaccurate information, and harass members of Congress, and thus the strategy was actually very top down. Although most supporters consider the movement to be populist, FreedomWorks, as mentioned earlier, is a well-funded, well-connected, DC-based think tank. The organization spent more than $10 million on the 2010 elections on campaign materials alone and set up a Super PAC through which it donates hundreds of thousands of dollars to politicians (Coffey 2012).

Despite these top-down tactics, Tea Party participants assert that the movement is a mainstream resurgence among powerless, ordinary citizens. Detractors, however, view their primary agenda as one attempting to preserve their collective privileges, as most activists are middle-aged, middle class, and white. They contend that the Tea Party engages in reactive rather than progressive politics, responding to threats to their sense of entitlement and sometimes engaging in racist or xenophobic rhetoric. An example of this is displayed in an e-mail sent out in August 2010 by Tea Party Nation to its 35,000 members, asking them to post their "horror stories" about undocumented immigrants on its (now taken down) website (Young 2010).

Thus, although Tea Partiers brand the movement as a grassroots uprising, others view it as a tool of the Republican Party that has been used and co-opted by powerful political actors connected with the political establishment in the Beltway (Pilkington 2011). MSNBC talk show host Rachel Maddow describes the movement in the following way: "They're called Fox News Channel tax day Tea Parties because all the big Fox News Channel personalities appeared at tax day Tea Party events. They were Fox News endorsed and promoted and, in some cases, hosted events. They didn't just cover the Tea Party protests. They ran ads for them. They used Fox News Channel staff production time and ad time on the air to promote the events. They ran tea party promotions" (MSNBC 2006). This free access to traditional media helped catapult the movement into national consciousness and related it to public sentiment of frustration with the government. MoveOn had done this earlier; however, it relied more on the Internet and digital media as a resource, as it does not have the connections to, or much support from, corporate-owned media.

Hybrid SMO

Regardless of these differences and criticisms, each organization extensively employs both e-activism and contentious street protests as a part of its repertoire, and both straddle electoral and contentious politics by taking advantage of the shifting political context to influence public opinion, which political mediation theory highlights the relevance of (Soule and King 2006). In sum, although the 2012 election did not bode well for Tea Party candidates and it appears that the organization may have lost its momentum, it is important to acknowledge that social movements ebb and flow, and the Tea Party might very well bounce back in the next election. Regardless of what the future brings, through their framing devices Tea Partiers have been able to persuade many citizens that the issues they raise are urgent, that alternatives are possible, that they have the moral high ground, and that citizens can be invested with agency. This has served well as a recruitment mechanism. Their injustice frames explicitly appeal to moral principles for organizational outreach by resonating with deeply held values and beliefs among the general population and linking them to movement's causes. Framing their grievances as a threat to the very existence of "everyday Americans" helps to create a sense of collective identity among Tea Partiers and their supporters who see changes in the economic, political, cultural, and social spheres—and

---

THEORY TOOLKIT

MOVEON AND THE TEA PARTY

We can apply a few of the theories discussed in Chapter 1 to the emergence and evolution of MoveOn.org and the Tea Party:

- **New social movement school of thought, cultural theories, resource mobilization theory, and political process theory.** These theories are all very useful in aiding our understanding of these new hybrid types of organizations. Each in some way informs us about how these two groups operate in both the realm of institutional politics (challenging vulnerable candidates for office; i.e. political process theory) and extrainstitutional politics (rallies, marches, the use of celebrities, house parties, etc.; strands of new social movement theories). Most important and applicable to these two cases are cultural theories that address the critical role of collective identity and framing.

- **Theories of new media.** As used in a complementary fashion to resource mobilization, these theories demonstrate (1) the importance of the peer-to-peer sharing of information within these two groups and across broader spectrums of society without heavy reliance on the mainstream media, (2) ways in which recruitment may be easier for contemporary social movement actors, (3) how weak ties forged in cyberspace can develop into strong ties with on-the-ground mobilization efforts and protest activity, and (4) nuanced forms of organizational flexibility that allow for more grassroots forms of participation and a broader spectrum for conversation and discussion.

---

specifically the changing demographics—as a threat to their entitlements. Although different groups work on different issues, there is a very strong emotional thread that holds them together, which indicates that a vehement sense of solidarity cuts across the various segments of participants. This is typical of Mann's (2000) conceptualization of contemporary social movements within the rubric of the new social movement theories that focus on forms of collective behavior that bring diverse groups together to support emotionally charged issues and promote new sets of values in a collaborative way.

The Internet and digital technology were essential resources for the emergence and outburst of Tea Party activism because it was in the virtual world that ordinary citizens first began to spread their message. By establishing weak ties in cyberspace, like-minded people were able to communicate with one another and show support for the causes that the Tea Party supports. This shows how the public sphere and sources of connectivity are changing because of the digital revolution, which allows for information to be created, disseminated, commented on, and circulated through diffuse networks. It also demonstrates how these in turn lead to on-the-ground local forms of participation in political and social issues. Therefore, theories of new media are important supplements to resource mobilization and cultural theories, in particular, their attention to what H. Jenkins (2006) calls the spillover effect.

CONCLUSION

Although different in their ideologies, tactics, and funding, what MoveOn and the Tea Party have in common is that they both take advantage of new ways of organizing and mobilizing their devotees through digital means. They both also rely heavily on different types of media in the hopes of influencing public opinion. Each has raised abundant amounts of money for advertisements and political campaigns. To impact the realm of institutional politics, MoveOn and the Tea Party have also pressured officeholders through e-mail and face-to-face lobbying efforts, and they have taken advantage of the vulnerability of politicians during election years. And, finally, both entities successfully used framing to pitch their concerns in a way that resonated with frustration among voters and citizens on both sides of the political spectrum.

MoveOn's and the Tea Party's mobilization endeavors therefore represent the growing symbiotic relationship between e-activism and local organizing, as they both work in the blogosphere as well as in real communities to impact institutional and extrainstitutional politics. Their strategies underscore the need to expand conceptualizations of Habermas's conception of the "public sphere" and participatory democracy.

DISCUSSION QUESTIONS

1. In what ways are MoveOn and the Tea Party hybrids when it comes to social change? Analyze another group that you consider to be a hybrid, and discuss how its tactics, strategies, and goals compare and contrast to those of MoveOn and the Tea Party.

2. How do the two entities resemble new social movements in some ways, but are actually top-down in other ways? Is either group really an outsider? Are there other advocacy groups you can locate that may be subject to similar criticisms?

3. Examine a social movement that utilizes cultural and symbolic tactics similar to those of MoveOn and the Tea Party. In your opinion, are these effective (especially groups that use somewhat "radical" tactics meant to shock or disturb). Do they do a better job of pulling people into the movement, or do they drive people away?

4. What other causes or social movements rely on celebrities to promote a cause? What are the pros and cons of using celebrities for political issues? How might this backfire? Give specific examples.

CHAPTER FOUR

Arab Spring

The Arab Spring, which broke out across parts of the Middle East and North Africa in 2010, took the world by storm. Entrenched dictators who had oppressed their citizens for decades suddenly were under siege, and a few were removed from power in a democratic wave that (at least temporarily) hit the region. These uprisings were originally greeted with great optimism throughout the world, yet what we have relearned from the Arab Spring is that democracy is not an easy thing to accomplish. To the contrary, in some cases protest has led to the revival of extremist Islamic groups striving to grasp political power, the transfer of political power from one authoritarian form of government to another, or protracted civil war, as the case in Syria. The long-term outcomes of the Arab Spring revolutions are uncertain, but what is clear is that new media platforms played a significant role (albeit complementary to traditional methods) in the planning and mobilization efforts that brought people onto the streets and posed serious challenges to existing political systems.

Giroux (2012, 39) emphasizes the importance of the communication field, and consequently the political environment, in motivating contentious politics. He summarizes, "Alternative newspapers, progressive media, and a profound sense of the political constitute elements of a vibrant, critical formative culture within a wide range of public spheres that have helped nurture and sustain the possibility to think critically, engage in political dissent, organize collectively, and inhabit public spaces in which alternative and critical theories can be developed." In essence, he argues that it is the media ecology that can either accelerate or impede serious political discussion and debate, and ultimately facilitate displays of collective behavior.

The Arab Spring social movements highlight the way the digital revolution has greatly expanded the parameters within which groups and individuals can voice concerns, share information, and organize protest activities. Innovative communication outlets have given social movement actors access to a political terrain within which they can discuss grievances and collectively make demands. The uprisings also require us to modify theories and conceptualizations of collective behavior. The resources, organizational processes and structure, and sources of connectivity and communication that activists rely on are different than they were in earlier eras, as new ICTs and other web-based tools have made self-organizing and flexible grassroots networks possible.

As we did in the previous chapter, we will evaluate the usefulness of the theoretical frameworks provided in Chapter 1 as they apply to the Arab Spring and its predecessors, acknowledging the role of public and traditional forms of organizing in conjunction with web-based strategies and tactics. Indeed, the case studies that we will examine in this chapter show that on-the-ground activities remain very effective, so we cannot dismiss them. However, the main thrust of this chapter is in analyzing the role that new digital technologies played. We will also address the additional question of how these analyses can contribute to and update traditional theories of social movements: in each of these countries disenfranchised youth took advantage of emerging wired technological formats in their respective countries to create mediated communities, networks, and identities, thereby expanding discourse in civil society.

To contextualize the Arab Spring (we will cover the cases of Tunisia, Egypt, Libya, and Syria), it is helpful to first examine the 2009 Green Revolution in Iran that preceded the Arab Spring. This chapter also assesses the complex ways in which the structural (why) and micro-level (how) mobilization efforts can sometimes be interconnected given the availability of new media.

IRAN'S GREEN REVOLUTION

One of the precedents of the Arab Spring, the 2009 Iranian Green Revolution highlights how the role of new communication technologies can assist rivals in political struggle. It also puts forth a model for attempting (the mobilization ultimately failed) to topple a dictator. First, let's go back in time to the 1953 US-backed coup that removed democratically elected leader Mohammad Mosaddegh after he tried to nationalize the oil industry. This incident is important to our understanding of the more recent revolution because media technology helped to fuel and support this earlier uprising as well. Mosaddegh was replaced by the Shah (Mohammad Reza Shah Pahlavi), who was very sympathetic to Western interests yet aggressively repressive of his own citizens (Abrahamian 2009). As a result, Iranian citizens rose up in opposition, and massive protests broke out in full force in 1978 (Kurzman 2004). Demonstrations and strikes continued, which eventually paralyzed the country, and in 1979 the Shah was forced to flee, and his challenger, Ayatollah Khomeini (a Muslim cleric who had been exiled in Iraq and later France in 1963 for fourteen years), took power.

As part of his strategy to oust the Shah, Khomeini smuggled cassette tapes into Iran to spread his sermons and messages during his exile (Hoveyda 2003). The Shah subjected much of the radio and television to censorship after installing a military government, and cassette tapes were cutting-edge technology at the time. Supporters spread Khomeini's sermons to followers from home to home (peer-to-peer in contemporary terms) among neighbors and eventually sold them in the markets. This new resource was to a large extent why the massive grassroots campaign gained momentum without its leader even being in the country. As part of a successful misinformation campaign, the opposition also circulated fraudulent cassette tapes with the recording of a voice that resembled that of the Shah, giving his generals orders to shoot at the peaceful protesters (Bakhash 1984). This further rallied people to participate in the burgeoning struggle.

This situation in Iran challenges traditional political process theory because the state was not necessarily vulnerable to attack in the late 1970s and there was no new or even valid political opening. The Iranian people indeed feared the state's coercive power and were subject to it time after time, but they believed that the strength of the revolutionary movement was superior to the oppression that they were experiencing (Kurzman 2004). In many of the participants' perspectives, not only was the revolution possible but it was deemed practically inevitable on the streets because of the precipitous energy that was generated by the challengers as the rebellion evolved. This did not occur *prior* to the revolution, as political process theory would suggest (Tarrow 1996; C. Jenkins and Perrow 1977), but on the streets amid a snowballing sense of collective identity. Once people were assured—even if only in their own minds—of a successful outcome, the opposition grew in popularity, a self-fulfilling prophecy of sorts. Thus, political mediation theory as espoused by Soule and King (2006) and theories for which collective identity plays a major role (Benford 1993; Gamson 1992; Tomlinson 1999) serve as a theoretical lens through which we can view both Iranian revolutionary outbreaks. These can be supplemented by new media and resource mobilization theories. Yet, as this case shows, technology can also be used by the target of dissent via misinformation campaigns.

Fast-forward thirty years. In 2009, Iranians used a different revolutionary form of communication, digital media, to mobilize marches and rebel against alleged electoral fraud in the presidential election that kept Mahmoud Ahmadinejad in power. Similar to the Green Revolution, resource mobilization theory is important in understanding the circumstances under which the uprising took place, because new technology and forms of communication were vital to the struggle.

During the Green Revolution, protesters supported Ahmadinejad's challenger, Mir-Hossein Mousavis, who requested that the results of the election be annulled given the obvious lack of regulation of the voting process (Shane 2011). Control over social media and the Internet was front and center during the attempted overthrow of Ahmadinejad. On June 13, while the election results were being announced, the government shut down all Internet access, filtered Facebook, and blocked mobile phone service. Even before the elections the government was censoring 21 percent of the secular websites and 11 percent of the reformist websites (Kelly and Etling 2008).

The virtual world was not the only space of repression, as the government also restricted traditional journalists from reporting on the events. On June 16 the Ministry of Culture banned all foreign media from leaving their offices or hotel rooms (Shane 2011). In Tehran it closed the offices of the English-language division of Al Jazeera, an Arabic (though relatively independent) news outlet that is highly respected for its approach to broadcasting different perspectives on sensitive regional and global matters (Habib 2011). It serves as an alternative to state-controlled news sources through its ability to circumvent embedded reporting and military press conferences—a situation unique to many countries in the Arab world (Whitaker 2003). The government also raided NBC News offices, confiscating cameras and other equipment (Mashayekki 2001), jammed the BBC World Service broadcast to the country, blocked websites affiliated with the BBC, and arrested BBC correspondent John Simpson and confiscated his material. ABC News also had material taken from its office, and two Dutch reporters were arrested and deported (Shane 2011). Once again these aggressive efforts to stifle independent journalism demarcate the significance of the media and communication tools to social movement actors (as depicted above, important to resource mobilization theorists) and the threat they can pose to those holding political power. Resource mobilization theorists have long argued that access to media to gain recognition, increase awareness about the issues they are promoting, and swaying public opinion are key in any political struggle.

To find the perpetrators of the revolution, the Iranian police followed the electronic traces left by activists, which led to thousands of arrests. The government also posted photos of demonstrators on the web and asked citizens to identify them, and it engaged in a misinformation campaign by posting false information that Mousavis had conceded the election and had therefore called off the protests (Shane 2011). This is another tactic at the state's disposal, which calls into question some of the more utopian theories about the Internet and digital media as outlined in Chapter 1 (Hindman 2007, for example). The digital insurgents, realizing the posting was from a government agent, in turn used Twitter to inform demonstrators where to gather for further demonstrations. The young rebels also blogged to encourage smart-phone users to change their personal information and time-zone settings to make it impossible for the government to identify or locate the participants. Opponents of the regime also used lists of open web proxy servers, as well as older communications systems such as fax machines and copiers, as a way to get around the restrictions. In addition, Mousavis's supporters engaged in acts of hacktivism by means of DDoS attacks against Ahmadinejad's website, and they exchanged attack tools through Facebook and Twitter (Considine 2011). Resource mobilization theory can help us account for the strategic and tech-savvy maneuvering by the challengers in the way new ICTs provide new types of civic engagement that are resistant to state regulation (Bennett and Iyengar 2008).

Abundant global support was another key resource for the Green Revolution. In the initial stages supporters, many of them outside of Iran, posted Twitter feeds and opposition websites that helped to build collective identity across national borders. New media allowed Iranians to report the events to the global community by uploading video, audio, and photos, and Al Jazeera and other media networks used the Internet and the 25Bahman Facebook group to globally broadcast information and cover events as they happened through live feeds (Mashayekki 2001).

This global, real-time exposure of what in the past would have taken weeks, if not months, to reach outsiders intensified global scrutiny of the Iranian government and generated sympathy for the demonstrators, both of which facilitated the social movement. The Green Revolution, therefore, gives us new ways to think about the importance of collective identity as addressed by cultural theories of social movements as well as by theories of new media. Perhaps most relevant is Kahn and Kellner's (2003) virtual public spheres and Bimber's (2003) accelerated pluralism that online tools make possible. This analysis also supports Polletta and Jasper's (2001) suggestion that collective identity can be based on a *perceived* shared experience and not necessarily on a concrete and material one. The Green Revolution exemplifies the role of collective identity in fostering international support and alliances, which can take place electronically as well as in physical space.

The Green Revolution thus demonstrated that new digital technology could be used to organize, distribute information, gain legitimacy and worthiness, and recruit members to the cause both locally and globally. The outcome of the social movement was not successful, however. After the death of seventy-two protesters during a military crackdown, the rebels aborted the revolution. Yet the mobilization in some key ways provided a model for activists in other nearby regions who also began challenging political corruption and demanding democracy and economic reform.

THE ARAB SPRING

The first glimpses of the Arab Spring began in December 2010. Some have linked the events of the Arab Spring to the revolutions of 1848 that were labeled "Springtime of the People." Others note the resemblance to the 1968 Prague Spring, a democratic awakening in Communist Czechoslovakia. Comparisons have also been made to the revolutions of 1989 (what many referred to as the "Autumn of Nations") that occurred in parts of Eastern Europe (Urban 2011).

The Arab Spring took place in a region notorious for a lack of institutional mechanisms to identify, take up, and respond to popular demands in a timely manner. In many of these countries, authoritarian regimes have ruled for decades without transparency and with little respect for rule of law, civil rights, or the formal realm of political processes. Thus, when their increasingly agitated and disaffected populace began to scrutinize and make demands of these dictatorial regimes, they were met with violent repression. In cases where the opposition was able to overthrow the regime, there was little political or civil infrastructure to make for a smooth democratic transition, and most of these countries are still trying to fill the political vacuum. We do not know what the future will bring, but we can make some theoretical sense of the developments and illustrate some commonalities and differences among the four countries where the Arab Spring was most pronounced: Tunisia, Egypt, Libya, and Syria.

Bishara (2012, 2) sums up these uprisings in the following way: "never has the power of people appeared so humane, so inspiring, so personal, so determined as in Tunisia, so daring as in Syria, so diverse as in Yemen, so humble as in Bahrain, so courageous as in Libya, or so humorous as in Egypt." Although this observation seemed quite accurate at the beginning of the revolutionary fervor, in hindsight, as the attempts at reform are stagnating or have been outright crushed, much of the original inspiration has been lost. Despite some of the ambiguous, if not disappointing, outcomes, these movements are important for several reasons. They demonstrated that people do indeed have agency, can hope and dream and act on implementing a better future, that governments and other authorities are susceptible to challenge, and that collective behavior and mobilization on the streets is one the simplest yet most powerful tactics in trying to affect social change.

In each of the cases we will explore, repressive regimes managed to sustain political power in large part through censorship or limiting access to news and information via state-run media (Howard and Hussain

2013). Under these circumstances there were few, if any, public channels for citizens to openly discuss grievances or dissent or to resist the ideological control that the political dynasties maintained through their monopoly on traditional media. Therefore, digital media and social networking sites played a critical role in bringing decades-old grievances to light in virtual and public displays of collective behavior. The more visible, or acknowledged, initial campaigns began through wired activism as citizens started to circulate among themselves information that was critical of the government. However, it is important to recognize that it was the occupation of physical space that really put concrete pressure on the authorities and gave the challengers leverage in the struggle by making the protests visible to their fellow citizens and to the outside world.

While not diminishing the public role of the collective struggles in each of the countries we will analyze, our main focus is on how digitally enabled communication systems enhanced the realm of public discussion, debate, and communicative action through the grassroots distribution of information. In fact, during the protests in Egypt and Tunisia (there is very little aggregate data available for Libya and Syria on the use of new ICTs), many citizens who participated in Arab Spring reported that they received their information about the revolutions from social media sites (or from others with social media access). Of those, 56 percent in Egypt and 59 percent in Tunisia said it had a positive effect in motivating them to sustain their participation in the social movement events. Almost 90 percent of Egyptians and Tunisians surveyed (again, of those who participated in the Arab Spring) in March 2011 said they were using Facebook to organize protests or spread awareness about them (Huang 2012). As the Dubai School of Government reported, the most popular Twitter hashtags in the Arab region during the first three months of 2011 (when the Arab Spring erupted) were "Egypt," "Jan25," "Libya," "Bahrain," and "protest," all of which provided information and updates about the growing revolutionary fervor across the region (*Arab Social Media Report* 2011). There was an international component of the digital activity as well. For example, an analysis of more than 3 million tweets that contained some of the most widely used hashtag codes pertaining to the Arab revolts, such as #Egypt and @sidbouzid, found that the major spikes in usage were driven by tweeters living *outside* of the Middle East (Stepanova 2011).

Tunisia

The driving forces behind the Tunisia revolution were a combination of the political corruption and nepotism of the dictator Zine el Abidine Ben Ali's regime, food inflation, high unemployment, and overall poor living conditions. The country also had a long history of suppressing citizens' political expression and a censored press. When Ben Ali came to power in 1987, all forms of media were forbidden until a small conservative television station was allowed to broadcast in 2003 (Pollock 2013). Later, in 2009 Ben Ali's son-in-law purchased a publishing house that printed four newspapers. Thus, when the revolution in Tunisia began most of the major news media sources were controlled by a member of Ben Ali's family. In other words, drawing on Habermas's (1989, 1993) work, the public sphere and the potential for participatory democracy and communicative action were extremely limited.

The conditions were ripe for political upheaval, especially when the global economic crisis, which began in 2008, affected large segments of the Tunisian middle class. At the time of the revolution, unemployment was 14 percent and youth unemployment was 23 percent. But what was needed was a spark. This occurred on December 17 when Mohamed Bouazizi, a twenty-six-year-old jobless street vendor, set himself on fire in the middle of the street in front of the Didi Bouzid regional council (Solnit 2012). Unable to find steady work and trying to support a family of eight, he had resorted to selling fruit and vegetables on the street until the police seized his produce because he did not have a license. His sense of desperation and indignity resonated with other unemployed and alienated youth immediately, and later with scores of other Tunisian citizens across all age groups.

Cultural theories as well as aspects of new social movement theories, for example Giddens (1991) and Johnston (1994), are informative in understanding the Tunisia uprising, because the activists were not necessarily utility maximizers. Rather, they had a shared set of grievances that they articulated through an injustice frame, which is a focal part of Ryan and Gamson's (2006) theorizing, which was embedded in moral principles—in particular, the sense of indignity that they felt subject to by the authorities. Additionally, the participants carefully framed their issues in ways that included not just the concerns of youth but of society as a whole, and in this way were able to recruit new members both online and offline to ultimately challenge the stability of the government. Thus frame bridging and frame amplification were key strategizing mechanisms (Snow et al. 1986).

The availability of new media, a critical tool that a renewed version of resource mobilization theory (McCarthy and Zald 1973; Gamson 1975) would highlight, helped to influence public opinion when the pictures of Bouazizi's self-immolation spread rapidly in cyberspace. Citizens recorded the tragedy on their mobile phones and posted them on the Internet and Facebook, which were then uploaded onto mainstream broadcasting sites by Al Jazeera (Laghmari and Kasseem 2011). The day after Bouazizi's death, Tunisians flocked to a common Twitter hashtag calling for a march the next day. Tweets mentioning Tunisia showed up in Twitter streams as many as 329 million times, reaching 26 million Twitter users. The most retweeted account, @VoiceofTunisia with its 496 followers, was retweeted over 400 times (Laghmari and Kasseem 2011).

This distribution of information and planning of the mobilization efforts in cyberspace resonates with McAdam and Paulsen's (1993) argument about the importance of weak social ties that develop in the virtual world and help spread messages across diffuse networks. These developments are also relevant to H. Jenkins's (2006) conceptualization of civic media and support, as well as Van Aelst and Walgrave's (2003) findings of how digitally networked individuals, as diverse as they may be, can use public media platforms to express common grievances that later lead to contentious politics at the local level. In other words, it is an example of the spillover effect transforming online to offline activism (H. Jenkins 2006).

For weeks Tunisians protested throughout the country, and on January 11 demonstrators reached the center of the capital city of Tunis. The police responded with a harsh and violent crackdown, and the images of the abuse, which were recorded in real time, provided more visual ammunition for bloggers and online political activists around the globe. International support encouraged the demonstrators to not only continue but ramp up the struggle. The next day tens of thousands took to the streets in Sfax, Tunisia's second-largest city. Blogger Majdi Calboussi recorded the protests and police violence on his Blackberry and then uploaded the footage onto Twitter and YouTube. The video got half a million hits the

Tunisian demonstrators rally in the streets after dictator Ben Ali fled the country.

first day alone and fueled the outrage (LeVine 2011). Diani (2000b), Verba, Scholzman, and Brady (1995), and Gould (1993) all emphasize the crucial role of relational ties in sharing information and recruiting individuals to a cause, thus giving theories of new media explanatory power in understanding these events.

Though the regime blocked YouTube during the month of unrest, it did not entirely block Internet access, and cyberactivists took advantage of this by playing bridging roles in the communication field. They reposted videos and Facebook content about protests from closed loops of private networks to Twitter and online news portals with greater reach. Additionally, during the first two weeks of January 2011, there was an 8 percent surge in the number of Facebook users, coupled with a shift from social use to more politically oriented use (Safranek 2012). Boulainne (2009) suggests that when citizens utilize digital media sites for political and knowledge-based reasons rather than for entertainment, the likelihood of political participation increases. This too is supported by the Arab Spring in Tunisia.

Alternative media sites such as *Tunisia Live* were also vital to the mobilization because they published stories, photos, and videos of the revolution that were not covered in the mainstream press. *Tunisia Live* served as a citizen media initiative that connected Tunisia with the English-speaking world and spread the story globally (Solnit 2012). Nawaat, the Tunisian blogging group, set up a website called TuniLeaks that widely distributed the cables to Tunisian citizens. This was significant because it allowed for a public platform for Tunisians to discuss issues and to post videos and blogs articulating their grievances and ways to mobilize. Once the protests gained momentum, the government completely blocked the Internet, Facebook, and YouTube. Although this development steered activists to other alternative news outlets such as Global Voices Online, gulfnews.comTunisia, and Canal France Internationale that became even more vital to the mobilization, the authorities' ability to at least temporarily obstruct cyberspace information sharing and organizing is illustrative of Hindman's (2007) caution of the potential caveats of relying on ICTs as a resource for protest activity.

Despite the government's attempt at censorship, activists found various ways to circumvent the blackout. They used landlines to phone in tweeted messages through Google's makeshift alliance with Twitter's Speak to Tweet service (Buhler-Muller and van der Merwe 2011). On every shift Al Jazeera dedicated personnel whose only duty was to keep the network's Twitter account updated while scanning social media forums for new content and information (Minnesota Prager Discussion Group 2011). This once again delineates the importance of controlling the narrative, in Nie's (2001) words, mediating the physical power of authorities by the soft power of new information technologies. Mann's conceptualization of interstitial locations through which activists, working at the grassroots level, can circumvent mainstream institutions and disseminate information and organize, is also pertinent to our understanding the unfolding of the Tunisian revolution.

The Tunisian regime eventually lost legitimacy as public opinion shifted in support of the young insurgents and galvanized their allies. Political mediation theory focuses on the importance of public opinion in shifting the momentum of a given social movement. Gamson (1990) specifically directs our attention to the role of public opinion and the *perception* of political openings, as well as belief in a possible victory despite a closed political system at the institutional level. His insights are useful in our theoretical understanding of how the social movement activity unfolded. One reason for the success of the revolution was the shift in public opinion in favor of the activists as they increasingly, and quickly, gained WUNC (Tilly 2004) and therefore legitimacy as a valid constituency promoting social change.

Responding to the common sentiment throughout Tunisia, Ben Ali promised to create 300,000 jobs in the next two years and not to run for re-election (after having ruled for twenty-three years). He also guaranteed more freedom and civil rights to Tunisians. However, thousands of protesters continued to demonstrate and demand that he vacate immediately. The president eventually announced the end of his reign and the dissolution of the government within six months, and he fled to exile in Saudi Arabia (Solnit 2012).

Resource mobilization theory is useful as a lens through which to analyze the unfolding of the revolution. For example, activists recognized the crucial role that social media tools played in the ouster of the regime in their celebratory gatherings. After the fall of Ali, banners and graffiti throughout the capital read, "We Love Twitter," and "We Love Facebook" (Solnit 2012). However, it is important to acknowledge that although technology played a major role in the uprising, there are other variables that enabled the mobilization efforts that social movement theory can help clarify.

After Ben Ali's departure Tunisian citizens held sit-ins, strikes, and riots throughout the country demanding legal recourse. The interim Tunisian government eventually issued an arrest warrant, charging Ali for money laundering and drug trafficking. He and his wife were sentenced to thirty-five years in prison on June 20, 2011 (Adetunji 2011). Again on August 15 protesters engaged in direct action by flooding the streets, calling for immediate reforms including the formation of an independent judiciary that could try corrupt officials and the killers of the twenty-three civilians, known as the of the "Revolution Martyrs" (Buhler-Muller and van der Merwe 2011). As a result, the prime minister resigned, the police force was dissolved, and political prisoners were released. The interim government announced a new constitution, and on October 21, Tunisians had the opportunity to vote in the first free and fair election in twenty-four years. The Islamist party Ennahda was voted into power yet agreed to step down in late September of 2013 because of months of political upheaval and discontent with the party, in particular its attempt to mandate that Islam be the official religion of Tunisia in the Constitution (Gall 2014).

There are currently plans for new elections in the spring of 2014, and in the meantime Ennahda has agreed to transfer power to an independent interim government. Though the political transformation is still a work in progress, Tunisian citizens were able to undermine the structural basis of the political system and therefore strategically gain leverage over the authorities, in what McAdam (1982) characterizes as one of the positive consequences of protest activity.

In sum, many of the protesters' demands were met, and Tunisian political power was significantly restructured. The death toll, at twenty-three, was relatively low in comparison to other revolutions that would ensue throughout the region. Though later rebellions in other Arab Spring countries would be more violent and lead to significant bloodshed, the robust and successful uprising in Tunisia provided a tentative model of how to overthrow a regime by using nonviolent means and organizing through social media. Tunisians lent their support to what would be the next major battlefield, Egypt. They sent information on how to occupy a public space and hold successful demonstrations, and they suggested forms of protection against tear gas, advised how to stop a tank, and offered other logistical strategies (Buhler-Muller and van der Merwe 2011). While the real work took place on the ground, in virtual sphere it was Facebook that served as the main channel of communication between the groups of activists in the two countries.

Egypt

The success story of Tunisia spread throughout the region via cyberspace, and as a result other regimes began to face similar challenges. As was the case in Tunisia, the list of grievances in Egypt under President Hosni Mubarak's tenure was long. A group of young individuals calling themselves the April 6 Movement, who had begun mobilizing years before the Arab Spring revolution, blazed the trail for the Egyptian Arab Spring. In fact, the labor movement in Egypt organized thousands of protests as early as 2004 in conjunction with the April 6 Movement. Workers held a strike on April 6, 2004 (thus inspiring the name of the movement), at a textile factory outside of Cairo run by the government. This initiated other strikes that activists advertised on a Facebook page, through which citizens began demanding Mubarak's departure (Souaiaia 2011). When the government attempted to break the strike by using riot police, labor activists, young Egyptians, and other sectors of the population formed the 6 April Committee. This coalition later organized the January 25 occupation of Tahrir Square calling for the end of Mubarak's rule, and Egypt soon exploded into a full-blown revolution.

Resource mobilization theory highlights the significance of networking among SMOs and other coalitions as a powerful organizing force in the early stages of the Arab Spring in Egypt, and it brings the use of traditional methods of protest politics to our attention. What is different here, however, is that during the beginning phase of the Arab Spring, ICTs allowed activists to reach a critical mass quickly through peer-to-peer networks and to create virtual public spheres (Kahn and Kellner 2003). As a result, Egyptian activists were able to establish avenues of civic engagement at the grassroots level (Bennett and Iyengar 2008; Castells 2001). These types of organizing tools give credence to theories of new media and their important function in today's social movements.

While occupying the square, activists expanded their list of grievances and demands. Complaints included Mubarak's role in maintaining the blockade against Gaza, his acceptance of the privatization measures imposed by the International Monetary Fund and the World Bank, the fact that half of the Egyptian population was sustaining itself on two dollars a day, the lack of freedom of expression, and excessive human rights abuses (Kuebler 2011). Amateur journalists, through their cellphone videos, circulated firsthand accounts of hundreds of cases of police abuse and disregard for citizens' rights and spread them globally. In this way they evaded state authorities and the mainstream media to get their story out and create their own account of the events, exemplifying the importance of interstitial locations (Mann 2000). This new transparency, developed and sustained through connective action via a digitally rooted politics, is also representative of Bennett and Iyengar's (2008) contention that new media has a profound impact on transmitting personal complaints into common demands.

As in Tunisia, disaffected youth make up a significant percentage of the population in Egypt; the average age in the country is twenty-four, and 60 percent of the population is under the age of twenty-five (Kuebler

A man works on a laptop during antigovernment demonstrations in Tahrir Square. Almost 90 percent of Egyptian protesters surveyed in March 2011 said they were using Facebook to organize protests or spread awareness about them.

2011). Like Tunisians, Egyptians had a martyr. On June 6 police pulled Khalid Said, a twenty-eight-year-old Egyptian and underemployed businessman, from an Internet café and beat and killed him because he had distributed evidence of police corruption by hacking into a police officer's cellphone. He also widely distributed a video of officers displaying drugs and stacks of cash. This incited the largest protests in the country in fifty years (Jennifer Preston 2011a)

Following the incident, Google executive and activist Wael Ghonim created a Facebook page, "We Are All Khalid Said," that commemorated Said by posting cellphone photos from the morgue and YouTube videos that juxtaposed pictures of him happy and smiling with those of him beaten and bloodied. This was the biggest dissident Facebook page in Egypt, and it helped spread the word about the upcoming demonstrations in protest of police brutality and lack of accountability (Preston 2011a). It was also through this digital site that activists began to build a sense of collective identity and organize contentious politics on the streets. The uprising, therefore, illustrates the spillover effect (H. Jenkins 2006).

For example, in the days preceding what organizers called "Revolution Day," 85,000 people committed online to participate in the protests (framed as a stand against torture, poverty, corruption, and unemployment) to be held on January 25. Activists picked January 25 as Revolution Day because it is a national holiday to commemorate the police forces, later calling it a "Day of Rage," thereby using the process of framing (Snow 1994) in a more dramatic way. That day more than 100,000 marched throughout the country—10,000 in Cairo alone, the largest demonstration to ever take place in the downtown area (Jennifer Preston 2011a). Police and demonstrators clashed, and the officers fired tear gas and used water cannons against the protesters. A few days later, after viewing the abuse, sixty political groups and political parties announced their participation in the upcoming protests, now framed as "Friday of Dignity," and the "Second Day of Rage" (McNally 2012).

Protests continued across Egyptian cities for the next several days. In an attempt to appease the insurgents, Mubarak dismissed his government and eliminated the cabinet, but he himself refused to step down. On January 31 about 250,000 people gathered in Tahrir Square, the European Union called for free and fair elections in Egypt, and investors worldwide withdrew large amounts of capital en masse (McNally 2012). This loss of support of former international allies and the change in international public opinion in favor of the dissenters are variables that both political process and political mediation theory address in explaining successful social movement outcomes (Soule and King 2006; Meyer 2005; Marullo and Meyer 2007; Tarrow 2001). This helped to sustain and fuel the occupation activities.

To keep the momentum going, Egyptian citizens used Twitter for planning discussions under the hashtag #25. Activists established the @TahrirSupplies link on Twitter to coordinate donations for medical supplies and other assistance to Tahrir demonstrators, something that in the past would have been very limited without the advantage of digital technologies and social media. Citizen journalists provided footage of the situation through mobile phones and circulated them through social networking sites, which helped to increase global awareness. The images were then broadcast on mainstream media, which influenced international public opinion in favor of the protesters, as many supporters outside of Egypt began to pressure their own governments to force Mubarak to cede power. In other types of symbiotic relations between mainstream and new media, Livestream viewers could watch the Al Jazeera channel on podcasts over the Internet and through its Facebook page and Twitter feeds. During the first two days of protests alone, viewership of the channel increased by 2,500 percent (Nir 2011).

The organizers also spread the information about the January 25 events through peer-to-peer sharing over a Facebook page that had about 400,000 members, which allowed them to elude the authorities (Hauslohner 2011). For example, to throw off the police, activists stated publicly that they would gather at a particular place while announcing the actual meeting place online. This is another example of how connectivity among social movement actors is being transformed by the grassroots forms of organizing and the decreasing reliance on formal SMOs described by new social movement theories (Van Aelst and Walgrave 2003; Kahn and Kellner 2003; Giugni 1998; Melucci 1996).

The framing of the revolution in the streets emphasized, in a playful way, the significance of social media and the Internet in fostering the uprising. Popular signs read, "Mubarak is offline," "Mubarak Failure," and "Delete Mubarak" (Brysk 2013). Ghonim explains the effectiveness of Facebook in motivating Egyptians to participate in these high-risk activities this way:

> This wasn't a page that tells people what to do; this was a page that asked people, 'What should we do?' and created surveys. Then, based on the most liked choices, actions took place. . . . Anonymity was critical—and not only for security reasons. . . . Contrary to what many people would think, the anonymity added a lot of legitimacy to the page. And why? Because people could connect directly to the cause. . . . The moment the footage started coming in, there was another lesson learned. People were very happy sharing their photos. Why? Because of the instantaneous feedback. The moment you upload the photo on the page, hundreds of likes, tons of comments, and it made everyone happy that they took part. So all of this played a critical role in building the DNA, the credibility between the page members and the page, despite the fact they didn't know who was running it." (McNally 2012)

Thus, similar to the case of Tunisia, access to new media venues for communication in Egypt was no longer constrained by political or economic forces as it had been with mainstream or state-controlled media. Through social networking sites, all citizens were free to participate in dialogue on equal terms. Ghonim's elaboration on the impact that Facebook had on the rebellion is an example of Castells's (2001) electronic grassrooting of democracy—activists exchanged ideas and information horizontally through geographically diffuse networks. His explanation also illustrates that new media outlets lend themselves to alternative organizational dynamics and structures that are often leaderless and based on peer-to-peer exchanges of communication to recruit new members and accelerate protest activity.

Thus, it is important that resource mobilization theory include these types of organizational structures in addition to formal SMOs (though, as stated, these were indeed crucial in the initial stages of the revolution). It is also vital to keep in mind that the real revolution occurred on the streets and was not a "Facebook revolution." Despite our focus on how ICTs impact SMOs and mobilization, we must exercise caution to not overstate the role of technology. As all of the Arab Spring uprisings illustrate, ICTs were significant in the organizing part of the struggle, but labor; energy; time; bodies; conviction; resisting violent reprisals by the police, military, and other government officials; the help of allies; and establishing and maintaining a sense of collective identity were essential complements to the use of digital technology.

Although the army was deployed in and around the square, it did not use violence against the occupiers. This may have been to increase its chances of staying in power after Mubarak's ouster, as it was clear the agitators had gained legitimacy, were gaining new allies, and were influencing public opinion in their favor. There was also concern that the military repression most likely would have further hampered the already dire economic situation, so most elites, of which the military is a significant part, allied with the protesters (Chivers 2012). As political process theory would suggest, activists were able to use this division between elite forces to their strategic advantage. The challengers manipulated fractures between high-ranking members in the political and economic realms and exploited some of the openings that resulted. This served to decrease the power discrepancy between the insurgent groups and the government, and diminishing this gap is a critical variable that theories of social movement outcomes point to.

Egyptians gather in Tahrir Square to call for the resignation of President Hosni Mubarak and the beginning of political change in Egypt.

When physical repression proved to be ineffective, the state undertook digital repression in the form of disinformation campaigns and e-activism to counter the visual ammunition that opponents had at their disposal. The crackdown began in earnest on January 28 when the government fully restricted the Internet, Facebook, Twitter, and cellphone access (Chivers 2012). Twitter and Blackberry Messenger services were disrupted, and Mubarak's regime eliminated Al Jazeera's government-controlled satellite, shut its bureau, seized its transmission equipment, and arrested much of its staff (Karr and Le Coz 2011). However, Al Jazeera was able to report news illegally with the aid of ten Arab satellite broadcasters. There were international collaborations too. For example, Nirus, a Boeing-owned surveillance technology provider, sold Telecom Egypt real-time traffic intelligence software that filters online communications and tracks them to their source.

In the ensuing weeks activists and authorities engaged in a cyberspace cat-and-mouse game. As was the case in Tunisia, to get around the blockade citizens accessed Google's app "Speak to Tweet." Organizers also encouraged supporters to use Twitter because it allows users to adopt pseudonyms and manually set their location or to choose "worldwide" to circumvent the blocking system (Snider and Faris 2011). However, technology, as noted, is a neutral tool. Authorities are not limited to blocking or disrupting services but can also manipulate and deceive through the anonymity that social media provides. For instance, when access to digital media was restored, pro-Mubarak supporters got onto the Khalid Said Facebook page and added wall posts and comments that criticized the protesters, demanded Mubarak be given a chance to remain in power, and claimed that the upcoming protests were cancelled (Karr and Le Coz 2011). In yet another international collaboration, British-owned Vodafone shut down its Egypt-based cellphone network following a request from the Mubarak regime and then restored it mainly to send pro-Mubarak propaganda to text-messaging customers across the country (Karr and Le Coz 2011).

An important point of comparison to the Tunisian case is that the alternative press provided a crucial resource in the struggle. Independent Egyptian newspapers such as *Al Shorouk* and *Al Masry Al Yorum* played a fundamental role in getting information out regarding the revolution. The former went from a distribution of 30,000 to 180,000 copies, and the latter doubled to 200,000 during the rebellion (Snider and Faris 2011). In these strategic ways demonstrators fought to manage the interpretation of the reality on the ground and relay it to the outside world, and in doing so petitioned the international community for support.

Amateur journalists countered government claims that the social movement actors were inspired and driven by outside forces with live images that they captured and uploaded onto YouTube, the Internet, and social networking sites, which permitted them to bypass editorial spin and the filter of state-controlled media. This further damaged Mubarak's credibility both domestically and internationally. Thus, Egyptians were able to prevent what has happened in many attempted but failed revolutions; atrocities go unnoticed by the global community until several years later when documents filter out past the governments' control of the media.

Back on the streets, despite the determination of the demonstrators to remain nonviolent, the government continued to accelerate the aggressive attacks on them. On February 2 police rode horses and camels into the crowds of protesters in what was the most violent day of the revolution up to that point, resulting in the "battle of the camels." Once again, akin to the situation in Tunisia, support for the opposition only grew in response to government violence. A coalition of youth groups called for another mass demonstration on February 4 called the "Day of Departure." In Cairo one million people protested, and by February 7 thousands were camping in Tahrir Square (Chivers 2012).

Both political process and political mediation theories (especially the work of Soule and King 2006; Meyer 2005; Meyer and Minkoff 2004; Tarrow 1996) can help to make theoretical and practical sense of the events during the Egyptian Arab Spring. The political mediation framework highlights how reading the political context can spur collective behavior and consequently alter the strategies and tactics participants choose, especially when there is belief in a conceivable triumph. Political process theory emphasizes the importance of a division among elites that activists can use to their strategic advantage as leverage. In the case of Egypt, the army's reluctance to use violence against the occupiers was likely the result of the fracture between the military and government.

The protest actions eventually led to the collapse of the regime when Mubarak resigned on February 11 and handed over power to the army. The military dissolved the Parliament, suspended the Constitution, and promised to lift the thirty-year emergency laws. In July more than two dozen officials were charged with murder, attempted murder, and terrorism. Mubarak was sentenced to life in prison on June 1 and charged as an accessory in the death of more than two hundred and forty demonstrators (Kirkpatrick 2012).

When the generals took over as the interim government, however, it was apparent that they were not competent to govern. In frustration with the slow economic and political progress, protesters returned to Tahrir Square, and Egyptian troops and police officers forcefully cleared the sit-ins, which drew thousands more (Kirkpatrick and Stack 2012). The following summer Egyptians voted the Muslim Brotherhood into power, and Mohammed Morsi became the first democratically elected leader of Egypt. Additional problems continued to loom, as many were suspicious of the intentions and agenda of the Muslim Brotherhood and what they considered to be Morsi's overreach of political power. Egyptian citizens responded with more demonstrations as they saw the country drifting toward a theocratic dictatorship, thus short-circuiting the promise of the

Arab Spring. Activists and journalists, in turn, were increasingly imprisoned and tortured.

The hopes of the Arab Spring continued to diminish as Parliament failed to pass any significant reforms, the economy continued to worsen, and tourism (a major economic asset) dropped by 20 percent. Frustrated citizens therefore forged another revolutionary attempt largely through the Tamarod ("rebellion" in Arabic) opposition, made up of a group of young organizers who began mobilizing against the new dictator. It distributed petitions throughout the country, noting the security failure, rising crime rates throughout Egypt, and increasing poverty (Finamore 2013).

An estimated 22 million Egyptian citizens signed the petition to oust Morsi and the Brotherhood (Finamore 2013). However, Morsi refused to back down and described those critical of his administration as "traitors" in his now infamous speech (Kirkpatrick and Hubbard 2013). This led to a rupture among some of his most high-ranking supporters, and following the speech his entire cabinet issued a statement on the government's official Twitter account: "The cabinet declares its rejection of Mr. Morsi's speech and his pushing the country toward a civil war. The cabinet announces taking the side of the people" (Kirkpatrick and Hubbard 2013). The foreign minister subsequently resigned his position, and six other ministers announced their resignations as well. On July 1, 2013, the military's leader, General Abdul Fattah el-Sisi, gave Morsi an ultimatum under which he had forty-eight hours to respond or else they would remove him from power, and when he failed to do so they forcefully removed him from office on July 3. Immediately after the coup, pro-Morsi supporters galvanized a potent oppositional force to the military takeover (Kirkpatrick and Fahim 2013).

As of this book's printing, the military is currently in control and the revolution has become unhinged. The Brotherhood is now officially banned and has been labeled a terrorist organization by the government. The members of the Brotherhood, suspected supporters of the group, as well as progressive organizations (in particular members of the April 6 movement) continue to be targeted for arrests and abuse. It appears that the main agenda of the military government is to avenge any apparent threats to its authority, consolidate power, and return to the status quo at all costs. Yet protests continue. The post–Arab Spring complications in Egypt remind us that revolution entails much more than overthrowing current leaders.

Libya

Inspired by the events in Egypt and Tunisia, protesters began agitating three days after the fall of the Mubarak regime in Egypt. The initially peaceful demonstrations that began on February 14 were coordinated through Facebook and blogs, and nonviolent direct action was the chosen tactic. The government responded immediately with violence: the military and police used live ammunition on the protesters, and President Gaddafi defiantly blamed "conspirators" for the dissent (Beaumont 2011). A "Day of Rage" was organized for February 17, and demonstrators held signs that read, "Freedom for the people" and "Down with Gaddafi." To tap into public sentiment and shame the government, protesters chanted, "traitors are those that beat their people" (Prashad 2012), in a skillful framing tactic to establish a sense of collective identity, as cultural-oriented theories of social movements emphasize (Ryan and Gamson 2006; Benford 1993),

Political process theory can illuminate the fractioning of support for the regime at high levels of governance that ultimately bolstered the opposition's cause and provided a key resource that they could use to their advantage (Tarrow 1996; C. Jenkins and Perrow 1977). A number of ambassadors stepped down from their positions once the protests picked up steam and the government used overly aggressive forms of retaliation, and there were several resignations from Parliament members as well (Lawrence 2013). These evacuations were complimented by large defections from the army.

International supporters of the Libyan rebels provided them a key resource by creating an additional schism and an opening for the rebels to exploit. For example, the International Federation of Human Rights and the Libyan League for Human Rights condemned the military response of intense bombings in civilian areas, and on March 10 France became the first country to formally recognize Libya's opposition (Prashad 2012). On March 19 the UN Security Council authorized a no-fly zone to protect civilians. A coalition of twenty-seven states from Europe and the Middle East eventually joined the intervention and began a collective bombing campaign. US and British warships and submarines fired cruise missiles at Libya's air defense systems in Operation Odyssey Dawn as part of the effort, allowing the rebels to counter the military (Whitlock 2011). This

A rebel with the Libyan flag and a Kalashnikov.

clear support for the insurgents provided them leverage and increased their perception of a possible victory, a factor that political mediation theory, perhaps most adamantly espoused by Gamson (1990), views as vital to sustain a political campaign.

As in the other cases we have reviewed, new technology was valuable to the cause, and therefore the use of ICTs can help inform resource mobilization theory. For example, what helped to draw the international community into the situation was a Twitter campaign. A Twitter feed was sent out that could be signed in a form of a petition by tweeting #NoFly-Libya, which had pressured the US State Department's Twitter to respond (Prashad 2012). These international alliances also exemplify elements of new social movement theories with the emergence of new forms of collective identity on a global scale. This resonates with Mann's (2000) interstitial locations as well as Tomlinson's (1999) shared values and visions for a better society that cut across geographical locations.

In addition to Twitter, other kinds of social media and alternative press proved significant to the eventual success of the opposition forces. Two of the most popular Twitter handles that covered the Libyan revolution were @feb17libya and @ShababLibya. The latter had more than

40,000 followers. Alternative media such as the *Muslim* and *Infowars* further exposed Gaddafi's actions, and Arab channels such as Al Jazeera and Al Arabiya, which closely covered the revolution, were watched widely. Additionally, Al Jazeera live blogging utilized video, audio, text, RSS feeds, tags, and recommendation feeds. The CNN blog also featured tags, text, video, and timestamps that provided various perspectives concerning the events (Beaumont 2011).

Digital technology not only was a crucial resource for the distribution of information and coordination of activities but also helped to build a strong sense of collective identity—some of it in cyberspace, thus resembling Kahn and Kellner's (2003) virtual public sphere. This new type of online informational politics and electronic grassrooting of democracy made available by digital communication technologies, in the case of Libya, resulted in a pouring out into the streets in protest action despite the government's violent reprisals. In sum, the spread of information among networks of friends, acquaintances, and other relational ties was essential to the recruitment efforts, which inspired people to participate in the struggle despite the very high risk of engagement.

Conversely, as Hindman (2007) warns, digital technology was also used as a tool of state oppression and attempts at censorship. The Gaddafi regime used extensive spying apparatus; monitored text messages, e-mails, and online chats; and ultimately shut down Internet communication (Morozov 2011). Human rights activists reported being presented with transcripts of their own text messages after they were arrested, in an effort to intimidate allies and sympathizers of the revolutionaries. Traditional journalists were also targeted. Four *New York Times* reporters were held in captivity for a week (Sorcher 2011). Unlike in Tunisia and Egypt, it was relatively easy for the Libyan government to block social media, the Internet, and cellphone service because they were all state controlled. In an example of an attempted misinformation campaign, the regime tried to depict that one protest rally as a progovernment demonstration. This was quickly discredited as counterfeit, which served to further shame the authorities. However, one Libyan journalist was shot in the head after exposing the Gaddafi government's false reports (Morozov 2011).

In the end, the UN-mandated military intervention was successful, although the revolution left more than 30,000 people dead. On October 20 Gaddafi was killed and cellphone videos and pictures went viral over the

Al Jazeera live blogging utilized various forms of social media to distribute feeds in its coverage of the Libyan revolution and Arab Spring.

Internet. However, the success of social movements is always hard to measure, and victories are never complete. The military forces did withdraw once the war ended, and some political prisoners were released, but the situation remains unstable. The borders lack control, militias are prominent and roam about at will, Islamist influence is increasing amid a weak and corrupt government that cannot control the chaos, and many political prisoners continue to face torture (Bennis 2012). On the positive side, citizens do not have to struggle with an entrenched police or military force, and they are not caught up in the midst of battles between secular and Islamist groups, as is the case in other Arab Spring countries (especially in Egypt and Syria). One of the shortcomings in Libya is that there is no unifying political force, which the Muslim Brotherhood in Egypt had been (if only for a short while), or civic or political institutions upon which to build.

Syria

What started in Syria as a nonviolent and nonsectarian protest in March 2011, framed by the slogan "Peaceful, Peaceful," soon turned into an armed rebellion and civil war (Toor 2011). The revolution surfaced after decades of escalating government suppression, stagnant employment rates, and police brutality. The Bashar al-Assad regime is the latest iteration of a de facto dynasty that began with his father, Hafez Assad, many years ago (Holliday 2011). Political parties have been banned for decades, and dissent was not only nonexistent but deemed impossible by most of the population, that is, until Tunisia and Egypt erupted. As with the other Arab Spring rebellions, emotion and the perception that revolution was not just possible but that success was probable anchored the momentum and was the main driving force of participation that sparked and maintained the mobilization. Therefore, we can also view this revolution through the lens of cultural theories of social movements.

The main tactic the rebels employed early on in the struggle was the occupation of public places, and this was facilitated by e-activism. Protests began on January 26 after a police officer assaulted a young man in the capital city of Damascus. About 1,500 people took to the streets (Holliday 2011). The police opened fire on the unarmed demonstrators and arrested fifteen children for graffitiing antigovernment slogans (*CBS News* 2011). The fact that the youths spent two weeks in prison led to more protests, and one month later the list of grievances expanded, calling for the release of all political prisoners. Police officers again fired live ammunition into the crowds, and the military used tanks and helicopters to put down the rebellion. In the city of Daraa, more than one hundred people were killed when troops fired on a mosque where protesters had gathered (Holliday 2011).

Thousands of Syrians then took to the streets to mourn the dozens of protesters who were killed, using the tactic of occupying public space to express their grievances, mobilize, and sustain a sense of collective identity and community. Fueled by the newly enabled Internet access (which the government tried to block at the start of the protests), the demonstrations quickly spread, growing from small, isolated incidents to mass forms of civil disobedience in the country's largest cities. On April 18, 2011, more than 100,000 Syrian citizens occupied Quwatli Square in Homs calling for the resignation of the president. In February 2012 the Syrian Army launched a massive bombardment on the city, and five hundred civilians were killed in a single day (Bhatti and Walker 2012).

Following the onslaught of violence against those engaging in civil disobedience, a group of online activists created a Facebook group that called for a peaceful "2011 Syrian Revolution" (Sandels 2012). They also initiated a Twitter campaign that called on Syrians to join the "Day of Rage" rallies (Toor 2011). After the "Day of Rage" and other ensuing protests, Facebook pages posted graphic video footage of police brutality against nonviolent demonstrators and sent out updates on planned marches and other civil disobedience activities (Sandels 2012). Live cellphone camera feeds provided additional images of the atrocities and human suffering, which were then transmitted by satellite link to the Internet (Bhatti and Walker 2012). The Shaam News Network and YouTube posted the cellphone pictures and Twitter feeds coming in from protests all over Syria, as well as the violent crackdown by the regime.

Opponents also used forms of hacktivism as part of their strategy. They created the Coalition of Free Syrian Hackers in Support of the Syrian Revolt and claimed to have hacked more than 140 government websites (Sandels 2012). The amateur videos posted online by mojos depicting the slaughtered civilians resulted in a surge of more antigovernment demonstrations across the country. Thus, Syria's power brokers, like other authorities in the region ensnared in revolutions by their populations, failed to understand that the violent attempts to quell civil disobedience would only bring about future self-perpetuating cycles of violence. It was digital technology and social networking sites that fuelled the recruitment drives, given the sympathy that was created for the protesters, as well as disgust for the actions undertaken by those in power. This had the effect of increasing participation in contentious politics.

Therefore, as with the previous three cases, theories of new media are applicable to the Syrian struggle. Castells's (2001) notion of information politics facilitated by online activism and McAdam and Paulsen's (1993) appeal to weak ties—many of which are pre-existing or that can be forged in cyberspace to help with recruitment efforts—and Van Aelst and Walgrave's (2003) attention to the effects of peer-to-peer sharing and its relationship to political activity are all useful theoretical frameworks within which we can situate and make sense of the Syrian Arab Spring.

These tools helped to build domestic and international networks of support, establish and maintain collective identity, accelerate the sharing and circulation of information and images, and coordinate the protest activities. They also assisted in creating WUNC (Tilly 2004) in the acts of collective behavior based on the above resources. Mojos fortified the legitimacy of complaints and helped gain compassion for the agitators by circulating pictures and videos of events as they evolved.

The importance of new media platforms in generating legitimacy and sympathy for the activists and mobilizing others to act on the behalf of the protesters cannot be overstated. Thirty years earlier, when Hafez Assad killed an estimated 40,000 citizens to thwart an uprising, it took months for the information of the atrocities to reach the international community, which was too little too late for those outside of the country (be they citizens or governments) to have an impact on the situation (Toor 2011). This time, however, armed with digital technology, mojos were able to expose the excessive actions taken by the government, police, and military immediately and internationally, as global television networks distributed the up-to-date, on-the-ground, in-real-time footage they took.

One protester who volunteered at the Shaam News Network (a website created by Syrian dissidents) underscores the significance of new media in the struggle. He explains, "Shooting videos is more punishable than carrying a weapon because video is the weapon of the protesters." Another Syrian described the usefulness of wired activism this way: "it has helped people inside Syria as well, more with motivation—when people see their videos on the Facebook page and thousands of people are watching them, it motivates them to go out the next day . . . because now people are hearing us and seeing us" (Bhatti and Walker 2012, A2).

The government realized the impact that social media and the Internet was having and responded with a rolling blackout of both. The regime also attempted to bar foreign journalists (Jennifer Preston 2011a). To try to regain a sense of legitimacy, it launched its own web-based campaign for self-promotion and utilized the Internet to create the Syrian Electronic Army, with its own media arm and a Facebook page listing the latest attacks by proregime hackers to counteract the Free Syrian Hackers (Sennitt 2011). Assad supporters also posted positive comments about the president on antiregime websites and included death threats against the opposition for treason.

In other misinformation campaigns, supporters of the formal establishment sent out thousands of reports challenging the cyberdissidents.

org website (launched by anti-Assad forces) and other Facebook pages. They also placed messages that called for violence and sectarianism online and on social networking sites and then then photocopied and posted them on the Facebook page as evidence of the opposition's incitement to violence (Sennitt 2011). In yet another attempt to prop up its image, the regime accused international satellite channels of exaggerating the size of protests and broadcasting unauthenticated footage. To verify the films and rebuke the government's accusations, protesters began carrying banners stating the date and neighborhood where the demonstrations were taking place and took shots of recognizable local landmarks.

Though there has been a substantial division among authorities within Syria, Assad has been able to cling to power in spite of the fact that his whole cabinet resigned and scores of soldiers (including some high-ranking officers and members of secret security agencies) have defected to the opposition (Nordland 2012). Many of the images of the generals and colonels departing from the regime were posted on YouTube (Chivers 2012). General Manaf Tlass's defection gained international attention because he was not only a high-ranking official but also a close friend of Assad (Nordland 2012). These defections can be viewed as moral and public relations victories and an acknowledgment of the validity of the protesters' demands.

Therefore, the revolution in Syria calls into question political process theory's anticipation of a collapse of the regime due to this severe rift, especially at such a high institutional level. A critique of this theory is that it focuses, almost exclusively, on the macro- and structural-unit level of analysis. Assad supporters, however, were driven by passion, anger, determination, and fear of being left out of the political system if the rebels succeeded in overthrowing their leader (as they are members of the ethnic minority Shia). Thus, a more micro-level analysis that looks at emotion and grassroots developments on the ground (for instance Melucci 1996 and Gamson 1992) is a theoretical necessity to understand the Syrian Arab Spring.

Political process theory, however, is useful in examining the international context. One of the difficulties regarding the Arab Spring in Syria is the complexity of the geopolitical context and the strategic clashes of interest. On one side, Saudi Arabia, Turkey, and Qatar are helping to arm the opposition because they are favorable to a pro-Sunni government. The

Unidentified rebels of the Free Syrian Army in Aleppo. The main tactic the rebels employed early on in the struggle was the occupation of public places, facilitated by e-activism.

United States and the European Union also support the rebels and have placed sanctions against Syria. In February 2013 the United States committed $60 million for food and medical supplies to the Free Syrian Army (M. Gordon 2013).

On the other side, Assad receives billions of dollars in military aid from Russia and is one of its major trading partners, particularly of Russian arms. Syria is also home to a Russian naval base and extensive Russian oil and gas investments (Cooper and Landler 2012). This allows the Syrian government to be more politically adept in terms of its survival and hinders international attempts to end the stalemate. The geopolitical context creates logistical problems because Russia's veto power in the United Nations presents a perhaps insurmountable stumbling block to any potential NATO intervention plan of the type that was successful in Libya.

Equally complicated are the sectarian issues that cut across different ethnic and religious groups. In neighboring countries Sunnis have become outraged by Assad's brutality, while Shiites have come to his defense. The Alawite sect, to which Assad belongs, is an offshoot of Shiite Islam, making majority-Shiite Iran a natural ally. Therefore, members of the Quds Force and the Iranian Revolutionary Guard are coming from Iran to try to keep Assad in power (Adnan and Gladstone 2013). Hezbollah, the powerful Lebanese militant Shia group that relies on Syria to provide a conduit for arms from Iran, is also supportive of the Assad regime and has joined in the struggle (P. Hubbard 2013).

The sectarian warfare and overall lack of unity among the insurrectionary forces, in addition to al Qaeda (a radical supporter of Sunni causes) now operating in Syria, has made the international community hesitant to arm the insurgents, as they did in Libya. This tentativeness is due to the fear that the factitious groups might turn on each other, and in addition to the threat that al Qaeda may gain a stronghold in the country. Finally, there is a concern that a victory in Syria could create a haven for Sunni extremists and destabilize Iraq, Lebanon, Turkey, and Jordan, all of which border Syria and where hundreds of thousands Sunni refugees from Syria have found safe harbor (Adnan and Gladstone 2013). Meanwhile, within the country the pattern of protest and reprisal continues in the now three-and-a-half year bloody civil war that has claimed, by some accounts, more than 200,000 deaths and countless others maimed and wounded.

The Emergence of ISIS and Further Complications for Syria Arab Spring

The situation in Syria continues to get more chaotic, especially with the emergence of the Islamic State of Iraq and Syria, sometimes referred to as the Islamic State of Iraq and Levant (ISIL), which is largely a product of the 2003 Iraq war, which increased hostilities between Sunni and Shiite Muslims in the region (B. Hubbard 2014). This is an extremist, fundamentalist, ultraconservative, and terrorist organization that is trying to build a caliphate, or sovereign Islamic state. Its headquarters are now in the city of Raqqa in northern Syria, which has become the center of extreme Islamist ideology. Religious and social laws ban alcohol, cigarettes, and casual dress; there are forced conversions to Islam and attempts at ethnic cleansing; and beheadings and crucifixions are now commonplace for those who threaten the strict order or are seen as enemies of ISIS (B. Hubbard 2014).

In addition to ISIS hundreds of Islamic militant groups with varying agendas came to Syria to assist the Free Syrian Army; some support ISIS and others do not. All of these groups are anti-Assad, but at the same time they are fighting each other. For example, there are many al Qaeda cells operating throughout the region, including the Nusra Front and Khorasan, but these are not aligned with ISIS. Though it originated as a cell that had its roots in al Qaeda, ISIS now competes with al Qaeda and al Nusra to form a caliphate. In fact, al Qaeda has disowned ISIS for being too radical (Baker 2014).

The United States has also become more involved, and in a direct way. On September 14, 2014, air strikes began in parts of northern Iraq, mainly to protect Kurdish refugees fleeing the wrath of ISIS to Mount Sinjar. The air strikes were conducted at the request of Iraqis to assist them in the fight against ISIS (Brook and Welch 2014). The United States began further air strikes against insurgent-dominated areas of Syria on September 23, 2014, in response to ISIS's aggressive seizure of much of the land in Iraq and Syria. The United States did so in conjunction with five Arab countries (Saudi Arabia, Qatar, Jordan, Bahrain, and the United Arab Emirates) to try to destabilize both ISIS and remaining cells of al Qaeda, the Nusra Front, and Khorasan in particular. In a speech to the nation on September 10, 2014, President Obama declared the intent was to "degrade and ultimately destroy" ISIS (Baker 2014).

The United States is working hard to form a broader coalition in addition to the five Arab countries. On September 26, 2014, Britain, Belgium, and Denmark agreed to assist with military operations in Iraq but declined to get directly involved with the intervention in Syria (Castle and Erlanger 2014). In preceding days France, Australia, and the Netherlands agreed to be part of the coalition. No European country, however, has taken part in military action inside Syria. With fear of growing regional conflict, public opinion within their own countries is not in support of direct involvement, and there are concerns that these efforts against ISIS may further empower President al-Assad.

On September 27, 2014, the United States initiated air strikes in Kobani, an area in Syria close to the border of Turkey where Kurds are under duress and where at least 150,000 refugees have crossed into Turkey fleeing the violence in Syria (Sanger and Barnard 2014). Kurdish militants in Turkey have been desperately trying to defend the Kurdish area of Kobani. The situation is incredibly complex. The Turkish government does not allow Kurds to cross into Syria to help the Kurds fighting there, and at the same time Syrian Kurds are crossing the border into Turkey to escape the civil war and ISIS. Thus, Turkey is caught in the conundrum of wanting to defeat ISIS in Syria but not wanting to enhance the power of Kurdish separatists in its own country (Barnard and Landler 2014). The Turkish government worries that the American-led attack on ISIS may strengthen the Syrian Kurds who work in alliance with Kurdish separatists in Turkey.

Other countries have similar fears that Assad will be the real victor as more countries get involved and ISIS, which is fighting Assad, is eliminated or at least significantly weakened. Another major concern is that the vacuum that might emerge if ISIS is defeated will also give pro-Assad forces more power. Furthermore, the air strikes may serve as a recruitment tool for ISIS and remaining al Qaeda cells by galvanizing Sunni Muslims throughout the Middle East who are anti-American (Kingsley 2014).

Far surpassing any other terrorist organization, ISIS is mounting a superior state-of-the-art digital propaganda campaign facilitated by social media and slick advertisements. It appears ISIS is being assisted by individuals educated in graphic design, marketing, advertising, and information technology. Ironically, as noted, this is a very conservative and reactionary group that in many ways shuns modernity, yet it is on the forefront of mastering new technologies to further its cause. For example, from its centralized Twitter account run by professionals, it distributes official statements and updates. These are complemented by provincial accounts through which supporters publish live feeds about local operations and events for each province where the group has a presence (Kingsley 2014). Those engaged in the fighting on the battlefield post their experiences on Twitter, Facebook, and YouTube to radicalize viewers, especially young ones, and offer advice how to best enter Syria and Iraq, with promises of assistance once they arrive. They also include pictures of normal, everyday activities to make it appear that they are regular folks, just like the viewers, but on a political mission. Other images they post are ISIS members delivering food to the community (Berger 2014).

Additionally, thousands of their Twitter followers, called the ISIS online "fan club," who work outside of centralized management, have installed and use the Arabic "Dawn of Glad Tidings" app, which allows the group to use their accounts to send out centrally written updates and post tweets that include links, hashtags, and images that are released all at once (Berger 2014). This is strategic because the quick inundation of messages through organized hashtag campaigns allows activists to repetitively and constantly tweet hashtags so that they trend on social networks, giving the impression that the group is larger and more popular than it really is (Kingsley 2014). The "fan club" also retweets the hashtags and translates Arabic members' messages into other languages, including English, to appeal to Western sympathizers.

ISIS also plays on global cultural events to attract attention. For example, during the World Cup ISIS put up a hashtag #WorldCup 2014 to get access to the global audience to spread its propaganda both in Arabic and in English (Marszal 2014). In a similar way it latched onto the trending hashtags that were popular during the Scottish independence referendum to widely distribute its material. It has used segments of the popular video game *Grand Theft Auto* to recruit and radicalize interested young Muslims (De Freytas-Tamura 2014).

ISIS is clever in coming up with new ways to use technology at major turning points in its struggle to increase its control in Iraq and Syria. For instance, the "Dawn of Glad Tidings" app was created in April 2014 on the day that ISIS invaded the city of Mosul in northern Iraq (the country's second-largest city). The day it was set up, it received 40,000 tweets (Berger 2014). The "Dawn" app helped pave the way for an easy victory because it widely distributed news of ISIS advances, along with horrific images of violence against its enemies including Syrian captives digging their own graves, and also posted on YouTube the video of its Hollywood-caliber *The Clanging Swords IV* feature-length video in the beginning of June 2014 (Kingsley 2014). These images give off the impression that ISIS is a dominant and invincible force. On Twitter it also posted images of the massacre of Iraqi soldiers in Saddam Hussein's hometown of Tikrit. This contributed to ISIS's military success: when the militants of ISIS arrived in Mosul waving their black banners, Iraqi soldiers abandoned their posts and fled en masse, petrified of the fate awaiting them if captured by ISIS (Kingsley 2014).

After securing Mosul ISIS then threatened to invade Baghdad, the capital of Iraq, releasing a high-end Photoshopped image of an ISIS member in the capital with the words "Baghdad, we are coming." The graphic design was undertaken by the independent volunteer "army" of tech-savvy ISIS supporters, without any request officially from ISIS. With the constant tweets of this message from supporters and affiliates, any search under "Baghdad" on Twitter returned this as the first search result—a great way to intimidate Iraqis, both soldiers and citizens (Kingsley 2014). Though ISIS by no means has the military ability to overtake Baghdad, it successfully affects people's perception of its numbers and strength.

ISIS is also determined to instill fear in citizens in the West. For example, when President Obama announced on August 7, 2014, that he had authorized strikes against Iraq, ISIS created the hashtag #AMessageFromISIStoUS, which threatened the United States with retribution against its involvement in Middle East matters. One tweet depicted an ISIS flag in front of the White House to reinforce the point. Another ISIS meme showed fighters posting with Nutella, a popular chocolate spread in Europe, a call to arms for recruiting Westerners to join ISIS in the battle in Syria. It also uses Instagram to spread its messages. One image of a high-tech gun with the message below read, "You only die once, Why not make it martyrdom?" This attracted seventy-two likes on Instagram (Kingsley 2014). In a video released a week before the Syria bombings, ISIS declared that it looked forward to the chance to draw the United States into another long war in the Middle East.

In addition to the beheading of two American journalists, James Foley and Steven Sotloff, and one British aid worker, David Haines, ISIS is shifting gears and using hostages as pawns and spokespersons to spread their message through social media. The latest victim is John Cantlie, who worked for the *Sunday Times of London* and the *Telegraph* as a freelance journalist. He was captured while traveling with James Foley on November 22, 2012, and they both spent time in the jail in Raqqa. On September 18, 2014, ISIS released a very high-quality three-minute video of Cantlie, sitting at a table in an orange jumpsuit—the same kind that Muslim prisoners held at Guatanamo Bay were forced to wear—claiming that the Western media "can twist and manipulate" truth about what is going on in the Middle East (Lackey 2014). Clearly under duress and having been told what to say, he elaborated, "After two disastrous and hugely unpopular wars in Afghanistan and Iraq, why is it that our governments appear so keen to get involved in yet another unwinnable conflict?" (Lackey 2014).

When the bombs started to fall on September 23, ISIS released another segment of its "lecture series," once again using British hostage Cantlie to deliver a message on behalf of ISIS. He compared the US intervention in the Middle East to the disastrous efforts that the US government undertook during the Vietnam War. At the beginning of the almost six-minute video, he pronounces, "In this program, we'll see how the Western governments are hastily marching towards all-out war in Iraq and Syria without paying any heed to the lessons of the recent past. Not since Vietnam have we witnessed such a potential mess in the making" (Callimachi 2014). This is a brilliant ploy of psychological warfare in the battle to influence public opinion by playing on reluctance of US citizens to get dragged into another unwinnable war, coming from a calm Western journalist rather than a black-clad militant threatening the lives of innocent hostages.

ISIS has released another video entitled "Lend Me Your Ears," again using sophisticated media imagery to try to influence American opinion in their favor. However, this taping goes further, as Cantlie quotes statements from US officials who disagree with President Obama's decision to get involved in the Middle East struggle. This could potentially create a schism among the American public in their support for military intervention in Iraq and Syria. For example, he quotes former CIA chief Michael Scheuer, who stated, "President Obama does not have the slightest intention of defeating the Islamic State," insinuating that United States has a broader and hidden agenda (Callimachi 2014). The video promises more to come, sounding like a mainstream news program, as Cantlie ends with, "Join me again for the next program" (B. Hubbard 2014).

There has been some online fight back against ISIS and its propaganda, in particular its ruthless public relations campaign by which the group recorded the beheading of two American journalists and posted them on YouTube, Facebook, and Twitter in September 2014. Twitter immediately suspended the accounts that shared the images in the English-speaking world and later began shutting down a number of key official and unofficial ISIS accounts such as @AsawirtiMedia, which consisted of several ISIS hashtag campaigns. It also discontinued ISIS's "Dawn of Glad Tidings" app. As does any digital service provider, it has the right to delete, suspend, or ban information or accounts that advocate violence or post controversial content. However, as soon as accounts are suspended or deleted, others quickly open up (Berger 2014). Individual subscribers have also created hashtags such as #ISISMediaBlackout that encouraged people to post photos and messages pertaining to James Foley's life and his work as a journalist (Kingsley 2014).

On a broader scale, there is an intense digital war going on between pro- and anti-ISIS factions. In the United States, for instance, the State Department has hired people to combat the messages coming out the Middle East. These efforts began in 2010 following the 9/11 attack on the United States to combat messages coming from al Qaeda and its supporters (Knowlton 2014). The State Department's intent is to engage youth (potential jihadists) on websites that are popular in Arab countries by publishing anti–Islamic State messages on Facebook, YouTube, and Twitter through the hashtag #Think Again Turn Away. Richard Stengel, the undersecretary of state for public diplomacy, works in conjunction with Arab officials to form what he calls "a communications coalition, a messaging coalition, to complement what's going on the ground" (Knowlton 2014). The communication center's slogan is "Contest the Space."

To try to beat ISIS at its own game and counter its propaganda, the center challenges claims made by ISIS, glorifies its setbacks, and highlights the brutality of the militant group. Some Twitter posts, which carry the seal of the US State Department, from Muslim scholars include "#ISIS murder of aid worker in violation of Islamic law," and another referencing a Turkish nurse stated "tired of treating #ISIS fighters so they can go behead people." In a speech at the UN General Assembly on September 24, 2014, Obama described the fight against militant extremists as "contesting the space that terrorists occupy—including the Internet and social media." Who is winning the digital war is up for grabs, but it seems ISIS has the upper hand because it is decentralized and has so many volunteers who constantly post and repost information, whereas several hours, or almost a full day, goes by without anything coming for #Think Again Turn Away (Knowlton 2014).

The Active Change Foundation has formed in Britain to refute both ISIS and also, more importantly, stereotypes about Muslims and Islam in general in response to the threat of the growing recruitment of youth by extremists. In September 2014 it launched a campaign around the Twitter hashtag #notinmyname in response to the beheading of British aid worker David Haines and other acts of violence committed by ISIS. The hashtag was tweeted tens of thousands of times within weeks, and a You-Tube video that promotes the campaign has had more than 200,000 view-ers (De Freytas-Tamura 2014).

The group has received a strong and satirical reaction from Muslims who feel stereotyped by the portrayal of Islam as a violent religion. Some are using the hashtag #MuslimApologies, tweeting fake apologies for Muslim accomplishments, pointing to a frustration about misconceptions about Muslims in much of the Western world; it was the leading hashtag trending on Twitter in Britain for a while. Some read: "Sorry for Alge-bra #MuslimApologies," "I'm sorry for inventing surgery, coffee, univer-sities, algebra, hospitals, toothbrushes, vaccinations, numbers, & the sort" (De Freytas-Tamura 2014).

CONCLUSION

The Arab Spring revolutions, though incomplete, originated from what Pilger (2011) refers to as the "theater of the impossible." The social, politi-cal, and economic contexts of each country are of course distinct, and re-sults of the revolutionary activity in each will take years to discern. What they all demonstrate, however, is that at least initially digital media—a new and critical resource—provided new venues of communication for expressing grievances, an activity that was previously unimaginable in these relatively shielded and oppressed societies. New web-based out-lets significantly enhanced the public communication sphere for citizens and led to combative forms of collective behavior that helped sustain the insurgencies. Young people in particular found a safe and anonymous platform for political conversation and discussion in cyberspace, which permitted them to collectively challenge the political and economic struc-tures and take to the streets en masse, where they gained recognition and sympathy and were able to alter public opinion, both nationally and inter-nationally, in their favor. Although these are hardly thriving democracies (Tunisia is much closer than the rest at this point), we can expect that the changes in the communication field will continue to serve as an invalu-able resource as the struggles continue.

THEORY TOOLKIT

HOW TO APPLY SOCIAL MOVEMENT THEORIES TO ARAB SPRING

We can apply a few of the theories discussed in Chapter 1 to the emergence and evolution of the Arab Spring:

- **Theories of new media.** These theories alert us to how ICTs can either enhance or hinder social movements, and they are pivotal in our theoretical comprehension of the Arab Spring. ICTs allowed for new communication venues through which activists could express grievances and formulate virtual weak ties and mobilizing strategies in a decentralized way. These led to contentious and disruptive forms of civil disobedience and protest politics on the streets. The application of new technology helped to sustain the uprisings and to sway public opinion both internally and externally in favor of the activists' demands. Mojos provided a new and valuable resource by circulating live coverage of government and police oppression and helped the protesters establish WUNC, thus altering the balance of power between challengers and the targets of their grievances through new media capabilities. New digital technology provided a critical resource to the struggles through the immediacy of the reports about retaliation by the authorities. Thus, the governments were not able to quickly abort attempts at social change as in the past.

- **Political mediation theory and cultural theory.** These theories fit the Arab Spring revolutions, as the uprisings were fueled largely by the subjective interpretations of what was possible—rooted in emotion more than a pragmatic assessment. Public opinion was then swayed in their favor once images of the peaceful protesters attacked by police were circulated globally. Framing and collective identity, as outlined, were also critical tools that activists used to pursue their agenda.

- **Resource mobilization theory.** This framework, with its focus on media connections, allies, formal organizations, and knowledge is also critical to our understanding of the Arab Spring. Additionally, in the Arab Spring described above, public opinion, institutional support, even if limited, from SMOs or other civil society groups, time, energy, labor power, and bodies on the streets were essential.

One of the things that allowed the unpopular dictatorships in Tunisia, Egypt, and Libya to survive for so long is that in the past, despite growing grievances among the masses, citizens had no way of knowing whether their own dissatisfaction or revolutionary passion was shared by others (apart from a small group they might know personally, i.e. with whom they have strong ties). It is essential, however, for a full-fledged social movement to emerge, that potential activists realize that others beyond these personal pockets of resistance are also willing to join the struggle. Social movement actors solidified weak ties in cyberspace through which they began building community and decentralized forms of organizing that fostered a sense of collective identity and erupted in revolutions on the streets, where strong ties were forged in the midst of the violent back-lash by the authorities.

The new media ecology creates new social and political spheres be-cause activists no longer have to depend on "open" political systems in the traditional sense of political process theory. Digital technologies are help-ing citizens to create new, albeit virtual, political openings and ways to participate in political discourse that were not available in the past. This, in turn, increases the vulnerability of authorities in different ways. As these Arab Spring cases depict, citizen journalists, or mojos, can influence public opinion by disseminating live coverage of events on the ground to which citizens both within and outside of the country respond to, and this sends a signal to the activists that they are succeeding and assists with recruitment efforts. The injustice frames that they circulated also gained them WUNC and invested the young agitators with a sense of agency. The new communication terrain, therefore, allows protesters to alter power relations, as the hard physical power at the disposal of the state can be un-dermined by the soft power of amateur journalists.

The availability of these new tools in activists' repertoire of conten-tion, therefore, assist in conceptually bridging the *why* and *how* of social movement activity (and in doing so highlights the interconnection be-tween structural and micro-level dynamics). Activists established weak ties through pre-existing social connections peer to peer, thus demon-strating the relationship between information sharing and protest activity in local communities and exemplifying the hybrid, or spillover effect, that new media enables. SMOs and traditional, external resources, as well as access to mainstream media are less critical (but still play a role) for contemporary social movement actors because grassroots mobilizations rely more on alternative and social media. Finally, these analyses also underscore the relevance of political mediation theory, because it was the subjective interpretations of what was possible that encouraged the protesters to continue their occupations despite the repression by authorities.

Another point to keep in mind is that social movement theory has historically been rooted in analyses that focus on Western European and North American countries. Such assessments have relied heavily on political process and resource mobilization theories, which focus primarily on openings in the political system that disaffected citizens can take advantage of to express their grievances, make demands, and push for reform. In contrast, these Arab Spring mobilizations illustrate that, in many cases, the *perception* of opportunities, the *framing* of issues, the formation of key *alliances* both locally and internally, as well as the creation of innovative tactics as part of a strategic repertoire of contention, can sometimes trump pre-existing mobilizing structures.

DISCUSSION QUESTIONS

1. In what ways did the 1979 Iranian revolution and the 2009 Green Revolution provide a context within which to understand the use of new technology at Arab Spring activists' disposal? How did new technology serve as a detriment to the Iranian, Tunisian, and Egyptian activists and challenge some of the overly optimistic views of ICTs for progressive causes?

2. What were the main grievances in the four countries that initiated the outbreak of the Arab Spring? What are the similarities and differences to other Arab Spring countries that witnessed revolutionary activity not covered in this book (for instance Bahrain, Yemen, Morocco, and others)? How can the political, social, and economic context inform our understanding of the commonalities and difference in these uprisings? In what ways were the strategies and tactics different, and why?

3. How does an analysis of the Arab Spring cases presented in this chapter highlight the difficulty of determining social movement

outcomes? In what ways did digital technology serve as a tool of state oppression and censorship? Cite other contemporary examples through your independent research.

4. Discuss the role of the international reaction to other social movements, past and present, and how this helped to sustain the mobilization efforts within the country you are covering in your own exploration of social movements.

CHAPTER FIVE

The Occupy Wall Street Movement and Its Precursors

On the other side of the world, the outbreak of Occupy Wall Street (OWS) events throughout the United States also caught many people by surprise. The Occupy social movement that began in 2011 was motivated by both the Arab Spring mobilizations and the Indignados movement (introduced in this chapter), and it borrowed many of the strategies and tactics employed by both. Occupy Wall Street would eventually result in a mutation into a variety of different spinoff groups, and while the overall movement has been rather dormant since 2012, whether it will once again blossom is unknown at this point. This chapter highlights a few ways in which recent social movements like OWS can inform resource mobilization theory by showing how the Internet and social media now serve as key resources for social movement actors. It also raises theoretical questions regarding new organizational styles of social movement activity as allowed for through new media and how they help us to update and inform other traditional theories of social movements.

Both OWS and the Indignados movement were enabled by new technologies and displayed a distinct organizational structure that set them apart from previous forms of collective behavior that embrace contentious politics. Traditional social movements tended to rely more on a hierarchical model, professional experts, formal and well-established SMOs, and charismatic leaders, and they provided a clear set of grievances and demands as the cornerstone of their mobilization efforts. OWS and the Indignados relied instead on a more horizontal infrastructure of connectivity that broadened the public sphere as participants and supporters shared grievances through peer-to-peer networks and coordinated political action at the grassroots level through the use of ICTs, the grassrooting of civil society (Castells 2001). The up-to-the-minute information sharing, organizing, and strategizing through new media facilitated both social movements in challenging their opponents. These two cases also demonstrate that it is now easier, cheaper, and faster for activists to get their message out, quickly reach a critical mass, and mobilize into a formidable political campaign, thus enhancing the explanatory power of theories of new media.

THE INDIGNADOS MOBILIZATION

To put OWS in perspective, we can first examine one of its key precursors, the Indignados movement, which coalesced in response to the global economic crisis that began in Europe and the austerity measures imposed by governments to address the financial fallout. The collective behavior against such measures originated in Spain with the M15 (May 15) movement and eventually became part of a broader, global movement. The organization began two weeks before the Spanish national elections in resistance to both of the two final candidates whom Spanish citizens feared would further the neoliberal agenda (rooted in economic policies that embrace privatization, deregulation, and cuts to social programs) that was currently in place (Amy Goodman 2012). More specific concerns were lack of political accountability among elected officials and their failure to represent citizen concerns, high levels of unemployment, cuts to public services, bank bailouts, and home foreclosures.

Social Media as Organizational Platform

In the spirit of the Tunisian and Egyptian revolutions, organizers of the Indignados movement, under the name Ya Democracia Real, called for an uprising via the #spanishrevolution hashtag on Twitter. Social media and the Internet provided the organizational platform after a few friends met in a local bar and shared their opinions about the dysfunctional political and economic systems in Spain (Baiocchi and Ganuza 2012). Truly grassroots in nature, and representative of what some scholars would refer to as a new social movement in terms of organizational structure (for example Melucci 1996; Giddens 1991), the participants were not affiliated with or supported by any political party or civic organization. As summed up by one of the protesters: "We are not a party. We are not a union. We are not an association. We are people. We want to expel corruption from public life . . . now, today, maybe something is starting to happen" (Amy Goodman 2012).

Resource mobilization theory can also provide a framework for understanding the development of the Indignados mobilization because it was the networking with other groups and building alliances that helped to launch the movement in both cyberspace and the real world. For example, Indignados joined forces with Youth Without a Future (Juventud Sin Futuro) to put out calls on Twitter and Facebook for the original and then subsequent protests (Rainsford 2011). Dozens of groups gathered in fifty-eight cities throughout Spain to demonstrate, primarily against the lack of job opportunities. At the time Spain had a 21 percent unemployment rate and a youth unemployment rate of almost 50 percent (Escobar 2011).

This diagnostic framing served as a critique of the 2010 bank bailouts that coincided with cuts in social programs (Snow et al. 1986; Ryan and Gamson 2006). The first M15 protest framed their central concern with the slogan "we are not goods in the hands of politicians and bankers." Later, through frame amplification, the motivational framing expanded to broader issues under the tagline "without work, without home, without pension, without fear" under the umbrella slogan of "Youth without a Future." Signs also read, "If we can't dream, you won't sleep," demarcating the lack of hope among young citizens (Escobar 2011). Framing the problem as a structural one protesters chanted, "It's not a crisis, it's the system" and, in a more humorous tone, "It's not a crisis, I just don't love you anymore" (Burns 2012).

Other participants painted the word GUILTY on bank offices and ministries as they marched, using the tactic of visibly shaming their target. Additionally, though the initial mobilization was very much youth centered, the young activists used frame bridging to resonate with mainstream concerns held among the population at large. These included concerns about austerity measures and the lack of a safety net, increasing rates of unemployment, and a lack of transparency and legitimacy with the political system. This enhanced recruitment efforts and ultimately impacted public opinion in support of the movement, giving it legitimacy on the basis of proven WUNC (Tilly 2004).

Activists promoted several types of disruptive nonviolent tactics as the mobilization efforts progressed. To establish collective identity, activists marched and occupied public spaces for months. According to Ya Democracia Real, about 50,000 demonstrated in Madrid alone on May 15. After the march the activists carried out a sit-in on a busy street and were met with police violence. Twenty-four were arrested following the melee (*El Mundo* 2011). Another rally took place after the arrests in opposition to the police response, and about twenty remained to camp out in Madrid's main plaza, Puerta del Sol. They stayed overnight but were removed the next day.

Word spread about the occupation through the hashtag #acampadasol, and this fast-paced flow of information led to further political strategizing (Day and Cobos 2012). The following day two hundred people showed up in the square. After the police removed them once again, activists used Twitter and Facebook to call for another occupation the next evening. Two days later almost a thousand Spaniards occupied the plaza, which was followed by a judicial injunction against the encampment (Burns 2012). In retaliation, tens of thousands of Indignados marched in eighty different cities across Spain.

The movement quickly garnered international attention and support. In acts of global solidarity, demonstrations were held in London, Amsterdam, Brussels, Lisbon, and elsewhere. On May 20 more than 10,000 camped out in Puerta Del Sol. In response to the police aggression intended to deter the protests on the next day, an estimated 20,000 showed up in solidarity (Silva 2012).

The squatters were soon accompanied by other tenters across Spain who gathered in Barcelona, Seville, and thirty other cities throughout the country in local acts of solidarity. The events were live-streamed on Ustream.tv as they unfolded, which served to enhance recruitment efforts (*EFE* 2011). Collective identity was easy to create and sustain, as youth initially made up the core of the contentious activities. However, because of the reality of the European economic crisis that was ravaging the lives Spaniards of all age brackets, the shared grievances provided a platform from which to extend collective identity among broad segments of the population regardless of age cohort.

Cultural theories and theories of new media give us a framework to analyze these events because it was new technology that helped to raise awareness about the mobilization, spread information through peer-to-peer channels, and recruit new members to the cause (Bennett and Iyengar 2008; Van Aelst and Walgrave 2003; Giugni 1998). Yet, similar to the Arab Spring mobilizations, the real difference happened on the streets, through the occupation of public spaces in local communities where activists forged strong ties after the initial weak ties were kindled in cyberspace and through virtual communities (McAdam and Paulsen 1993).

The Indignados as a New Social Movement

The Indignados mobilization also displayed elements of what some theorists classify as new social movements, operating in an ad hoc fashion and leaderless in nature (Melucci 1996; J. Cohen 1985). The one-day demonstration that the students orchestrated on May 15, which initiated the Indignados movement, quickly and spontaneously transitioned into open-ended sit-ins and a months-long self-governing encampment. This would serve as a template for a new type of communal resistance. Additionally, both the international and national support is representative of Tomlinson's (1999) distantiated identity.

The Indignados movement continued to press on as Spain's economic situation became worse. On February 19, 2012, hundreds of thousands protested across the nation in fifty-seven cities against economic reforms that would decrease workers' bargaining rights and social services. Long-established squatter networks joined forces with members of the M15 movement in protest of the hundreds of thousands of evictions that had taken place across the country beginning in 2011 and ending in 2012 (Burns 2012). This collaboration has led to highly effective "squatting offices" in major cities that coordinate information on empty buildings and offer consultations to people who want to squat. The movement right now is dormant, however, and there has been no visible activity since 2012.

A peaceful demonstration of several thousand Indignados in the Plaza Catalunya in Barcelona, the epicenter of the M15 movement.

Despite its now apparent inactivity, 8 million people claimed to have participated in at least one event hosted by the Indignados during the outbreak of activity in the streets (Day and Cobos 2012). As we will see later in the chapter, the Indignados' tactics were borrowed and implemented by occupiers in the United States, including using the Internet and social media tools as an organizational platform to propel the mobilizations and recruit new members across diffuse networks in both the virtual and real world. They also relied heavily on Twitter and Facebook to arrange meetings and facilitate online, and later offline, discussions and meetings to plan strategies. Similar to the Indignados uprising, OWS participants relied heavily on the device of framing to promote their agenda in a way that would resonate with mainstream concerns. Finally, the use of ad hoc civil disobedience through marches, sit-ins, rallies, occupying public spaces by means of tenting, and the relatively leaderless nature of the resistance were essential tactics that the US-based mobilizations emulated, representing what some scholars (in particular Melucci 1996) consider to be new social movements.

The Indignados Movement Spreads

Ten days after the Madrid protests began, the contagion of unrest spread to Greece. Sparked by similar economic factors as those Spain was experiencing, 80,000 citizens congregated in Athens's main square in June 2012 in opposition to the austerity measures proposed by the government. They waved banners in solidarity with the Indignados of Spain and other European countries (Ouziel 2011). Organizers used Facebook and other social media sites to organize the efforts. The Indignados then traveled to various city squares throughout Mexico to further engage in grassroots organizing. Combining new and old types of media and tactics, as well as cyberactivism and street protest, students collected proposals and suggestions, using blackboards to allow people to write their ideas or proposals, and then posting photos of the suggestions on social network sites and in street exhibitions (Bacon 2011).

In Mexico, they expressed grievances similar to those articulated in the Spanish and Greek outbreaks of collective behavior. Over 7 million young people in Mexico are unemployed, and the country has the third-highest rate of unemployment among fifteen- to twenty-nine-year-olds in member countries of the Organization of Economic Cooperation and Development. The Indignados in Mexico spent two months camping in front of the Mexican Stock Exchange following a forty-two-day hunger strike by university professor Edur Velasco, who set up a tent outside the building on October 11 (Appel 2011). He demanded that the government guarantee greater access to higher education among youth, and a few days later students and other activists joined him in setting up tents. Though there are many recent uprisings over the government's inability to curb the drug cartels, the Indignados movement in Mexico was particularly concerned with political corruption and lack of economic opportunities. It shows that physical forms of protest in real communities are the main driving force in struggles for social change, which are assisted in key ways by new information technologies and media.

Mexican Spring

Then there was the Mexican Spring in preparation for the July 2012 presidential election. The organic uprising began at the elite Iberoamerican

University on the day that Pena Nieto, the Institutional Revolutionary Party candidate, was scheduled to speak. After organizing through Facebook and Twitter, 20,000 marched in Mexico City, and thousands demonstrated in six other cities throughout Mexico shouting, "Down with Televisa" and, "This is not a soap opera" (Johnson 2012), in reference to Nieto's wife, who is in a telenovela soap opera on Televisa (Kennis 2012).

Highlighting the significance of the marches and the role social media played in their organization and turnout through horizontal information exchanges among peer networks, one high school student explained, "This is the digital age, and you don't find out about leaders appearing on the television; you hear about it from the Internet and your friends on line" (Kennis 2012). This statement also illustrates the tendency of contemporary social movements to forego vanguards or spokespersons and their often-sporadic nature (Melucci 1996).

One of the biggest demonstrations, consisting of about 10,000 Mexicans, took place outside of the headquarters of Televisa. Cognizant of the significance of the public sphere as an arena to shape common perceptions, the main complaint was the unfair media coverage provided by the two main TV stations, Televisa and TV Azteca. Together, the two stations have a 95 percent Mexican media share, and protesters claimed that both manipulated the information through coverage biased in favor of Nieto. Participants insisted that the mobilization was nonpartisan and targeted only the television monopolies. These concerns, having a free exchange of ideas at the grassroots level without state or market control, are at the crux of certain new social movement theories. Nieto accused students of being dupes of the leftist candidate, Andres Manuel Lopez Obrador. The media labeled the contentious activities a conspiracy. In fact, Televisa reported that "they didn't look like Ibero students," "they are anti-democratic," and "they had to be paid protesters" (Kennis 2012).

Mexico's largest newspaper chain, *El Sol*, also assisted the state by claiming external infiltrators were behind the disruptions. To counteract these accusations, supporters of the cause put out a call on Facebook pleading for student support. Minutes after the message was posted, a response showed up on the student's screen that had sent the message saying, "We have 131," that 131 students responded to the original student who put out the call (Molina 2012). In a showcase of how quickly challengers can respond to attempts at elite repression given new media platforms, the Indignados posted a YouTube video that displayed the 131 students who participated in the demonstrations flashing their student ID cards. The video had more than a million hits and served as a great recruitment tool to get more students involved in the protest activity.

Students then created the hashtag #YoSoy132 on Twitter that exploded in popularity and led to the creation of a campaign and a social movement called Yo Soy 132, meaning that they surpassed the original number of 131. They also created a website to announce future planned marches. The evening before the election, Yo Soy 132 organized the largest student march since the infamous 1968 student protests advocating for democracy in the Tlatelolco Plaza that resulted in a brutal massacre by the authorities. Online activity spread onto the streets as protesters gathered on July 2 to continue with their demands regarding economic and political corruption and more precisely to rebel against *El Sol*'s allegations that they were outside agitators. To succinctly frame the issue and foster collective identity among challengers, protesters held signs stating, "If there's an imposition, there will be revolution. Isn't that what we said?" (Molina 2012). These are the primary variables that cultural and sociological theorists, such as Ryan and Gamson (2006), point to.

The tech-savvy Mexican youth also employed digital technology to support their cause during their election itself. Prior to the election the Indignados, with the help of mojos, circulated a video that asked citizens to observe the polling stations, record instances of fraud with their video cameras or cellphones, and send them the official Yo Soy 132 e-mail address (Molina 2012). On July 5 the site showed clips revealing people receiving prepaid supermarket cards from the Nieto staff in exchange for their vote, among other violations. The Yo Soy Observer Commission received more than 1,000 reports of irregularities. Thus, new media and the capabilities they offer to hold authorities accountable and expose corruption is something that resource mobilization theory can include in these activists' repertoire of contention.

Additionally, these documented observations challenged the official narrative put forth by the state and the mainstream media. The unrest continued after the election, as much of the population was convinced that it was corrupt, a claim supported by international election observers (Molina 2012). Though Mexico is infamous for electoral fraud, this was the first time citizens organized collectively to fight what has typically been viewed as business as usual.

Mexican agitators engaged in more contentious politics on July 7 when they occupied many public plazas throughout the country and put out a call for international supporters to demonstrate outside of Mexican embassies. In Mexico City more than 90,000 marched to the chant of "No to imposition!" Activists in the Indignados movement also successfully translated their original grievances of the high cost of education and unfair media coverage to broader political issues of corruption and economic injustice at the societal level as the cause gained traction through frame amplification (e.g., Snow et al. 1986). Dignity became the rallying cry. One member of the Yo Soy 132 movement explained, "We should continue organizing and fighting for the country that we want, but first we must regain our dignity, become indignant, and transform this country" (Molina 2012). On July 7 and 8, Yo Soy 132 held a National Summit of Students to strategize for the future.

The main goal was to seek out allies among other SMOs to establish horizontal links, and both work in conjunction with active groups and organize dormant sectors of civil society. These include groups working on issues of human rights, education, social violence, indigenous rights, public health, environmental issues, freedom of speech and equal access to media, gender issues, and cultural issues. Through these efforts they have linked with international groups in more than thirty countries including the UK, Spain, Italy, Canada, China, the United States, Portugal, and Argentina (yosoy132.wordpress.com). This too is symbolic of how new social movements operate—at the grassroots level, without recognizable representatives, and forging alliances with other groups through frame bridging and frame amplification. Yet again, as resource mobilization points out, and though we are witnessing different types of organizational structures and forms of connectivity that digital technology enables, traditional SMOs and forms of organizing are still an important resource for sustained social and political mobilizations.

The Indignados in Europe and Mexico were harbingers of the subsequent Occupy Wall Street movement in the United States. The declining US economic conditions and the shared grievance of a lack of political representation by elected officials helped to spark this social movement. Below we will examine the underlying frustrations that led to the mobilization;

the strategies and tactics that activists applied; how they framed their issues, forged collective identity, and created networks of resistance with other allies; and how activists utilized digital tools to initiate and sustain the campaign, as well as the consequences of Occupy Wall Street.

OCCUPY WALL STREET IN THE UNITED STATES

Both the Arab Spring and the Indignados movement sparked revolution across the United States in the fall of 2011. Then–New York mayor Michael Bloomberg anticipated this occurrence because the declining economic conditions in the United States were hitting youth particularly hard: "You have a lot of kids graduating college, can't find jobs. That's what happened in Cairo. That's what happened in Madrid. You don't want those kinds of riots here" (Einhorn and Siemasko 2011). The members of OWS did not riot in the United States, but tens of thousands did orchestrate and maintain ongoing protests, demonstrations, and encampments across the country. Similar to most contemporary social movements, OWS activists organized using digital technologies that allowed them to circumvent professional experts, charismatic leaders, or formal SMOs. Instead, they shared grievances and planning strategies in a horizontal fashion through new media to quickly and cheaply get the word out about their campaign and reach a critical mass.

The OWS social movement was made up of an assortment of activists. Many were young, many had been foreclosed upon, and many were unemployed or underemployed. Though left-leaning, they were not officially associated with any political party yet shared a concern for the current economic and political predicament in the United States. Though they worked cooperatively, the various groups were only loosely connected and had no central leadership or spokesperson. The lack of any central form of leadership or concise diagnostic frame was a strategic tactic because it welcomed inclusivity and participatory democracy and was an enhancement of the public sphere. This, in turn, opened up avenues for alliances with other advocacy groups that would prove critical to the sustainability of Occupy Wall Street in various formats once the tenters were decamped.

Under the rubric of the We Are the 99 Percent campaign, Occupy participants began discussions about the essential nature of the political and economic systems that they participate in and thus help legitimize. The US economic and political climate was ripe for protest at the time. For example, at the start of the 2008 recession, the collective wealth of the richest 1 percent of Americans was greater than that of the 99 percent combined. The United States now has the largest concentration of wealth since 1928 and is the most unequal of any industrialized country. While CEOs' compensation rose 36 percent during 2010, wages stagnated for the rest of the population, and people were losing their homes at alarming rates because of Ponzi schemes carried out by the major banks (Sherter 2011).

In September 2011 the OWS campaign swept across the country with hundreds of occupations in various forms. The first to take place was the occupation of physical spaces including parks, plazas, and public spaces outside of federal buildings. These forms of nonviolent civil disobedience resulted in more than 7,000 arrests in 114 cities as citizens engaged in large-scale disruptive activities that have been absent in this country for decades (OccupyArrests.com). It only took a few months (in some cases weeks), however, for most tenters to be forcibly removed by the police. After the disencampments, participants in OWS found other venues through which they could continue their protest activities.

In many popular accounts OWS is portrayed as a spontaneous, youthful unleashing of collective behavior that seemed to come from nowhere. The reality is somewhat different. The roots of OWS first began in July 2011 when the soon-to-be occupiers (mostly young and with little social movement experience) met with veterans and organizers of the Indignados (Milkman, Lewis, and Luce 2013). Resource mobilization theory (McCarthy and Zald 1973) addresses how both leaders and formal organizations, in addition to media attention, are key requisites for successful and sustained social movement activity, thus giving us a lens through which to evaluate and make sense of the origins of OWS.

A case in point is that it took the large-scale protests against Wisconsin Governor Scott Walker and the events of the Arab Spring to begin the planning of the protests in the United States. Another misconception is that Occupy was born on the Internet (similar assumptions have been made about the Arab Spring, both of which have been dubbed the "Facebook Revolution" by some journalists). This is also false. In the aftermath of these initial meetings with OWS, planners held a conference

A young man meditates amid the Occupy Wall Street demonstration near the New York Stock Exchange on September 21, 2011, in New York City.

encouraging people to meet at a park near Wall Street to begin the more formal and broader strategy of mobilization. The encampments were also inspired by the Canadian magazine *Adbusters* when the editors put out a call to occupy Wall Street in their July edition. The ad asked, "WHAT IS OUR ONE DEMAND? #OCCUPYWALLSTREET SEPTEMBER 17.

BRING TENT" (Milkman, Lewis, and Luce 2013). The same message was sent to the 900,000 people on its listserv. Taking a cue from Arab Spring, *Adbusters* also sent out an e-mail that read, "America needs its own Tahrir," and on July 4 it tweeted, "Dear Americans, this July 4 dream of insurrection against corporate rule." On August 30 the hacktivist group Anonymous (discussed in Chapter 2), released a video in support of this call, urging its members to "flood lower Manhattan, set up tents, kitchens, peaceful barricades and Occupy Wall Street."

Social Media Fuels the Flames

A distinguishing characteristic of the Occupy movements that parallels the Indignados and the Arab Spring uprisings was that revolutionary communication tools and mobile technological devices enabled citizens across the United States to break out of their isolation, raise awareness of the issues that concerned them, and take their rage onto the streets in a collective cause. The recognition that they were not alone by sharing their stories through new media, on the streets, and in the camps imbued citizens with a sense of agency. Tumblr.com was instrumental in sparking the protests by publishing the "We are the 99 percent" blog: personal stories of lost jobs, lost homes, crippling debt, and a lack of government support or accountability (Jacobs 2011). This sharing of stories and grievances aided in constructing a sense of collective identity through weak ties that become strong ties (McAdam and Paulsen 1993; Boulainne 2009). Bimber's (2003) accelerated pluralism accounts for the broadening formats for political discussions, communicative action, and the public sphere in general. Theories of the Internet, therefore, are pertinent to an analysis of this outbreak of collective behavior.

The "We are the 99 Percent" slogan summarized the main motivational frame and further helped to solidify collective identity among participants in the movement. This framing technique also made reference to the sheer numbers of those affected by the growing inequality, thus dramatizing the cause. Additionally, the OWS movement's use of framing was unique because participants did not make specific demands but wanted collectively, through dialogue and debate, to create an alternative to the current economic and political systems. Some of the signs that reflected this sentiment, again relying on the tactic of clever framing (while injecting humor), were "Wake Up From the American Dream. Create a Livable American Reality," "Lost my Job Found an Occupation," and "Dear Capitalism, It's not You it's Us. Just Kidding, It's You" (occupy-wallstreet.org). These injustice frames are something that constructionist theories promote as being effective in drawing in new recruits, creating sympathy for a cause and swaying public opinion, and ultimately creating social change).

OWS was also characterized by a yearning for new ways of living by establishing novel types of relationships and ways of interacting, which is emphasized by certain schools of thought in new social movement theory (e.g., Johnston 1994). For example, general assemblies were held in the spirit of what this new system might look like. The assemblies were open to the public with the intention of giving everyone a voice in the decision-making process (Jennifer Preston 2011b). The goal was to foster genuine communicative action, or in Habermas's terms, "ideal speech situations," and to open the public sphere to individuals oftentimes excluded. There were other concrete forms of creating community as well: basic needs like food, shelter, medical care, sanitation, security, education, and culture were handled by working groups, copying the organizational structure of the Indignados encampments in Spain and Tahrir Square in Egypt, as well as the earlier occupation of the State Capitol in Madison, Wisconsin. By borrowing these tactics, OWS demonstrated that social movements tend to build on strategies that have proven successful in the past and that this replication provides an important resource for social movement actors.

2.0 Technology Sustains Occupy

Digital technology was a driving force behind the OWS campaign because the shared stories provided citizens with a sociological imagination—an understanding that their personal problems were rooted in social issues and structural flaws in the economic and political systems. In addition to Tumblr there were dozens of wikis and web pages where citizens could further engage in the discussions and planning of Occupy Wall Street.

Three of the most popular websites were howToOccupy.org, take thesquare.net, and especially OccupyWallst.org, which raised thousands of dollars from dozens of groups and hundreds of individuals and provided food, shelter, and gas mask protection to occupiers (Jennifer Preston 2011b). While ICTs are clearly changing some aspects of collective behavior and contentious politics, which resource mobilization theory now must take into account, traditional resources are still relevant. To organize the various protests, activists also used Meetup.com and Foursquare, two location services that people can download and use on their cellular devices to track schedules of marches, location changes, and alternative routes (Glantz 2011).

Online activity quickly translated into interest, motivation, and street activity. On September 17 about 1,000 people gathered to occupy the financial district in New York City. One week later they undertook an unpermitted march that began at Zuccotti Park (renamed Liberty Plaza by the occupiers), and the number of participants soared to more than 2,500 as marchers made their way through the streets of Lower Manhattan (Moynihan 2011). Riot police met the demonstrators, and, in the first incident of police violence, a commander was filmed pepper-spraying in the face women standing on a public sidewalk after being "kettled" along with many others (the term kettled refers to ordering protesters to disperse but using orange nets to capture small groups of demonstrators in isolated spaces with no escape route).

The video of these women falling to the ground and screaming in pain went viral, promoting anger and triggering sympathy and support for the activists. Thus, the aggression used by the police authorities backfired and gave the mobilization a boost in terms of recruitment, sympathy, media coverage, and shaming the target of resistance. At the end of the assembly, a total of eighty protesters had been arrested (Moynihan 2012). In yet another instance the public, on-the-ground mobilization efforts of activists in circulating these images was key.

The next major event occurred on October 1 when 700 activists were arrested on the Brooklyn Bridge for blocking traffic (Pilkington 2011). This resulted in a class-action lawsuit against the New York Police Department, and after the mass arrest several major labor movements endorsed the occupiers. Service Employees International Union organizers and healthcare workers' Local 1199 in Manhattan, for example, not only marched and camped out with the occupiers in the park but also delivered blankets, ponchos, food, and water to help them sustain the encampment. This fit well with one of the most common signs that were visible throughout Zuccotti Park which read, "Compassion is our new currency," a good example of how the successful framing of issues can foster and nurture collective identity and propel social movement activity. The assistance of formal organizations in terms of resources and strategic alliances most strongly emphasized by resource mobilization theory and to a lesser extent by political process theory.

Another example of compassion under the umbrella of solidarity in action was when a call for pizza went out and $2,600.00 worth arrived in less than an hour. Wisconsin's state house was supplied with pizza in a similar fashion, including some paid for and dispatched by Egyptian revolutionaries (Solnit 2012). These cross-national and international networks of support could not have happened without digital media, which underscores the importance of cross-fertilization among organizational supporters as a key resource for timely social movements.

The Role of Traditional, Alternative, and Social Media

On November 16 police moved in and cleared Zuccotti Park. Acknowledging the importance of media coverage and its critical role in the public sphere and civil society in exposing wrongdoing by the authorities, police attempted to make filming of the event difficult if not impossible through physical obstruction and "frozen zones." In this way they prevented even credentialed journalists from entering the area (Julia Preston 2012b) under the guise of security (for their own personal safety). However, activists got around police obstacles by live-streaming the events from their cell phones, and a live chat window ran alongside the video player of both Livestream and Upstream which allowed users to comment on events as they unfolded (Stelter 2011). The Occupystream.com site also provided links to real-time online streams following OWS and protests abroad. There were more than seven hundred Occupy-related channels, 70 percent of the live-streaming content was created on mobile phones, and 89 percent of it viewed on mobile phones (Jennifer Preston 2011a). Thus, through novel technological devices activists circumvented the dominant institutions to voice their concerns and organize their agenda in an example of Mann's (2000) interstitial locations. This is a critical component of new social movements and is what Habermas (1993, 1989) would consider an invaluable asset in ordinary citizens' attempt to regain control over the public sphere and aspects of communicative action. It is also demonstrative of Melucci's (1996) intermediate public space through which individuals can politicize issues through dialogue outside of the influence of authorities. It is also indicative of Castells's (2001) grassrooting of civil society. Therefore, theories of new media provide a good lens for understanding and analyzing the developments of Occupy Wall Street.

Additionally, throughout the encampments New York City organizers continuously updated Livestream news in the form of videos and photos onto the Twitter account, #OccupyWallST, with more than 90,000 followers and liked by more than 300,000 Facebook users worldwide (Saba 2011). There were also more than one hundred accounts on Twitter pertaining to Occupy Wall Street with tens of thousands of followers that collaborated under the hashtag #OWS. The main account, @occupywallstnyc had more than 100,000 followers (Kelley 2011).

#Occupy and #occupywallstreet hashtags organized events through websites such as Occupytogether.com. YouTube also helped to keep the Occupy Wall Street movement sustainable. There were 1.7 million YouTube videos tagged with the key word "occupy" in YouTube's news and politics section that were viewed 72 million times (Berkowitz 2011). There were also more than four hundred Facebook pages for Occupy and 2.7 million fans around the world (Jennifer Preston 2011a). Protester Craig Juedlman posted a photo of his bruised face on Facebook containing the message, "just got punched in the face like 5 times by NYPD . . . guess they saw my earlier post" (Berkowitz 2011). Similar to the Arab Spring, the brutality exercised by the authorities only provoked more activists to join the protests out of a sense of compassion and empathy under the rubric of Jasper and Polletta's (2001) perceived shared status, or feeling of collective identity, thus once again giving relevance to cultural theories to make sense of how the events of OWS transpired.

In one of the cleverest challenges to police attempts to suppress leaks, activist Tim Pool acquired a Parrot AR drone, which can be purchased (cheaply) on Amazon.com, that he named the "occucopter" (Sharkey and Knuckey 2011). It is controlled with an iPhone and has an onboard camera, which Pool modified to stream live video to the Internet. This increased support for the social movement actors because the police and other authorities had a more difficult time manipulating the narrative to discredit the dissenters in yet another example of how new technology is expanding Habermas's idea of the public sphere and of participatory democracy.

Protests and acts of civil disobedience continued on December 17 outside of the World Financial Center, whose owner, Brookfield Property, also owns Zuccotti Park. On New Years' Eve OWS called for Occupy 2012 in an attempt to retake Zuccotti Park. What began peacefully turned into a mêlée when protesters breached the park's barricades and police arrested several people. On the six-month anniversary of the first occupation, on March 17, police arrested dozens more in Zuccotti after hundreds gathered following a march (Moynihan 2012).

The police, it turns out, have not completely escaped accountability. For example, in April 2013 Michael Premo, a longtime housing activist was found innocent of charges of assaulting a police officer because of the work of a mojo. Premo was arrested in 2011 when he, with other members of OWS, tried to occupy a vacant lot in lower Manhattan. When police prevented them from doing so, they began a march and were subsequently kettled. The video taken by the amateur journalist clearly showed the officer tackling Premo as he tried to get up after falling down during the skirmish (Kane 2013).

Thus, while resource mobilization usually acknowledges the role of the media in terms of gaining access to mainstream media, mojos turn this dynamic on its head. Access to, and utilization of, new digital tools gives contemporary activists leverage that social movement organizers and participants did not have in the past. This is one of the ways in which theories that account for the role of new media can nicely supplement resource mobilization theory in understanding OWS.

The Agenda Diversifies

As the movement developed, OWS participants shifted their priorities from forming outdoor, self-sustaining communities and holding general assemblies to focus on more concrete issues such as the housing crisis, lack of regulation of the financial system, and the sharp increase in student debt (discussed in the depth in the next chapter). One spin-off group, Occupy Our Homes, for example, has occupied homes of families facing eviction, hoping to get media attention by humanizing and dramatizing the evictions. It has had numerous successes in warding off foreclosures and evictions throughout New York City (Anderson 2011).

Another subgroup, Occupy Wall Street New York, has also held what they label "move your money relays." In March 2012 activists began escorting people from Bank of America branches, where members closed out their accounts and transferred their money into community banks and local credit unions. Supporters of the cause created a website called FTheBanks.org, which provided instructions for transferring money, as well as information regarding when collective efforts to do so were taking place. On another front, the Fight BAC (Bank of America campaign) went nationwide after being advertised on the alternative news provider *AlterNet.org*. During "Move Your Money," or "Bank Transfer Day," activists helped more than 40,000 Americans remove their money from large banks, and more than 65,000 citizens switched to credit unions in October alone (Maharawal 2012). Religious groups moved $55 million out of the Bank of America by November 2012, and a San Francisco interfaith group moved $10 million from Wells Fargo in observance of Lent.

Occupy Oakland

Occupy Oakland was the most violent of all the encampments. The first clash between activists and police occurred on October 15 and gained international attention when an eighty-four-year-old retired schoolteacher was pepper-sprayed at the encampment at Frank Ogawa Plaza and the image went viral over YouTube. Five of the participants were arrested for camping violations (Ash 2012). After police cleared the camp, many of those who were ejected planned a street march for later that afternoon in protest of the closure. When approximately 30,000 protesters tried to re-establish the encampment, another confrontation resulted. This massive and spontaneous show of support was made possible by information sharing through the Internet.

Two days later several videos circulated showing a protester being punched in the face at the follow-up demonstration by a deputy inspector. Once again the police attempted to clear the area, only to have demonstrators come out in even larger numbers, thus setting in motion a cycle of protest, violence, and retaliation through bigger and bigger demonstrations. Outrage only escalated when Iraq marine veteran Scott Olsen was badly injured after being hit by a projectile dispersed by the police (Ash 2012). The peer-to-peer distribution of information helped build collective identity and frame the grievances in a way that would disgrace certain members of the police force.

For example, the Occupyoakland.com website consistently and thoroughly provided details about the events as they unraveled. One thread, regarding the raid on the park read: "this morning at 5 am over 500 police in riot gear from cities all over central CA brutally attacked the Occupy Oakland encampment . . . the police attacked the peaceful protest with flash grenades, tear gas and rubber bullets after moving in with armored vehicles" (Seltzer 2011). Dramatizing the events in an attempt to sway public opinion is a main concern of political mediation theory (Soule and King 2006).

Allies across national borders also developed, made possible by digital technology. For example, in a display of international solidarity and collective identity, Egyptian activists held a march from Tahrir square to the US Embassy in Cairo to show support for the Occupy Wall Street actors. Within the United States protesters marched in Manhattan, for instance, chanting, "New York is Oakland, Oakland is New York" in solidarity (Nir and Flegenheimer 2012).

Calls to regroup after the raid went out over Twitter immediately, as did a call to e-mail the office of the mayor with complaints. A few weeks later, on November 2, more than 5,000 people watched the Oakland Police Department raid during a one-day general strike that activists held, thanks to mojos distributing the images virally (Romney 2012). More than 10,000 protesters shut down the port (which is the fifth busiest in the United States). One resource that enhanced the efforts of the insurgents was the organizational support that helped build and sustain the infrastructure of the movement. Prior to the strike Occupy Oakland began networking with one of the strongest trade unions, the International Longshoreman and Warehouse Union, which became a key ally and helped with recruitment efforts (Romney 2012). Working in conjunction with allies and formal organizations of course is one of the important variables that enhances political struggle according to resource mobilization theory.

Following the raid the Occupy Oakland website encouraged activists to fight back stating, "Reconvene today at 4pm at the Oakland Library on 14 and Madison" (Romney 2012). That evening there was a second

During Occupy Oakland, information shared online helped to build collective identity and frame grievances to disgrace certain members of the police force. © Steve Rhodes/ Demotix/Corbis.

confrontation following a rally at the Oakland Public Library. The battle continued on December 12 in a second general strike, fortifying collective identity. Thousands of OWS protesters blocked access to several major West Coast ports from San Diego to Anchorage in synchronized demonstrations. This brought work to a standstill in Oakland, California, Longview, Washington, and Portland, Oregon (Romney 2012). A diagnostic frame on one sign read, "Sorry for any inconvenience while we fix our democracy."

City Hall was shut down a few days after the general strike when two dozen Occupy Oakland protesters tried to storm the building. Members of Occupy Oakland's interfaith coalition had called for protesters to take over the mayor's and city administrators' offices after police arrested twelve in Frank Ogawa Plaza the day before in an attempt at another encampment (Gwynne 2012). On January 28, four hundred people were arrested once again outside of City Hall after police engaged in a mass kettling maneuver. In fact, they were waiting in riot gear before the activists arrived, declaring they were alerted by media sites that described the actions as "antipolice." This exemplifies how digital technology can be both detrimental as well as helpful to activists' mobilizing strategies, as Hindman (2007) warns.

There are other examples that demonstrate how the authorities are also quite savvy in using new technology in counteractions to contentious politics. Members of the Oakland Police Department, for example, collected photos of occupiers at demonstrations and sought out those individuals at subsequent protests, specifically protesters with prior arrests. In one instance on January 4, an Occupy Oakland media committee photographer, Adam Katz, was singled out by the police. He had been arrested while filming the raid of the disencampments and charged with obstruction of justice. He contended, "Officers who knew my name, and knew that I took pictures, deliberately went after me and arrested me under completely false pretenses." In another occurrence, during a January 15 general assembly in the plaza, police approached an occupier and showed him his photo in a book they had and informed him that they knew he was on probation (Cagle 2012).

Occupy Events in Other Cities

While the mass arrests in New York and Oakland received most of the media attention, in large part because of the violence that occurred, other actions took place from coast to coast across the United States that received less notice. All in all, more than 1,600 cities were occupied during Occupy Wall Street (Barsoumian 2011). Occupy Los Angeles was one of the most peaceful of the occupy movements and among the least disruptive disencampments. In fact, the mayor initially welcomed the encampment outside of City Hall and on a rainy day handed out ponchos to the campers, and the Los Angeles City Council adopted a resolution in support of the movement (Wilson 2011). Police looked on passively until the camp was cleared in April, purportedly because of health and safety concerns, as declared by the city. Though the camp was cleared, the initial receptivity afforded activists time and space to raise awareness, gain visibility and media attention, and debate issues both informally among campers and more formally in the general assembly meetings.

In July 2012 activists pushed the boundaries of more traditional tactics and regathered to hold a "Chalk Walk" in direct response to people being charged with felony vandalism for writing political messages on sidewalks (much of this outside of major banks). In the "free chalk for free speech" event, organizers handed out chalk to passersby, warning them that they may be arrested for writing on the sidewalk (Ebright, Castelan, and White 2012). This tactic can be viewed as a way to augment the public sphere that allows for free expression of political ideas and sentiments—literally "free." Many made chalk drawings and were arrested, and police used tear gas, rubber bullets, and batons to disperse the crowd, in some ways recalling the regimes in the Arab Spring countries that tried to block the Internet and social media to stifle free speech, which was viewed as a threat to the status quo.

International Solidarity Facilitated by Digital Platforms

After the tent evictions across the United States, the Coalition for the Political Rights of Mexicans Abroad, which is part of the Indignados movement, sent a letter of support to OWS activists under attack. It declared, "We greet your movement because your struggle against the suppression of human rights and against social and economic injustice has been a fundamental part of our struggle, that of the Mexican people who cross borders and the millions of Mexican migrants who live in the United States" (Bacon 2012). In an effort to bolster future transnational collaborative efforts in the Occupy struggle there has been much online activity to try to establish a shared, yet loose, agenda. Recently, an international assembly consisting of members of Occupy groups on all six continents released a declaration of intent. The meeting was held online and included thousands more over e-mail. The statement emphasized that it is both a work in progress and that it represents a global movement. It was distributed publicly for more input and suggestions (*AlterNet* 2012).

Alvaro Rodriguez of the Indignados movement in Spain and one of the drafters of the statement elaborates:

> This is the beginning of a new global process of bringing the opinions of many people around the world together. It represents the beginnings of a form of global democracy in its infancy which is direct and participatory— of the people, by the people, and for the people. While the statement does not represent the position of local and city assemblies, the next step is to

present it to assemblies around the world for consideration, discussion and revisions, as part of a dialogue of the "Global Spring" movements taking place across six continents. . . . The process of writing the statement was consensus based, open to all, and regularly announced on our international communication platforms, that are also open to all (e.g. the "squares" mailing list, the weekly global roundtables and the "international" Facebook group).

In a statement printed in the *Guardian* on October 25 and circulated in cyberspace, one Egyptian activist wrote,

To all of those across the world currently occupying parks, squares and other spaces, your comrades in Cairo are watching you in solidarity. Having received so much advice from you about transitioning to democracy, we thought it's our turn to pass on some advice . . . As the interests of government increasingly cater to the interest and comforts of private, transnational capital, our cities and homes have become progressively more abstract and violent places, subject to the casual ravages of the next economic development or urban renewal scheme. An entire generation across the globe has grown up realizing, rationally and emotionally that we have no future in the current order of things."(*Guardian* 2011)

This international collaboration, which is leading to a sense of collective identity that crosses borders, is possible only through the use of new media tools, especially considering how quickly and efficiently it was being organized in a decentralized fashion. This gives us notice of the relevance of theories of new media in affecting social change. This cross-national sense of solidarity also gives support to theories of new social movements (Giddens 1991; Tomlinson 1999; Johnston 1994).

CONCLUSION

Although it is a bit difficult to generalize across the various Occupy events and settings, and although the political and theoretical ramifications are yet to be sorted out, there are some notable achievements secured by OWS as a social movement. In addition to the global fermenting of

THEORY TOOLKIT

THEORY TOOL KIT TO UNDERSTAND OCCUPY WALL STREET

We can apply a few of the theories discussed in Chapter 1 to the emergence and evolution of Occupy Wall Street:

- **Political mediation theory.** The OWS social movement, though now dormant, showed the relevance of political mediation theory by altering the conversation about and impacting public opinion on class inequality in the United States.

- **Theories of new media.** These theories are also relevant to understanding how ICTs helped to influence the mainstream media to cover the story and therefore raise awareness about the grievances of the occupiers. New media is transforming contentious politics, as evidenced in OWS's peer-to-peer online sharing of images and video captured by mojos of the often violent reaction by the authorities, which helped the OWS participants to sustain their cause, at least for a while. Incorporating these theories of new media with culturally oriented theories of social movements shows how collective identity can emerge in cyberspace and result in the spillover effect on the streets.

- **New social movement theories.** Certain aspects of these theories are also important in making sense of the OWS encampments. These encampments were decentralized and leaderless organizational structures that operated in a more horizontal fashion in terms of power sharing and decision making, made up of citizens attempting to have a stronger voice in determining how the political, economic, and social spheres should function.

organizational networking, the movement has altered the media and political narrative about economic inequality in the United States. A Pew Research Center survey of 2,048 adults, for instance, found that 66 percent of Americans now believe there are "very strong" or "strong" conflicts between the rich and poor, a 19 percent increase from 2009. Thirty percent say there are "very strong conflicts" between poor people and rich people—double the proportion that offered that view in July of 2009 (*Common Dreams* 2011).

This shift in attitude is partially a consequence of the media coverage that OWS activists secured. For example, the word "protest" appeared in newspapers and online exponentially more in 2011 than at any other time (Power 2011). A LexisNexis search showed that US newspapers published 409 stories with the word "inequality" in October 2010. In October 2011 it swelled to 2,269. In October 2010 there were 452 stories that covered issues of greed, as opposed to 2,285 in 2011 (Heuvel 2012). Also in October the Nexis news-media database registered almost 500 mentions of "inequality" each week; the week before OWS started there were only 91, and there was a seven-fold increase in Google searches for the term "99 percent" between September and October (Stelter 2011).

Other analyses by Pew Research Center's Project for Excellence in Journalism found that the Occupy Wall Street movement accounted for 10 percent of national news coverage in the week of October 9 and 10 percent of the mainstream media's news coverage in the week of October 10 to 16 (Pew Research Center 2011). In November *Time* magazine ran a cover story entitled "What Ever Happened to Upward Mobility?" (Foroohar 2011). In January the *New York Times* ran a piece on mobility and inequality in today's America as well as a front-page story entitled "Harder for Americans to Rise from the Lower Rungs" (Blackwell 2012).

In addition to other factors and resources, ICTs helped to influence this shift in the national narrative and propelled the mainstream media to cover these issues, which until the OWS uprising had ignored for the most part. It was the online organizing and information sharing that got people onto the streets, which increased the visibility of the encampments. Supporters of OWS garnered the attention of the mainstream press, swayed public opinion in their favor, and increased momentum because mojos distributed the episodes of unprovoked violence by the authorities against nonviolent protesters. Though at first mainstream media either ignored or trivialized the mobilization, the spillover effect onto the streets facilitated by ICTs forced mainstream journalists to report on the happenings and take OWS, and the grievances of the participants, seriously.

The events of OWS show that online activity not only informs individuals about certain events but also motivates people into action in certain circumstances and thus serves as a hybrid of online and offline participation in political causes. Therefore, theories of new media are well suited to comprehend OWS because they suggest that collective identity can be established, at least originally, through weak ties in cyberspace and can lead to activity in the real world to forge a stronger sense of collective identity in tangible community settings.

This analysis can also help to update resource mobilization theory by taking into account the new digital tools that activists have in their current repertoire of contention. It expands the ways we can envision political openings as discussed by the political process model. Furthermore, the ambitions and formations of the encampments fit within the contours of theories of new social movements, which focus on democratizing new areas of social life and allowing for marginalized voices to be heard through horizontal chains of communication. The communities that were created and maintained (albeit short lived) in the occupation of public spaces were intentionally designed for this—to allow for dialogue and to foster new ideas about how to reclaim citizens' role in political, economic, and social life.

DISCUSSION QUESTIONS

1. In what ways did the Arab Spring, the Indignados, the Mexican Spring, and the Wisconsin battle lead to Occupy Wall Street? Do some research and update what is happening now for each of these cases. What theories best apply to recent developments? Do you agree that leaderless social movements are a good strategy for activists to employ? Make a case for and against this new development with specific examples not addressed in this book.

2. What role did mojos play in sustaining the causes that this chapter describes? Summarize how they are playing critical roles in other social movements through your own independent research.

3. How was the emergence of OWS misrepresented in some popular accounts? Compare and contrast how the media distorted outbreaks of contentious politics in this situation to other social movements.

4. Track further mutations of OWS. What is going on now in your local community in terms of Occupy events, issues, or discussions?

CHAPTER SIX

Occupy Student Debt and the Dreamers

This chapter analyzes three recent student-led social movements that address issues in higher education. The first two center on the reaction to increasing student debt and proposed tuition hikes at universities across Canada and the United States. The third mobilization focuses on the DREAMers (supporters of the Development Relief and Education for Alien Minors Act), which is a movement that consists of students without proper citizenship status who are challenging federal and state laws that prohibit them from obtaining most types of financial assistance to attend college.

The case studies in this chapter inform social movement theory because they illustrate that with the digital revolution (1) the parameters within which groups and individuals can voice concerns, share information, organize protest activities, and forge collective identity are expanding dramatically; (2) the resources, organizational processes and structure, and sources of connectivity and communication that activists rely on are different than in earlier eras; (3) the material resources and access to mainstream media of well-established SMOs are less relevant (but not completely unimportant) today; and (4) protesters have increased leverage over authorities through new methods of holding them accountable for hostile or unconstitutional responses to protest activity.

PROTESTS IN CANADA

The first large-scale student protests in Canada began in the spring of 2012 when students engaged in disruptive activities in the province of Quebec. The original grievance was a planned tuition hike by the government, but student activists incrementally broadened and amplified their demands and reached out to the Canadian citizenry for support. They did so through frame bridging and frame amplification (Snow et al. 1986) to link their grievances to the broader economic hardships that all Canadian citizens were facing, including cuts in social services, factory closures, union busting, and an increase in retirement age (Heath 2012). Thus, they tapped into other pre-existing issues under the rubric of economic injustice, which helped to nurture a sense of collective identity among much of the public.

From the outset activists publicly discussed student debt as a problem rooted in class struggle and inequality and used digital technology to promote their cause. On the "Fight Tuition Increase" website, for example, students emphasized the fact that the financial sacrifice that the citizens of Quebec were asked to abide was not shared fairly but hit the middle and lower classes disproportionately hard (Heath 2012). The website specifies, "In 2007, the Canadian government transferred more than $700 million in additional federal funding to the Quebec government. The Charest government could have invested this money in education, which would far have exceeded the $325 million currently collected by tuition fee increases. Instead, the richest individuals and corporations got a tax cut and students got left with nothing" (Leier 2012). This site helped to engage students by increasing awareness of the rising level of student discontent. Theories of new media, therefore (Castells 2001; McAdam and Paulsen 1993; H. Jenkins 2006; Kahn and Kellner 2003; Van Aelst and Walgrave 2003), are pertinent to our understanding of the emergence of the Canadian student protests.

Through new media the student activists issued a rallying call for a strike at the University of Montreal, one of the largest universities in Canada. Their efforts were successful. On May 14 Line Beauchamp, the Quebec education minister and deputy premier, resigned after failing to reach an agreement with students (Banerjee 2012). The university cancelled classes and ended the semester early because of the constant disruptions

Students in Montreal march behind a banner during a demonstration demanding free education. The Canadian student protests used frame bridging and frame amplification to gain wide public support for their cause.

following the collapse of the talks among students, university administrators, and government representatives. The contentious tactics included sit-ins in front of government offices and entrances to universities, blocking main highway entrances, and massive marches and demonstrations on college campuses and in surrounding neighborhoods (Dolphin 2012).

These events at the University of Montreal were only an indicator of what would transpire in the upcoming months. As other universities joined in the resistance labeled the "Maple Spring," activists undertook widespread actions throughout Canada in the longest and largest student strike in North American history (Marshall 2012). The use of the Internet and social networking sites was central to accelerating mobilization efforts in the upcoming months. The original Fight Tuition Increase website ignited the cause, and organizers planned the activities almost exclusively in cyberspace to enlist new supporters, which eventually resulted in spillover activity in public spaces (H. Jenkins 2006).

The stakes were high because the police met the peaceful actions with violence in the form of beatings, pepper spray, and tear gas, and universities used court injunctions to try to end the strikes (Marshall 2012). Boulainne's (2009) research is useful because these peer-to-peer interactions in the virtual world created collective identity prior to protest activity. The organizing also indicates the utility of virtual public spheres sustained in cyberspace despite the geographic distance separating individuals interested in a cause (Khan and Kellner 2003).

The number of participants swelled as the students' ability to remain nonviolent in the face of harsh treatment by the police won over public approval, particularly because the evidence was circulated widely through a variety of digital media platforms (Banerjee 2012). This peer-to-peer circulation of images of police brutality through multiple social networking sites highlights the emergence and flourishing of collective identity in the virtual world through weak ties. Giugni (1998) argues that young activists in particular rely on social media for much of their information about social and political events, and these tools of civic media (H. Jenkins 2006) alert us to how electronic media can lead to a participatory culture in local communities. The students' use of new ICTs also demonstrates Nie's (2001) contention that state power can be counteracted with digital resources in the hands of ordinary citizens to ultimately hold authorities accountable for their response to civil disobedience.

As the campaign surged the public increasingly recognized the student activists as a valid constituency and challenger to government policies because the students demonstrated the concept of WUNC (Tilly 2004). On May 16, the second day of major protest activity, police used more aggressive tactics when thousands of students and their allies marched to resist the government's attempt to end the strike by fining anyone trying to block entrances to universities (Dolphin 2012). Within a few months, what began as a specific complaint against rising tuition costs was transformed into broader Canadian support for sweeping reform in both the economic and political spheres. One of the major points of contention was the passing of Law 78, which made it illegal to participate in an unpermitted assembly of more than fifty individuals, punishable by fines ranging from $5,000 to $125,000 for individuals and unions (Maharawal and Gluck 2012). On May 22, after the government passed the bill, tens of thousands of Canadians marched through the streets, and more than one thousand were arrested for deviating from the prearranged route the police had dictated (Dolphin 2012).

The next day an estimated 350,000 students and their allies marched wearing what became the ubiquitous red square, a symbol that students (as well as many of their fellow citizens) were "squarely in the red," that is, debt. This protest was the largest act of civil disobedience in Canadian history (Leier 2012). While the protests snowballed and grievances accumulated, activists transformed the red square into a symbol of a lack of political freedom in addition to economic hardship. Violent clashes broke out once again, and the police arrested 122 demonstrators (Marshall 2012).

After the bold reprisal by the authorities, the students broadened their framing of the issues (Snow et al. 1986; Gamson 1992). They expanded their list of grievances by questioning the government's failure to invest in the future of its youth coupled with its willingness to set the police on them in a violent fashion, challenging the very authority and legitimacy of the government. For example, Gabriel Dubois, student and spokesperson for the Coalition of the Association for a Student Union Solidarity (CLASSE), the union that represented the striking students, summarized, "The bill that the government is proposing to table is an anti-union law, it is authoritarian, repressive and breaks the students' right to strike. . . . This is a government that prefers to hit on its youth, ridicule its youth rather than listen to them" (Marshall 2012).

On the CLASSE webpage entitled "Somebody Arrests Me," thousands of students posted photos of themselves breaking the law (Lindsay 2013). The site asked visitors to sign an e-petition opposing Law 78. The final statement of the declaration reads, "I disobey. Somebody arrest me." Such strategies demarcate how activists can utilize new media to further their agenda and recruit new supporters, thus giving credence to theories of new media that extend some of the basic premises of resource mobilization theory.

As McAdam and Paulsen (1993) suggest, weak ties that activists forge in cyberspace can help disseminate information, foster dialogue, and convince people to get involved in contentious activity as the social ties spread and create new forms of collective identity. Collective identity and a sense of determination, which students initially developed online, were solidified amid police repression in local public spaces, which organizers transformed into a powerful part of their repertoire of contention. The Canadian uprisings also demonstrate that digital communication devices make organizational activity amenable to leaderless and ad hoc forms of strategizing, thereby decreasing obstacles to organizing. Theories of new social movements and of new media apply here (Melucci 1996; Bimber 2003).

Political mediation theory is also applicable because the activists reacted to the shifting events on the ground, altering their tactics on the basis of signals they interpreted from the police response. Their growing awareness of support among Canadian citizens also influenced their strategies and tactics and the alliances that they forged. Activists effectively altered their relationship with the target of their challenges by gaining sympathy and support for their cause. Political mediation theory (Meyer and Minkoff 2004) and theories that focus on the consequences of social movements (McAdam 1982) consider this ability to be an important variable in enhancing recruitment efforts. Furthermore, political mediation theory argues that the *perception* of a possible victory, rather than how open or closed the formal political context is in reality, helps to sustain social movements. Clearly, throughout the struggle the Canadian government did not show a high level of tolerance for contentious politics, but rather the opposite.

For example, authorities continued their crackdown when, on May 26, police arrested a record high 560 protesters, the largest single mass arrest in Quebec history. By June the total number of arrests was more than 2,500 (Maharawal and Gluck 2012). Yet, Premier Charest's dismissal of the students' demands and the use of excessive force by the police only emboldened the student activists. Theoretical frameworks that focus on cultural and psychological accounts of collective behavior, such as collective identity and framing, are therefore useful in understanding the dynamics as they unfolded. These theories propose that citizens participate in contentious politics for reasons embedded in emotion and commitment rather than on a utilitarian assessment of the situation. Furthermore, the dissemination of the videos of police brutality that ordinary citizen journalists captured and spread through digital media formats fuelled the emotional appeal and sense of worthiness of the cause.

Activists also attracted international support by globally circulating the digital feeds of the protest events. Participants in the OWS movement in New York City, for example, marched in solidarity with the citizens of Quebec three times, and on October 15 supporters of the Canadian movement demonstrated in nine hundred cities across the globe in acts of solidarity (CBS News 2011). Another valuable resource that the students relied on was their collaborative work with other community groups and unions, as they had established relationships and networks of support prior to the strikes. For example, CLASSE worked with the student and employee unions Fédération Étudiante Universitaire du Québec, Confédération des Syndicats Nationaux, and Canadian Union of Public Employees (Maharawal and Gluck 2012). Resource mobilization theory points to these kinds of ties across SMOs as decisive for successful social movement efforts. Thus, although ICTs are changing the landscape in some important ways, traditional SMOs are by no means irrelevant to contemporary political struggles.

The outcome of the mobilization was relatively successful. In the fall 2012 elections, a majority of students supported the candidate from the Leftist Party, Pauline Marias, who ran on a platform of halting the tuition increase. Once elected, he kept his promise through a ministerial decree, and the students then voted to return to class (Lindsay 2013).

OCCUPY STUDENT DEBT IN THE UNITED STATES

Students in the United States also organized in a proactive effort to stop planned tuition hikes. However, the mobilization was in some ways different from the Canadian situation because the grievances included the debt they had *already* accumulated, in addition to the proposed rising costs. In the United States the volume of student loans grew by 77 percent between 2002 and 2012, and during this same time frame the average debt for full-time students increased by nearly 60 percent to more than $5,500 (Greenstone and Looney 2013). Now, the average student debt is currently $30,000 for US college students (Denhart 2013) and this can be attributed to three factors. First, over the past thirty years the average price of attending college has more than doubled at four-year schools (Honan 2012). Second, between 2007 and 2012 forty-eight states reduced funding for higher education. And, third, federal funding for higher education has been drastically cut over the past several years, a trend which began in the 1970s under the neoliberal project (Malcolm and McMinn 2013). It is in this context that Occupy Student Debt emerged as a social movement.

Similar to the Canadian case, the resistance began online. In the hopes of reaching a critical mass quickly and efficiently, organizers of Occupy Student Debt (a spin-off group of Occupy Wall Street) encouraged fellow students to sign an e-petition pledging to stop paying off their loans on the (now defunct) website, http://occupystudentdebt.com/owsdebtday. The online statement declared, "We were told to work hard and stay in school, and that it would pay off. We are not lazy. We are not entitled. We are drowning in debt with few means of escape. The student loan bubble may not burst with a bang, but it is slowly suffocating us. Please share your story. We stand in solidarity with the 99 percent" (a reference to the framing used by participants in the Occupy Wall Street social movement). The site's Pledge of Refusal asked students to refuse to make payments toward their debt until reforms, such as free public education, were met. This refusal to pay would only happen once they reached one million signatures. Although they fell short of their goal, the website served the purpose of increasing awareness about the growing social movement and helped to form a virtual community through online forms of collective identity.

As was the case in Canada, online tools were integral in the organizing stages of the social movement and the sharing of grievances. However, as was also the case in Canada, it was the public occupations that put direct and real pressure on the target of discontent, propelling the movement into a sustainable campaign. The reprisals by officials and the police force are another commonality. Some of the most controversial on-the-ground events took place in the University of California and state school systems. In November 2011, at the University of California, Berkeley, approximately one hundred students pitched tents outside one of the main administrative buildings (in the spirit of the OWS encampments) after thousands had gathered earlier in the day to protest planned tuition hikes (Berton and Jones 2011). Police warned students that they would be arrested if they did not decamp, yet many decided to stay. During the dismantling of the tents, many students were beaten with batons, and video images of the abusive police conduct went viral, with more than one million viewings on YouTube. This not only bolstered the efforts of activists on the Berkeley campus, but also sparked forms of resistance on other US campuses (Medina 2012).

For example, that same month at the University of California, Davis, police officers pepper-sprayed and clubbed peaceful protestors, arresting almost a dozen of them. Students recorded the incident and distributed the images on YouTube, Twitter, and Facebook, and it then became a major news story in the mainstream press (Heestand 2012). After an investigation, the Kroll Security consulting firm detailed "a cascading series of errors," and UC Davis agreed to pay damages of $30,000 to each of the twenty-one participants who was pepper-sprayed (L. Gordon and Megerian 2012).

This exemplifies how mojos, enabled by smart phones with video capabilities, provide a critical resource for protesters and can supplement resource mobilization theory's account of professional expertise, established SMOs, money, and support from elites in social movements. Like their counterparts in Quebec, the student organizers and participants at the UC schools relied little on any of these (though as mentioned, the assistance of labor was instrumental in the Canadian struggle). Instead, it was amateur journalists who sparked widespread interest in the cause and energized recruitment efforts.

Furthermore, this case, as well as the student mobilizations in Quebec (and the Arab Spring events covered in the previous chapter), also illustrates that with access to digital media and smart phones flagrant police violations can no longer be swept under the rug. Activists can record episodes of excessive force by the authorities and upload them onto a variety of media outlets and social networking sites in real time. This type of civic media (Castells 2001), enhanced by new electronic media, assists actors engaging in protest activities and supports the contention that ICTs play a significant role in political struggles (Bennett and Iyengar 2008; Boulainne 2009; H. Jenkins 2006; Giugni 1998). The fact that they created collective identity prior to the events also supports new media's role in expanding participatory democracy through virtual public spheres (Boulainne 2009).

The unprovoked abuse by authorities at both Berkeley and Davis gave the protesters leverage by earning them approval and support among the public, especially when the images were circulated throughout the mainstream media and press. The exposure of police brutality also allowed students to frame their issues through the prism of moral principles and injustice, therefore increasing their standing in relation to the target of their dissent (McAdam 1982; Marullo and Meyer 2007). Here, cultural theories of social movements are useful with their emphasis on putting forth a clear and concise frame pitched in moral or ethical terms (Ryan and Gamson 2006).

The mobilizations that began in California soon spread nationwide, and for the next several months activists engaged in public forms of resistance. For example, students organized a nationwide "One Trillion Day" protest on April 25, 2012, as student debt cumulatively reached the $1 trillion mark in the United States (Goodale 2012). Many set fire to debt-related documents, and some held signs reading, "Education in America: Don't Bank on it." During graduation ceremonies across the country, students tossed inflatable debt balls, wore plastic chains, and wrote the amount of their debt on graduation caps instead of the more celebratory messages that students typically express. On June 22, 2012, about one hundred students marched around the New York City campus of the City Universities of New York and Washington Square Park and then staged a debtor's die in. In a clever play on words, activists held signs that read, "You are not a loan." On November 20 students and faculty dressed in caps and gowns at Liberty Plaza in New York City handed out debt bills instead of diplomas (Honan 2012).

These symbolic displays of anger, frustration, and emotion once again support social movement theories that focus on cultural interpretations of the dynamics collective behavior and the motivation of citizens to participate in a campaign. Activists established collective identity by applying an injustice frame of banks preying on students and also by framing their issues in conjunction with larger structural issues of economic injustice, a lack of accountability among political elites, and demands for an alternative future.

Resource mobilization theory and theories of new media illuminate the role of digital media in Occupy Student Debt's ability to pursue its agenda, organize activities in local communities, and facilitate collective identity among participants. Student organizer Yates McKee describes how the early establishment of collective identity allowed for a deeper understanding of the structural reasons for their personal troubles:

A major development in the past month was the staging of the first New York City Debtors' Assembly in Washington Square Park on June 11. The format was simple, and the facilitation was minimal. Seated around a banner reading "Strike Debt," affixed with the red felt square familiar from

Occupy Student Debt protesters organized a nationwide "One Trillion Day" protest in April 2012 in reference to the fact that student debt had cumulatively reached the $1 trillion mark in the United States.

student struggles in Quebec, those assembled were invited to step up to publicly share their "debt stories" through a cardboard "debtors' mic." In two hours, several dozen people from a wide range of backgrounds and generations delivered emotionally charged, first-person testimonials about the experience of debt servitude to Wall Street and its intermediary institutions. Whether speaking of the ruinous effects of student debt, credit card debt, healthcare debt, or mortgage debt, almost all of the speakers remarked that this was their very first time speaking publicly about their status as debtors. To speak as a debtor, and to address others as debtors, was an empowering process in its own right: the simple act of speaking built community and solidarity based on a shared experience of breaking with debt shame—the insidious sense that to be indebted is an individual moral failure rather than an enforced condition of life under contemporary capitalism." (McKee 2012)

This spillover activity (H. Jenkins 2006) increased awareness of the activists' legitimate grievances and demands by means of civic media and participatory democracy that students and their supporters initiated on-line and through the electronic grassrooting of democracy (Castells 2001).

McKee's statement demonstrates how students and US citizens transformed the topic of personal debt into a political issue, funnel-ing individual troubles into a critique of the capitalist system. This is what sociologist C. Wright Mills (1959) refers to as the sociological imagination—viewing personal troubles as rooted in structural and systemic societal forces. Debt was framed as a common thread to help groups and individuals forge new alliances, which then served as a re-cruitment tool by giving legitimacy and worthiness to the grievances (quite similar to the strategies Canadian students employed). This ul-timately strengthened a sense of community and collective identity, in other words WUNC (Tilly 2004).

In terms of the immediate outcomes of the student protests, the UC students were successful. There have not been any tuition increases in the UC system over the past three years (M. Gordon 2013). The students pro-testing the CUNY system were less successful in the short term because administrators voted to implement tuition hikes despite the resistance among students. In the broader scheme, however, they were able to raise awareness about their dire economic situation through their participation in contentious tactics on the street and use of digital tools to disseminate their message of disapproval with the system.

THE DREAMERS MOBILIZE

The mobilization of the DREAMers is another student-related effort for social change but one that cuts across the dimensions of both economic and racial injustice. Breaking the silence imposed by their undocumented status, the DREAMers held demonstrations and prayer vigils, they fasted outside of the White House and their congressional representatives' of-fices, they blocked buses that attempted to deport undocumented per-sons, and they held sit-ins in congressional offices. Through these tactics they have transformed the discussion of immigration reform based on policy changes into a formidable social movement and demonstrate how important the public dimension is to social movements, no matter what new media technology strategies are used.

This social movement is in some ways an extension of the mobilization efforts in Canada and the United States, though articulating additional grievances of *undocumented* students in their inability to afford higher education. This movement evolved out of the broader issue of immigration reform in the United States, and though a complete analysis of the issue of immigration is beyond the scope of this book, a brief summary of recent developments will help situate the DREAMers mobilization in a broader context. Large-scale hostility toward immigrants escalated in the 1990s as federal and state governments attempted to pass anti-immigration legislation. Things really heated up at the federal level in 2002 when Congress passed the Secure Communities measure, which stipulated that state and local law enforcement agencies cooperate with federal immigration authorities (Ginger 2010).

Later, in 2005, Milwaukee representative James Sensenbrenner (R-Wisconsin) introduced a bill to the House that sought to make it a felony for anyone to reside in the United States without legal papers (presently a civil violation) and for others to hire or assist anyone undocumented (Garcia 2013). After the House passed the bill December 10, the largest Latino demonstration in US history was held while the Senate debated the policy (Nowicki 2010). Between March and May 2006, nearly 5 million people protested the proposed legislation in more than 160 cities.

Organizers and participants in the contentious undertakings used signs and slogans as framing devices to challenge popular rhetoric about immigrants not wanting to assimilate and being an economic and social drain on society. Banners and chants consisted of messages such as "We are America," "We come to this country not to take from America, but to make America strong," and "Today we march, tomorrow we vote" (Chavez 2008). This reminder that immigrants do indeed hold political power was decisive in the 2012 presidential election. President Obama presented himself as much more compassionate about immigration reform than the Republican contender, Mitt Romney, and in return he received 71 percent of the Latino vote (Julia Preston and Santos 2012).

The 2006 demonstrations caught police and the residents of California (where by far the largest protests took place) off guard because the planning and discussion took place almost exclusively through the Spanish-language press and radio, and to a lesser extent through the Internet and social networking sites (Julia Preston 2012b). These outlets served as public venues through which citizens could share common grievances, disseminate information, and organize. Resource mobilization theory points to the significance of media access to successful social movement outcomes, and in this case social movement actors circumvented mainstream press and relied on new and internal media forums. The bill was defeated after the massive demonstrations put pressure on elected officials, dramatizing the potential political influence Latinos held given their numbers and willingness to organize collectively (Gonzalez 2011).

The rash of protest activity in 2006 challenges some of the presumptions of political process theory in that there was no real political opening at this time. In fact, an anti-immigration sentiment was formidable throughout the political institutions at the federal, state, and local levels. Political mediation and theories that acknowledge the role of culture in expressions of collective behavior provide better explanations for these contentious events. As with the student debt protesters, a pivotal aspect of this mobilization was the increasing awareness among participants that those who are undocumented are not isolated migrants trying to survive economically and keep family members from being deported but a well-represented segment of the population. It was the activists' determination through their perception of the *possibility* of victory that extended the campaign. There was also a growing sense of WUNC (Tilly 2004) among participants, and this sense of belonging, rooted in a demand for dignity, galvanized their support.

The DREAMers emerged as a subset of this broader mobilization for widespread immigration reform in their support of the DREAM Act. The proposal was first introduced in the Senate in the summer of 2001 and was designed to provide conditional permanent residency to "illegal aliens" of "good moral character" under the age of thirty-five who arrived as minors (before the age of sixteen), do not have proper visa/immigration documentation, have attended school on a regular basis, have graduated from an American high school, meet in-state tuition and GPA requirements, and have lived in the United States for at least five consecutive years (Adam Goodman 2012). After completing two years in the military or two years at a four-year institution of higher learning, these individuals would have an opportunity to obtain a temporary six-year residency. During this six-year conditional period, however, they

DREAMer students employed a variety of tactics to influence politicians to support the act. They organized mass demonstrations, lobbied politicians, and shared their personal stories with the mainstream and alternative press.

would not be eligible for federal higher education grants (such as Pell grants) nor be able to apply for student loans and work-study (this would later be challenged at the state level and is discussed below). After the six years, those who have met at least one of the conditions—either serving in the military of fulfilling the educational requirements—are eligible to apply for permanent resident status, which would allow them to eventually become US citizens.

Students employed a variety of tactics to influence politicians to support the act. They organized mass demonstrations, lobbied politicians, and shared their personal stories with the mainstream and alternative press. Again, they took advantage of an important resource of mobilization theory, the media. This was a wisely calculated initial strategy, because given their undocumented status they could not vote and use the formal institutional process to voice their opinion and promote an agenda. Though there was danger of arrest or deportation given their choice of tactics, many considered this one of the few available in their repertoire at that particular time.

There are other commonalities between the Canadian and US student debt protests and the DREAMers in terms of not only online activity, but offline endeavors as well, most notably in the occupation of public spaces. DREAMers were also bold in their tactics, protesting in front of the Alabama Capitol, outside the home of Arizona sheriff Joe Arpaio (notorious for his anti-immigration stance), in front of federal immigration courts, and inside of Immigration and Customs Enforcement offices, processing centers, and detention centers (Adam Goodman 2012).

Though the proposal did not make it through Congress, in its wake students pivoted and began to mobilize at the state level. In California students petitioned state legislators in 2006 to introduce the California DREAM Act. This mandated that all students who had completed high school in the state, regardless of immigration status, would be eligible for in-state tuition and have access to all financial assistance (both public and private) for higher education at California state colleges and universities. The legislation was vetoed by Governor Arnold Schwarzenegger but reintroduced later in a bill that allowed undocumented students to apply for privately and publically funded money, which was signed into law by Governor Jerry Brown in 2011 (Lee 2011). There were similar mobilizations in New York, Maryland, and Rhode Island, which were successful in the latter two states (Hing 2012). The New York resolution has yet to be decided. The choice of strategy and tactics helps to inform political mediation theory because this framework recognizes the importance of activists responding to fluid situations, either on the ground or as policy is being debated in the formal setting of institutional politics (e.g., Meyer and Minkoff 2004).

The successful outcomes that students achieved were largely due to direct action tactics that students undertook through the rallying call of "Undocumented, Unafraid, and Unapologetic," which put immediate and direct pressure on authorities. On March 10, 2010, they held the first "National Coming Out Day of Action" as part of their newly organized Coming Out of the Shadows campaign. Student activists held civil disobedience events in many major cities including Chicago, Los Angeles, Phoenix, Miami, New York, and Washington, DC, most taking place in front of federal buildings and consisting of teach-ins, sit-ins, marches, rallies and demonstrations, and hunger strikes.

Furthermore, DREAMer activists relied heavily on social media to pressure Congress to pass the proposed bill. They posted videos online of their personal stories and used YouTube to promote a video in which students stated their names and held signs that read that they were undocumented (Escalona 2011). The United We Dream campaign was also organized online in 2008 with a list of individuals interested in taking action to support immigration reform (Kantrowitz 2013). Those who signed up could be immediately contacted through e-mail exchanges, texting, and social media sites. Requests were sent out to make calls to their political representatives and to raise money in support of the cause. Social media also helped to spread share-ready stories, demonstrating strength in numbers.

Social movement theories that focus primarily on the political environment cannot adequately assess the emergence of the DREAMers and the tactics they used in the *early* part of the campaign. For students in the country without proper legal status, their participation cannot be classified as exclusively rational based on their interpretation of the political and social context. Rather, the early development (as well as the later stages) of the movement was grounded in emotion, commitment to moral and ethical concerns, and solidarity, thus reinforcing cultural theories as well as new social movement theory (Tomlinson 1999; Giddens 1991; Polletta and Jasper 2001).

At the crux of the protests was a demand for immigration policies that include the right of students, many who came to the United States at a very young age and have no firsthand knowledge of their country of origin, to attend college with the same financial opportunities that native-born students enjoy. One of the latest manifestations of this sentiment is the National Immigrant Youth Alliance's online "Coming Out Guide." This is a forum through which students share advice, organize, and announce upcoming events in local communities (Bogado 2012). The guide is an extensive document that includes YouTube coming-out videos, encourages individuals to come out either on a personal level to someone they know or by hosting a coming out meeting or house party to foster relationships with allies and other DREAMers in a safe environment, and recommends creating a Google group so that there are regular discussions to plan on-the-ground activities that will follow.

This use of online platforms supports Gould's (1993) contention that invitations through personal ties among people of trust is a strong predictor of individuals' engagement in activism, and ICTs enhance this capacity through the formation of weak ties in the virtual sphere across dispersed networks. It also highlights that mediated forms of communication often complement face-to-face interaction as suggested by Boulainne (2009) and H. Jenkins (2006), resulting in the spillover effect as new ICTs assist in these hybrid forms of activism. Through these kinds of peer-to-peer information sharing, new forms of connectivity also facilitate the development of community and grassroots civic engagement regardless of physical distance (Bennett and Iyengar 2008).

Additionally, this type of organizing demonstrates that new media also allows for organizational structures through spontaneous, virtual, leaderless infrastructures of networked and coordinated activity. The organizational processes and kinds of connective action that digital networks enable are transforming the political environment because they no longer rely exclusively on traditional and external resources such as access to mainstream media or professional leadership that resource mobilization theory stresses, and they allow individuals to collectively address common problems that can lead to collective behavior.

Political process theory is also relevant in assessing the latter part of the struggle as the political context shifted for the DREAMers after Barack Obama's re-election in 2012. The overwhelming support he received from Latinos was widely acknowledged in the mainstream press, and in this new environment DREAMers reconsidered their original strategies and alliances. Both political process and political mediation theories (Soule and King 2006; Meyer 2005; Tarrow 2001) recognize that when politicians are running for office, or are up for re-election, they are often vulnerable and more attuned to significant constituencies. With the changing demographics throughout many parts of the United States, students and organizers within the Latino community are seizing the new political opportunities afforded by their sheer numbers on the voter rolls by focusing on electoral politics in addition to contentious politics. Tarrow (1996) and C. Jenkins and Perrow (1977) argue that the broadening access to institutional participation and support of elites gives challengers

leverage over their opponents and can shift the balance of power in political struggles. Their hypotheses therefore fit the development of the
DREAMers' strategies since Obama was re-elected.

To take advantage of the new political terrain, for example, organizers
began to build infrastructure in 2009, following the election of Obama in
2008, by forming two groups, United We Dream and Voto Latino. In the
spring of 2012, the two organizations held demonstrations in more than
twenty cities, combining institutional and extrainstitutional politics. In
late May DREAMers gathered signatures from more than ninety immigration law professors on a letter to President Obama denoting the legal precedents he could invoke to defer deportations (Julia Preston 2012a). Latino
organizers, students, and other volunteers went door to door encouraging
voters to go the polls, and they also held workshops and citizenship fairs
to register eligible voters. As a result, on June 15, 2012, President Obama,
through an executive action, passed the Deferred Action for Childhood
Arrivals bill. The legislation allows approximately 800,000 young people
to remain in the United States without threat of deportation and grants
them the right to work (Julia Preston and Cushman 2012).

Despite this victory, however, students and other community activists continue to push for broader immigration reform to make citizenship
possible for undocumented persons. They are making progress toward
this goal but have not achieved it entirely. On October 5, 2013, Governor
Jerry Brown signed eight bills that addressed immigration reform in the
state of California (which included the right of those living California to
attain a driver license despite immigration status and support of the Trust
Act, which limits the ability of authorities to deport undocumented per-
sons). The newly elected University of California president, Janet Napol-
itano, allocated $5 million in university funds to support undocumented
students attending the University of California system (M. Gordon 2013).

In February 2014 more than five hundred young immigrants gathered
for the annual meeting for the United We Dream Network. This gathering came in the wake of disappointment in both Congress and President
Obama to move the immigration agenda forward (Julia Preston 2014).
What is amazing is that this organization in the early years of its founding conducted meetings in the shadows in fear of Immigration and Customs Enforcement. In 2014 they met publicly at the Sheraton Hotel in the
center of Phoenix, making a point to contest Governor Jan Brewer (R-AZ)

THEORY TOOLKIT

THEORIES WE CAN USE TO UNDERSTAND THE MOVEMENT FOR IMMIGRATION REFORM

We can apply a few of the theories discussed in Chapter 1 to the emergence and evolution of the student-led social movements discussed in this chapter:

- **Theories of new media.** These theories are most relevant to providing a framework within which to interpret and assess these student- and youth-based social movements. They highlight how activists can connect with one other, have discussions, and mobilize without formal access to the institutional realm of politics by establishing virtual public spheres that are created in cyberspace. These theories also inform us of the importance of weak ties, often created online or through social networking sites, which then lead to a sense of collective identity and is an integral resource for on-the-ground mobilization efforts.

- **Cultural theories.** These theoretical frameworks are necessary because of the emotionally charged nature of the campaigns. As this chapter depicts, framing served a very important purpose in providing clever slogans and signs, raising awareness about the cause, drawing in new recruits, and gaining public sympathy and support for the activists' agenda.

- **New social movement theories.** The organizational structure of each campaign was decentralized and allowed for more spontaneous actions than past forms of collective behavior.

- **Resource mobilization theory.** Relatedly, mojos' astute use of new media helped influence public opinion, assist in recruitment efforts, and hold the authorities in check, therefore providing a critical resource that can help inform resource mobilization theory.

- **Political process and political mediation theories.** These are relevant in interpreting the macro-level dynamics of the movements. For the DREAMers in particular, the changing political context greatly affected their choice of tactics and strategies.

who has denied passing legislation that would allow those who qualify for Deferred Action for Childhood Arrivals to apply for driver's licenses. Rallying outside of the Department of Homeland Security center they chanted, "Obama, Obama, don't deport my mama!" (Julia Preston 2014).

CONCLUSION

These three case studies contribute to the recent literature on contentious politics and social movements. Each illustrates that emerging ICTs create new social and political spheres within which to communicate and organize because activists no longer have to depend on open political systems in the traditional sense that political process theory refers to. The innovative media terrain helps citizens craft new, albeit virtual, political openings and participation in political discussion that were not available in the past. This, in turn, increases the vulnerability of economic and political authorities to challenges among ordinary citizens. By finding creative ways to voice their grievances and occupy public spaces across parts of Canada and the United States, student activists successfully generated support for their cause outside of institutional politics despite the repressive tactics authorities employed. For any social movement to emerge and evolve it is necessary that potential activists realize that others are also willing to join the struggle. By sharing information and solidifying weak ties in cyberspace, citizens in these two countries built community and forged a sense of collective identity that erupted in displays of contentious politics on the streets.

The analyses further illustrate that macro-oriented theories that focus on the *why*, or emergence, of political struggle can be applied to certain aspects of mobilizations, although in some instances they need to be accompanied by cultural theories that target the *how* of social movement activity. Political mediation theory nicely complements political process theory with its acumen regarding how activists' perception of available opportunities intersects with the strategic choices they make and the tactics they employ. A key signal that activists gauge is public opinion, and this is influenced by how well they can demonstrate Tilly's (2004) concept of WUNC. Citizen journalists, as these cases illustrate, can influence this perception and therefore public opinion by disseminating live coverage of events on the ground to which citizens both within and outside of the country respond to, which sends a signal to the activists that they are succeeding and assists with recruitment efforts. This new communication field is also vital in that it allows activists to at least influence, if not control, the narrative and to hold authorities accountable for their actions as events transpire on the streets.

The student mobilizations in Canada and the United States also support culturally oriented theories because the protest efforts were emotionally charged, and a calculated cost-benefit assessment of the situation as utility maximizers, especially given the backlash among the authorities, cannot account for the high levels of participation. Resource mobilization theory, however, can serve as a bridge between macro- and micro-level analyses by distinguishing the role of new media as a key resource. As noted, by sharing grievances in the virtual world, activists created a sense of collective identity, which helped to create a new political opening within which to challenge the existing political and economic structures and led to successful collective behavior in real locations. This in turn altered the political context and helped to sustain the campaigns at the grassroots level.

Finally, these student-led outbreaks of contentious politics, enabled by new technologies, display a distinct organizational structure that allows for more spontaneous actions than past forms of collective behavior. Activists, particularly young ones, are finding new ways to share information through peer-to-peer networks, inform one another of both online and offline contentious activities, organize and plan for upcoming events, and create virtual forms of collective identity that serve to initiate and facilitate face-to-face interaction in local communities. In sum, they help document the ways in which ICTs accelerate social movement activity, play a role in decentralizing mobilizations, improve recruitment efforts through virtual forms of collective identity, and hold authorities accountable.

DISCUSSION QUESTIONS

1. Compare and contrast the student protests in Canada and the United States. How and why did their demands snowball? Analyze another student protest not related to debt. What are some of the similarities and differences in terms of tactics, strategies, and demands?

2. Why is collective identity central in the midst of police repression? Look up other social movements where activists were subject to harsh responses by the authorities. What did the demonstrators do to maintain a sense of solidarity and resistance? Was it successful?

3. Explain how the debtors' mic facilitated the sociological imagination. Find other campaigns that use the "open-mic" forum to support a cause. What are the results?

4. How did mojos hold police accountable on UC campuses? Do some follow-up research on these cases, and compare and contrast them to other events occurring on college campuses.

5. What tactics did the DREAMers engage in and how did they change with the political context? How is their campaign changing and diversifying as the immigration debate continues? What role do symbolic forms of resistance play in the struggle?

The Digital Future of Social Movements

The arsenal that activists have in their repertoire of contention is a key component to any social movement. Social movements have always been shaped by the availability of, and access to, the latest technology, which then influences the tactics that social movement actors employ and how they mobilize their campaigns to facilitate recruitment efforts. In the past, it was primarily mainstream media that influenced public opinion in reaction to outbursts of contentious politics. Activists also relied on mass media as an essential resource to gain exposure for their cause. Today, however, although access to mainstream media is by no means insignificant, it is no longer the most important ingredient in making for a successful campaign in terms increasing awareness about an issue, getting recognition, influencing public sentiment, achieving legitimacy, and recruiting new supporters.

There have always been drawbacks to relying on traditional sources of media to cover and disseminate information about protest events. One is that the mainstream press has typically focused on violence perpetrated on behalf of the participants, tending to discredit social movements. Another is that, because much of the media is state and corporate controlled, it may choose to ignore anything that challenges the interests of these elite groups. Furthermore, if we look at the cycle of protest activity, historically traditional media sources tend to gravitate toward events that offer spectacle and drama, and then decrease the reporting, or cease reporting altogether, when the entertainment factor is no longer on display.

177

For example, although there was abundant television and press coverage of the events during the height of Occupy Wall Street, after the decampments when the activists shifted toward less sensational types of organizing, coverage fizzled out.

Media fatigue may also play a role as the public loses interest in ongoing struggles that seem to have no clear end in sight (the cases of the protracted war in Syria and the ongoing strife in Egypt between the military and Islamist groups are good examples of this). However, it is important to recognize that, regardless of the withdrawal of media attention, activists do go back to the day-to-day task of building a stronger movement to sustain their campaign, in large part outside of public view until the next major outburst of public dissent. Sometimes these movements morph into other social justice causes as well (the OWS movement, for example, later began addressing the housing crisis in certain cities, Hurricane Sandy relief efforts in New York and New Jersey, and the soaring rate of student debt).

NEW WAYS TO CONCEPTUALIZE THE PUBLIC SPHERE

This book raises important questions about Jürgen Habermas's definition of communicative action (dialogue, debate, and information sharing among citizens) and the public sphere (where such exchanges take place). Habermas was critical of what he viewed as the overreach of elite-dominated media, which stifled authentic civic discussion and critical thinking. Today, however, social movement actors can gain WUNC (Tilly 2006) under new conditions that can circumvent mainstream media. The newly emerging digital media platforms provide a new source of political energy and communicative action, and they create distinct ways for individuals to engage in political discussion (in virtual public spheres) and organize collectively. Because the communication field is vastly expanding, sources of connectivity among activists now evolve through diffuse networks of peer-to-peer information sharing and commentary.

The innovative forms of communication in this new technological landscape also result in new kinds of journalism and whistle-blowing (e.g., the cases of Chelsea Manning, Edward Snowden, WikiLeaks, Disturbance Theater, and the Yes Men). New digital capabilities allow for novel terrains within which to capture and leak sensitive information to the public, something that the mainstream press is often unwilling to do, or incapable of doing. Additionally, several of the assessments in this book show how technologically sophisticated mojos are altering the communication field and ultimately the political and social landscape by documenting on-the-ground events in real time. They were particularly critical throughout the Arab Spring and Indignados revolutions, the OWS encampments, the Occupy Student Debt protests, and the DREAMers social movement.

More precisely, the analyses in this book illustrate some common characteristics of activists' use of digital technology to promote social change. For example, we have examined tactics that include the use of hacktivism, e-petitions, memes, digital whistle-blowing, misinformation campaigns, and Facebook, Twitter, and YouTube postings—all of which have proven to be successful tactics of virtual methods of resistance. Some individuals and groups have focused on short-term goals, and others have employed web-based activism to organize and propel long-term strategies that result in sustained campaigns. Although collective or individual uses of digital technology to pursue a short-term cause are not technically considered social movements because they are not *sustained* campaigns, flash campaigns, based on clicktivism, can yield tangible results, as we have seen. The examples of civilian protest against Disney's treatment of *The Lorax* movie, confronting the airlines to address passenger concerns, questioning corporations and banks regarding excessive fees for certain services, or critiquing the mass media's use of derogatory terms when referring to minorities have all had positive results for concerned citizens.

Other cases illustrate that technology is a tool that can be used by anyone and for any particular cause. It may be utilized in the spirit of social justice and progressive causes or, in other instances, quite the opposite. Both, however, can have political and legal implications, as web-based 2.0 technologies are not as anonymous as some may assume. For instance, as we have documented in the Steubenville rape case, technology can be used to assist the police in tracking those guilty of physical or cyberspace crime through the suspects' digital fingerprints. Additionally, the Tunisia, Egypt, Libya, and Syria cases elaborate on how ICTs can be used by both activists as well as by the targets of protest—in many cases the government traced Internet use and e-mails and monitored cell phone activity

Technologically sophisticated mojos are altering the communication field and ultimately the political and social landscape by documenting on-the-ground events in real time.

to locate organizers of, and participants in, dissident politics. The Arab Spring revolutions further depict how authorities can block or limit service and manipulate protesters in ways that discredit them by engaging in disinformation or propaganda campaigns.

However, the Arab Spring uprisings showed that with the advent of new media platforms, authoritarian forms of government, which had for decades violently suppressed their citizens' exercise of free speech and peaceful assembly with impunity, were now subject to scrutiny from the outside world. Mojos circulated their atrocities worldwide and in real time throughout cyberspace, and the mainstream media eventually disseminated those images. This, in turn, put pressure on the governments and military to use more caution (at least in some cases) when dealing with the protest events. The circulation of the documented, unprovoked violence created sympathy for opposition groups and helped with recruitment efforts, allowing the protesters to alter power relations, as they were able to take command of the narrative and hold the police, military, and government accountable for their actions. Thus, the soft power of amateur journalists successfully challenged the violent physical power at the disposal of state authorities.

IMPLICATIONS OF ICTS AS A KEY RESOURCE
FOR SOCIAL MOVEMENT THEORY

This text has set out to examine various strands of social movement theory in a complementary fashion to help analyze and explain the outbreak of protest activity over the past ten years. The social movements under investigation in this text help to refine our understanding of contentious politics as they both challenge and contribute to the recent literature on collective behavior. They emphasize the *unquestionable* role that new digital technology has on mobilization efforts. In each of the case studies we can see that by using theories from the disciplines of political science (political process and political mediation theories), sociology (resource mobilization and culturally oriented theories), and media studies (which examine the role that technology has on collective behavior), we can better understand contemporary forms of contentious politics and see that wired activism does not replace, but rather adds to, traditional forms of protest activity.

As political process and political mediation theories recognize, the political environment in which social movement actors organize influences the strategies and tactics they employ and is an important factor to consider in understanding outbreaks of collective behavior (especially for understanding why revolutions take place). Political process theory in particular focuses on political openings in the formal, institutional arena that activists can exploit. Because of the new technology that activists have at their disposal, we should view these openings in different ways. The case studies in this book highlight that the new media permit citizens to create new, albeit virtual, political gateways and ways to participate in political discourse outside the formal openings available in the past. This, in turn, expands the public sphere of communication and available platforms for activism both in cyberspace and on the streets.

For instance, throughout the Arab Spring, Indignados, Occupy Wall Street, and immigration- and student debt–related uprisings, digital media provided new, safe venues to communicate grievances. Online tools were also used to organize and build networks of support. Facebook, Twitter, and the Internet all played a role in community building and served as organizing outlets to identify and alert citizens about high levels of discontent. What citizens were once whispering about secretly behind closed doors became a call to action on the streets, and oftentimes (especially in the DREAMers and student debt mobilizations), the sharing of personal stories online emboldened individuals to organize and take to the streets by applying the sociological imagination—seeing personal troubles not as individual failures but as social problems rooted in the structure of society (i.e., Habermas's reference to critical thinking).

These new modes of communication were also vital for most Arab Spring countries, given the authoritarian and repressive nature of the political systems and lack of freedom of speech and other basic civil rights. For a full-fledged social movement to emerge, it is essential that potential activists realize that others are also willing to join the struggle, particularly if the struggle may turn violent. Leading up to many of the Arab Spring outbreaks, it was social media that provided the context within which citizens were assured they had WUNC. Finally, this new media terrain helps to bridge the "how" and "why" of social movement activity by considering the social and political environment in which activists organized (much of it online by opening up new possibilities for discussion), while also providing a key resource through which to strategize and mobilize in local spaces.

Numerous studies in this book also question some of the basic premises of resource mobilization theory, in particular the importance of SMOs and material resources for successful campaigns. Indeed, SMOs have taken on a very new kind of structure as assisted by the Internet and new media. For example, MoveOn and the Tea Party are structured as social movement *communities* rather than formal groups based on membership and mandatory membership fees, a development that requires a reconceptualization of SMOs. Furthermore, the Tea Party is a reminder that it is not only progressive or left-leaning groups that are utilizing technology for political leverage. MoveOn.org and the Tea Party are also two of the earliest hybrid forms of mobilizing that straddle the line between offline and online activism, and they have had a significant impact on both the institutional and extrainstitutional political climate. Both pressured office holders to accommodate their demands, and both were successful in recruiting a solid membership base through cyberspace organizing and outreach, face-to-face lobbying, and canvassing efforts. In essence, they represent the growing symbiotic relationship between e-activism and local organizing as they simultaneously operate in the blogosphere and in real communities.

Similarly, the Indignados, the Arab Spring revolutionaries, the Occupy Wall Street participants, and the DREAMers reinforce the declining relevance of existing SMO mobilizing structures, given the recent paradigm shift toward grassroots mobilization, spontaneous operation, leaderlessness, reduced reliance on money, and less labor-intensive approaches. Young wired activists often serve as the forerunners in the horizontal infrastructure of connectivity of many of the current and ongoing campaigns, which tend to rely on decentralized self-organizing and flexible networks made possible through new communication flows and web-based tools. Additionally, new ICTs allow activists to alter their demands and tactics as protest activities unfold, as allowed for by the transmission of up-to-the-minute information sharing and organizing.

We must also rethink culturally based theories of social movements in regards to how we define strong and weak ties, as well as the ways in which these ties relate to forging a sense of collective identity. The Indignados in Spain, Greece, and Mexico, OWS, the Arab Spring rebellions, struggles against student debt, and the DREAMers highlight the ways activists can establish weak ties through pre-existing peer-to-peer social connections through technology such as Facebook, Twitter, YouTube, and e-mail. Later, it was their mobilizing and tenting on the streets that transformed weak ties into strong ties. This exhibits the relationship between information sharing and protest activity in local communities—the spillover effect—and new ways of creating solidarity that digital media platforms enable.

Strong ties and an emerging sense of collective identity are particularly important amid violent backlash by the authorities; therefore, collective behavior must be grounded in *place* and not just in the virtual world to be truly representative of a social movement over the long term. Finally, the analyses in this book highlight the alignment of technology with certain aspects of new social movement theory, as virtual information sharing can politicize new areas of social life and help translate personal troubles (shared in cyberspace) into social issues that ultimately lead to local organizing in concrete communities.

In sum, the combination of various theoretical frameworks, updated to include theories of new media, are necessary for a comprehensive understanding of the case studies in this book. For instance, social movement theory has historically been rooted in analyses that focus on Western European and North American countries, which relied heavily on political process and resource mobilization theories. Yet the Arab Spring mobilizations teach us that in many cases it is the *perception* of opportunities and the subjective interpretations of the possibility of achieving a successful outcome (which political mediation theory emphasizes), the *framing* of issues, key *alliances* both locally and internationally, and innovative tactics as part of a strategic repertoire of contention that are sometimes more pertinent than pre-existing mobilizing structures. The new media played a crucial role in influencing this perception, assisting with framing efforts, helping to build alliances, and facilitating the strategies and tactics that the activists carried out.

SOCIAL MOVEMENT ACTIVITY IN THE FUTURE: WHAT CAN WE EXPECT?

The case studies examined in this book validate that there are two very pertinent issues social movement scholars and students must consider regarding contemporary and future mobilization efforts: access to the public sphere (in both local communities and in cyberspace) and control of technology. The cat-and-mouse game between activists and the authorities is indicative on an underlying fear among people in power of continued unrest, both in the United States and across the globe.

One of the most recent examples of this is the Russian government's crackdown in Ukraine and its annexation of Crimea in March 2014. The now sixth-month war between Ukraine and Russian-backed separatist rebels, as well as the Russian forces themselves, is in full force. Though President Putin denies Russia is playing a role in the fighting other than trying to facilitate peace, Ukrainians insist they come into constant contact with Russian troops (Gall 2014). More than 3,000 people have died in the struggle, and ceasefire is in place (Herszenhorn and Odynova 2014).

There have been strong critiques of the Russian government for its use of force, especially in Ukraine, as well as the manipulation of information coming out of the region through the state-owned media. In one attempt to stifle political dissent, Russian president Vladimir Putin signed legislation that allows the government to regulate the use of mass media and social media and to clamp down on bloggers. The government also designated a watchdog group called Roskomnadzor with which bloggers must register before posting anything online.

State-run television channels have demonized Russian opposition politicians and citizens who have spoken publicly in support of Ukraine, and Mr. Putin warned in a speech in September 2014 of "national traitors" who could bring down Russia from within (Herszenhorn and Odynova 2014). Despite the propaganda and the "official line" the Kremlin is putting forth, Russian troops deployed to Ukraine are using social media to share information about their deployments and deaths of their fellow soldiers, posting photos of themselves and fellow soldiers on the battle lines, many hurt or dead (Herszenhorn and Odynova 2014). Many soldiers have posted news on Facebook pages, disturbed that they were ordered to the Ukrainian border.

However, the Kremlin still tries to control the narrative and stifle dissent, particularly that coming from media sources. For instance, on September 18, 2014, a BBC crew was attacked in southern Russia in a city called Astrakhan for interviewing the family of a soldier who died in Ukraine (Herszenhorn and Odynova 2014). Putin insists that Russian "volunteers" may have gone to Ukraine to fight but they are not being ordered to serve there. Yet stories from Russian military soldiers continue to appear online, some posted by relatives and friends who are reluctant to speak publicly in fear of retaliation from the government. One Russian activist, Yelena Vasilyeva, created a Facebook group clearinghouse where people could share information. A Ukranian computer programmer created a searchable database called lostivan.com after seeing that information about Russian fighters in Ukraine was disappearing from social networking sites (Gall 2014).

Although this clampdown and the propaganda and misinformation campaigns coming from the Putin regime are blatant, a good critical-thinking exercise for those of us in the United States and elsewhere is to examine whether similar developments (though perhaps on a smaller and more subtle scale) are occurring in our own societies. For example, there are growing concerns about the limited ability of people to peacefully protest, as we have witnessed in the cases of the Arab Spring and OWS, accompanied by trends of militarizing societies in a formidable backlash against civil disobedience tactics. Also, as the case of OWS and the student protests in Canada and the United States illustrated, the police can use city ordinances at their own discretion to outlaw protest activities and ban demonstrators from public spaces. Mainstream journalism has not been immune to these trends. In the New York–based OWS events, for instance, the press was barred from trying to document police abuse, and reporters were assaulted when trying to record events, take pictures, or gain access to public facilities such as courthouses. The violence used during the decampments by the police during OWS and on university campuses also showed the repressive side of the US government. This fear of dissent among the police and other authorities, and their attempts to neutralize protest activity (including violating aspects of the First and Fourth Amendments) at any cost is telling, and in fact it jeopardizes the democratic system itself.

Furthermore, we can look at the situation in Russia and some of the other authoritarian governments in Arab Spring countries and argue that Big Brother is not only operating in local communities but is invading cyberspace as well. The case studies in this book note the ways in which mojos have been deterred by authorities from using their mobile devices to share information or record injustice. Though tracking personal information that is stored digitally is not necessarily new and access to certain sites has been limited or blocked in the past as well, these measures are escalating. For example, in 2012, Apple, Inc., received a patent that allows it to limit, or to shut down altogether, the ability of individuals to use their smart phones, phone cameras, or any wireless device during certain events, including those that pertain to protest activity (Whittaker 2012). This can be done by putting digital devises in "sleep mode" or by other measures. Given the critical role of mojos in capturing live footage of events and challenging the story line put forth by the mainstream press or by the authorities themselves, this poses an obvious threat to protesters' freedom of expression to record images at protest rallies, demonstrations, or the occupation of public spaces, and it could have a crippling effect on forms of collective behavior.

Yet, as we have seen time and time again, wired activists usually find creative measures to provide a way around whatever obstacles are put in their path, and we can anticipate—and hope for—more of this in the future.

Abouzeid, Ranai. 2011. "Tunisia: How Mohammed Bouazizi Sparked a Revolution." *Time*, January 21. Available at http://www.time.com/time/magazine/article/0,9171,2044723,00 .html. Accessed June 5, 2012.

Abrahamian, Ervand. 2009. "Mass Protests in the Islamic Revolution, 1977–79." In *Civil Resistance and Power Politics: The Experience of Non-violent Action from Gandhi to the Present*, edited by Timothy G. Ash and Adam Roberts, 162–178. New York: Oxford University Press.

Addley, Esther, and Josh Halliday. 2010. "Operation PayBack Cripples MasterCard Site in Revenge for WikiLeaks Ban." *The Guardian*, December 8. Available at http://www .theguardian.com/media/2010/dec/08/operation-payback-mastercard-website -wikileaks. Accessed January 3, 2011.

Adetunji, Jo. 2011. "Ben Ali Sentenced to 35 Years in Jail." *The Guardian*, June 20. Available at http://www.guardian.co.uk/world/2011/jun/20/ben-ali-sentenced-35 -years-jail. Accessed June 6, 2012.

Adnan, Duraid, and Rick Gladstone. 2013. "Massacre of Syrian Soldiers in Iraq Raises Risk of Widening Conflict." *The New York Times*, March 5. Available at http://www.nytimes. com/2013/03/05/world/middleeast/fighting-escalates-in-syrian-city-opposition-says .html?pagewanted=all&_r=0. Accessed March 5, 2013.

Agence France Presse. 2012. "Tens of Thousands Throng to London to Protest Iraq War." October 17, p. 22. Available at http://rense.com/general58/prorot.htm. Accessed September 28, 2014.

Alami, Mona. 2012. "In Bahrain, the Spark Behind the Pearl Revolution Still Glows." *USA Today*, May 13.

Al Jazeera. 2011. "Clashes erupt as protests spread across Syria." December 31. Available at http://www.aljazeera.com/news/middleeast/2011/12/201112301351830614.html. Accessed June 5, 2012.

AlterNet. 2012. "'Global May Manifesto': Statement from International Activists with Occupy, Other Groups." May 10. Available at http://www.alternet.org/newsandviews /article/928183/'global_may_manifesto'%3A_statement_from_international_activists _with_occupy,_other_groups. Accessed May 11, 2012.

Alvarez, Lizette. 2013. "New Breed of Cuban Dissident Finds Changed Miami." *The New York Times,* April 1. Available at http://www.nytimes.com/2013/04/01/us/yoani-sanchez -cuban-dissident-welcomed-in-miami.html?_r=0. Accessed April 1, 2013.

Amenta, Edwin, and Neal Caren. 2004. "The Legislative, Organizational, and Beneficiary Consequences of State-Oriented Challenges." In *The Blackwell Companion to Social Movements,* edited by David Snow, Sarah Soule, and Hanspeter Kriesi, 461–488. Malden, MA: Blackwell.

Amenta, Edwin, and Michael P. Young. 1999. "Making an Impact: The Conceptual and Methodological Implications of the Collective Benefits Criterion." In *How Social Movements Matter,* edited by M. Giugni, D. McAdam, and C. Tilly, 22–41. Minneapolis: University of Minnesota Press.

Anderson, Michelle D. 2011. "Occupy Wall Street Re-occupies Foreclosed Home in East New York: A Report from the Scene." *The Village Voice,* December 7. Available at http:// blogs.villagevoice.com/runninscared/2011/12/occupy_wall_str_37.php. Accessed May 31, 2012.

Appel, Abrahim. 2011. "Mexico City: Starving for Education." *American Accents,* November 22. Available at http://abrahimappel.wordpress.com/2011/11/22/mexico-city-starving -for-education/. Accessed June 23, 2012.

Arab Social Media Report. 2011. Available at http.www.arabsocialmediareport.com/home/ index/aspx/News/description/aspx?NewId=11&Primenodid+15&mno=Pri. Accessed August 1, 2013.

Archibold, Randal C. 2010. "Foe and Supporters of New Immigration Law Gather in Arizona." *The New York Times,* May 29. Available at http://www.nytimes.com/2010/05/30 /us/30immig.html. Accessed July 30, 2013.

Arnowitz, Leora. 2013. "Victoria's Secret Nationwide Protest Planned by Parenting Organization Boasting 50,000 Members." *Fox News,* March 29. Available at http://www .foxnews.com/entertainment/2013/03/29/victorias-sectret-bright-young-things/. Accessed July 2, 2012.

Arquilla, Hohn, and David Ronfeldt. 2001. *Networks and Netwars: The Future of Terror.* Santa Monica, CA: Rand Corporation.

Arsu, Sebnem, and Rick Gladstone. 2012. "Eighty-Five Syrian Soldiers, Including a General, Defect en Masse to Turkey." *The New York Times,* July 2. Available at http://www .nytimes.com/2012/07/03/world/middleeast/dozens-of-syrian-soldiers-defect -en-masse-to-turkey.html. Accessed July 2, 2012.

Ash, Marc. 2012. "A Witness to the Violence in Oakland." *Reader Supported News,* October 26. Available at http://www.readersupportednews.org/news-section2/316–20/8096 -focus-a-witness-to-the-violence-in-oakland.

Assange, Julian. 2012. "Two Years of Cablegate and Bradley Manning Still Awaits Trial." *Common Dreams,* November 30. Available at https://www.commondreams.org /view/2012/11/30–5. Accessed August 3, 2013.

Associated Press. 2012. "Thousands in Egypt Mark First Anniversary of 'Friday of Rage.'" *New York Daily News,* January 27. Available at http://articles.nydailynews.com/2012– 01–27/news/30672053_1_egyptian-protesters-tahrir-square-muslim-brotherhood. Accessed June 23, 2012.

Bacon, David. 2011. "From Planton to Occupy—Unions and Immigrants and the Occupy Movement." *Truthout,* December 6. Available at http://www.truth-out.org /unions-and-immigrants-join-occupy-movement-1323183717. Accessed June 5, 2012.

_____. 2012. "Mexico's 'Indignados' Have Had It Up to Here." *Truthout*, September 10. Available at http://truth-out.org/index.php?option=com_k2&view=item&id=3244 :mexicos-indignados-have-had-it-up-to-here.

Bai, Matt. 2012. "The Tea Party's Not-So-Civil War." *The New York Times*, January 15. Available at http://www.nytimes.com/2012/01/15/magazine/tea-party-south-carolina .html?pagewanted=all. Accessed June 5, 2012.

Baiocchi, Gianpaolo, and Ernesto Ganuza. 2012. "No Parties, No Banners." *Boston Globe*, February. Available at http://www.bostonreview.net/BR37.1/gianpaolo_baiocchi _ernesto_ganuza_spain_indignados_democracy.php. Accessed June 5, 2012.

Baker, Peter. 2014. "Paths to War, Then and Now, Haunt Obama." *New York Times*, September 13. Available at http://www.nytimes.com/2014/09/14/world/middleeast/paths-to -war-then and-now-haunt-obama.html?. Accessed October 10, 2014.

Bakhash, Shaul. 1984. *The Reign of the Ayatollahs: Iran and the Islamic Revolution*. New York: Basic Books.

Banerjee, Sidhartha. 2012. "Quebec Student Protests: 2,500 Arrests and Counting." *The Canadian Press*, May 25. Available at http://www.huffingtonpost.ca/2012/05/25/quebec -stdent-protest-arresnts_n_1544938.html?ref=canada. Accessed January 1, 2013.

Barnard, Anne, and Mark Landler. 2014. "Turkey Inching Toward Alliance with U.S. in Syria Conflict." *The New York Times*, September 27. Available at http://www.nytimes. com/2014/09/28/world/europe/turkey-hesitant-to-ally-with-us-in-syria-mission. html. Accessed September 28, 2014.

Barsoumian, Nanore. 2011. "Barsoumian: Armenian American Voices in 'Occupy' Movement." *The Armenian Weekly*, October 28. Available at http://www.armenianweekly. com/2011/10/28/barsoumian-armenian-american-voices-in-'occupy'-movement/. Accessed June 22, 2012.

Beaumont, Peter. 2011. "Can Social Networking Overthrow a Government?" *The Sydney Morning Herald*, February 25. Available at http://www.smh.com.au/technology /technology-news/can-social-networking-overthrow-a-government-20110225 -1b7u6.html. Accessed June 6, 2012.

Benford, Robert. 1993. "Frame Disputes Within the Nuclear Disarmament Movement." *Social Forces* 71(3): 677–702.

Bennet, Daniel, and Pam Fielding. 1999. *The Net Effect: How Cyber-Advocacy Is Changing the Political Landscape*. Washington, DC: Capitol Advantage.

Bennett, William. 2003. "Communicating Global Activism." *Information, Communication and Society* 6(2): 143–168.

Bennett, William, and Shanto Iyengar. 2008. "A New Era of Minimal Effects? The Changing Foundations of Political Communication." *Journal of Communication* 58(4): 707–731.

Bennis, Phyllis. 2012. "Syria: No to Intervention, No to Illusions." *ZNet*, June 28. Available at http://www.zcommunications.org/syria-no-to-intervention-no-to-illusions-by -phyllis-bennis. Accessed June 28, 2012.

Berger, J. M. 2014. "How ISIS Games Twitter." *The Atlantic*, June 14. Available at http:// www.hollywoodreporter.com/news/iraq-war-anniversary-hollywoods-anti-429697. Accessed September 25, 2004.

Berkowitz, Ben. 2011. "From a Single Hashtag, a Protest Circled the World." *Brisbane Times*, October 19. Available at http://www.brisbanetimes.com.au/technology/technology -news/from-a-single-hashtag-a-protest-circled-the-world-20111019-1m72j.html. Accessed May 31, 2012.

Berman, Ilan. 2013. "The Brotherhood's Agenda, Cairo's Catastrophe." *Forbes*, January 14. Available at http://www.forbes.com/sites/ilanberman/2013/01/14/the-brother hoods-agenda-cairos-catastrophe/. Accessed August 30, 2014.

Bernstein, Richard, and Kym Rice. 1987. *Are We to Be a Nation? The Making of a Constitution*. Cambridge, MA: Harvard University Press.

Bernstien, Viv. 2012. "Occupy Movement Looks Toward Political Conventions." *The New York Times*, April 23. Available at http://www.nytimes.com/2012/04/24/us/politics /occupy-movement-prepares-for-democratic-convention.html. Accessed April 24, 2012.

Berton, Justin, and Carolyn Jones. 2011. "Protesters Guard UC Berkeley's New Occupy Camp." *San Francisco Chronicle*, November 17. Available at http://www.sfgate.com /bayarea/article/Protesters-guard-UC-Berkeley-s-new-Occupy-camp-2289240.php. Accessed May 22, 2012.

Bhatti, Jabeen, and Portia Walker. 2012. "Activists Ensure That the World Sees Syria's Bloodbath." *USA Today*, February 22. Available at http://www.usatoday.com/news/world /story/2012-02-22/syria-bloodbath-video-journalists/53213498/1. Accessed May 31, 2012.

Bimber, Bruce. 1998. "The Internet and Political Transformation: Populism, Community and Accelerated Pluralism." *Polity* 31(1): 133–160.

———. 2003. *Information and American Democracy: Technology in the Evolution of Political Power*. Cambridge, MA: Cambridge University Press.

Bimber, Bruce, and Richard Davis. 2013. *Campaigning Online: The Internet and US Elections*. New York: Oxford University Press.

Bishara, Marwan. 2012. *The Invisible Arab: The Promise and Peril of the Arab Revolutions*. New York: Basic Books.

Blackwell, Angela. 2012. "Mobility and Inequality in Today's America." *The New York Times*, January 4. Available at http://www.nytimes.com/2012/01/15/opinion/sunday /Sunday-dialogue-mobility-and-inequality-in-todays-america.html. Accessed August 1, 2013.

Bogado, Aura. 2012. "Undocumented Youth Infiltrates Another Immigration Issue." *The Nation*, April 12. Available at http://www.thenation.com/blog/173825/undocumented -youth-infiltrates-another-immigration-issue/. Accessed May 5, 2013.

Bottari, Mary. 2012. "Walker Raises and Spends More Money than Any Other Candidate in Wisconsin History." *PR Watch*, May 2. Available at http://www.prwatch.org /news/2012/05/11494/walker-raises-and-spends-more-money-any-candidate -wisconsin-history. Accessed August 30, 2014.

Boulainne, Shelley. 2009. "Does Internet Use Affect Engagement: A Meta-analysis of Research." *Political Communication* 26(2): 193–211.

Boyd, Andrew. 2003. "The Web Rewires the Movement." *The Nation*, August 4. Available at http://www.thenation.com/article/web-rewires-movement. Accessed March 30, 2004.

Bradley, Tony. 2010. "Operation Payback: WikiLeaks Avenged by Hacktivists." *PC World*, December 7. Available at http://www.pcworld.com/article/212701/operation_pay back_wikileaks_avened_by_hacktivists.html. Accessed July 20, 2013.

British Broadcasting Corporation (BBC). 2011. "FBI Claims Arrest of Key LulzSec Hacker." September 23. Available at http://www.bbc.co.uk/news/technology-15035151. Accessed May 17, 2012.

———. 2012. "1979: Exiled Ayatollah Khomeini Returns to Iran." February 1. Available at http://news.bbc.co.uk/onthisday/hi/dates/stories/february/1/newsid_2521000/2521003 .stm. Accessed May 31, 2012.

Britt, Douglas. 2010. "The Yes Men Infiltrate Diverse Networks." *Houston Chronicle,* April 30. Available at http://www.chron.com/entertainment/article/The-Yes-Men-infiltrate-DiverseWorks-1712890.php. Accessed August 2, 2013.

Brook, Tom Vanden, and William Welch. 2014. "U.S. Blasts Terrorists in Iraq." *USA Today,* September 16, p. 1A.

Brownstein, Ronald. 2004. "MoveOn Works the Hollywood Spotlight to Amplify Its Voice." *Los Angeles Times,* July 4, p. B7.

Brysk, Alison. 2013. *Speaking Rights to Power: Constructing Political Will.* New York: Oxford University Press.

Buhler-Muller, Narina, and Charl van der Merwe. 2011. "The Potential of Social Media to Influence Socio-political Change on the African Continent." *African Institute of South Africa,* briefing number 6, March. Available at www.ai.org.za/wp-content/unloads2011/11/NO-46. Accessed January 3, 2013.

Bulwa, Demian, Kevin Fagan, and Carolyn Jones. 2011. "Dozens of Occupy Protestors Arrested at Bank Sit-In." *San Francisco Chronicle,* November 17. Available at http://www.sfgate.com/news/article/Dozens-of-Occupy-protesters-arrested-at-bank-2290021.php. Accessed May 31, 2012.

Burns, Rebecca. 2012. "No Vacancies: Squatters Move In." *In These Times,* April 19. Available at http://www.inthesetimes.com/article/13037/no_vacancies_squatters_move_in/. Accessed April 23, 2012.

Burress, Charles. 2003. "Making Their Move." *San Francisco Chronicle,* February 9, p. A23.

Cable News Network (CNN). 2004. "Bhopal Hoax Sends Dow Stock Down." December 3. Available at http://articles.cnn.com/2004–12–03/world/bhopal.hoax_1_dow-chemical-dow-stock-bhopal?_s=PM:WORLD. Accessed May 31, 2012.

Cagle, Susie. 2012. "'Empty Buildings Are the Crime': Occupy SF Commune Evicted After One Day." *Truthout,* April 30. Available at http://truth-out.org/news/item/8294-occupy-sf-commune.

Callimachi, Rukmini. 2014. "As U.S. Bombs Fall, British Hostage of ISIS Warns of Another Vietnam." *The New York Times,* September 22. Available at http://www.nytimes.com/2014/09/23/world/middleeast/as-us-bombs-fall-islamic-states-british-hostage-warns-of-another-vietnam.html?_r=0. Accessed September 25, 2014.

Campbell, Bradley 2014. "The Story of Edward Snowden Is So Unbelievable, Sometimes You Forget It's Nonfiction." *PRI,* February 14. Available at http://www.pri.org/stories/2014/-02–14/story-edward-snowden-is-so-unbelievable-you-sometimes-forget-it-is-nonfiction. Accessed February 20, 2014.

Carr, Coeli. 2011. "Black Friday vs. Cyber Monday: The Rivalry Is Over." *CNBC,* November 18. Available at http://www.cnbc.com/id/45278120. Accessed December 6, 2013.

Carter, Jimmy. 2012. "The Tea Party and Me." *USA Today,* September 20. Available at http://www.cartercenter.org/news/editorials_speeches/tea-party-092910.html. Accessed August 1, 2013.

Carty, Victoria. 2010. "Bridging Contentious and Electoral Politics: How MoveOn Is Expanding Public Discourse and Political Struggle." In *Engaging Social Justice: Critical Studies of the Twenty-First Century Social Transformations,* edited by David Fasenfest, 58–81. Boston: Brill.

Castells, Manuel. 1989. *The Informational City: Information Technology, Economic Restructuring and the Urban Regional Process.* Oxford: Blackwell.

———. 2001. *The Internet Galaxy: Reflections on the Internet, Business and Society.* Malden, MA: Blackwell.

_____. 2007. "Communication, Power and Counter-power in the Network Society." *International Journal of Communication* 1: 238–266.

Castle, Stephen, and Steven Erlanger. 2014. "3 Nations Offer Limited Support to Attack on ISIS. *The New York Times,* September 26. Available at http://www.nytimes.com/2014/09/27/world/europe/british-parliament-vote-isis-airstrikes.html?_r=0. Accessed September 28, 2014.

Catholic PR Wire. 2011. "iMissal Launches on iTunes: The First Catholic Missal/Missalette for iPhone and iPod Touch." *Catholic Online,* March 25. Available at http://www.catholic.org/prwire/headline.php?ID=6271. Accessed June 5, 2012.

CBS News. 2011. "'Occupy' Protests Go Global, Turn Violent." October 15. Available at http://www.cbsnews.com/stories/2011/10/15/501364/main20120893.shtml. Accessed May 31, 2012.

Ceasar, Stephen. 2012. "Police Response to UC Berkeley Occupy Protests Is Criticized." *Los Angeles Times,* June 7. Available at http://articles.latimes.com/2012/jun/07/local/la-me-0607-uc-berkeley-20120607. Accessed June 8, 2012.

Center for Responsive Politics. 2006. "Moveon.org Independent Expenditures." *Opensecrets.org.* Available at http://www.opensecrets.org/pacs/indexpend.php?cycle=2008&cmte=C00341396. Accessed April 7, 2009.

Chang, Cindy. 2013. "Immigration Cases Make up 40% of Federal Prosecutions, Study Says." *Los Angeles Times,* May 21. Available at http://www.articles.latimes.com/2013/may/21/local/la-me-ff-immigrationprosecutions-20130522. Accessed June 1, 2013.

Chapman, Stephen. 2011. "LulzSec Releases Deluge of Private Arizona Law Enforcement Information." *ZDNet,* June 23. Available at http://www.zdnet.com/blog/security/lulzsec-releases-deluge-of-private-arizona-law-enforcement-information/8892. Accessed September 25, 2014.

Chavez, Leo. 2008. *The Latino Threat: Constructing Immigrants, Citizens, and the Nation.* Palo Alto, CA: Stanford University Press.

Chivers, C. J. 2012. "In Fleeing Pilot, Hints of Trouble for Syria's Assad." *The New York Times,* July 14. Available at http://www.nytimes.com/2012/07/15/world/middleeast/syrian-pilots-defection-signals-trouble-for-government.html?pagewanted=all&gwh=58E3A8D3CC97089A62ECCDE9957B715A. Accessed July 15, 2012.

Christian Science Monitor. 2012. "WikiLeaks to Release Five Million E-mails Stolen from Stratfor." February 27. Available at http://www.csm.com/World/latest-news-wire-2012/0227/wikileaks-to-release-five-million-e-mails/. Accessed August 1, 2013.

Cleaver, Harry. 1998. "The Zapatistas Effect: The Internet and Rise of an Alternative Fabric." *Journal of International Affairs* 51(2): 621–640.

Coffey, Brenda. 2012. "Koch Brothers Exposed." Available at http://www.kochbrothersexposed.com/protest_movement_starts_rebranding_billionaire_koch_brothers. Accessed December 8, 2012.

Cohen, Jean. 1985. "Strategy and Identity: New Theoretical Paradigms and Contemporary Social Movements." *Social Research* 52: 663–716.

Cohen, Noam. 2006. "That After-Dinner Speech Remains a Favorite Dish." *The New York Times,* May 22. Available at http://www.nytimes.com/2006/05/22/business/media/22colbert.html. Accessed May 31, 2012.

Common Dreams. 2011. "Rising Awareness in Class Divide, Many Point to OWS: Report." January 12. Available at http://www.commondreams.org/headline/2012/01/12-0. Accessed June 5, 2012.

_____. 2012. "Students Protest Debt as Student Loan Debt Collectors Make a Billion." March 26. Available at http://www.commondreams.org/headline/2012/03/26-5. Accessed June 5, 2012.

Conant, Jeff. 2012. "Police-Occupy Stand Off at the Gill Tract Farmland in SF Bay Area." *AlterNet,* May 10. Available at http://www.alternet.org/newsandviews /article/928181/police-occupy_stand_off_at_the_gill_tract_farmland_in_sf_bay_ area/. Accessed May 11, 2012.

Considine, Austin. 2011. "For Activists, Tips on Safe Use of Social Media." *The New York Times,* April 1. Available at http://www.nytimes.com/2011/04/03/fashion/03noticed. html. Accessed June 5, 2012.

Cooper, Helene, and Mark Landler. 2012. "US Hopes Assad Can Be Eased out with Russia's Aid." *The New York Times,* May 26. Available at http://www.nytimes.com/2012/05/27 /world/middleeast/us-seeks-russias-help-in-removing-assad-in-syria.html?page-wanted=all. Accessed May 27, 2012.

Corn, David. 2010. "Sarah Palin's WikiLeaks Fail." *Mother Jones,* November 19.

Crawford, Amy. 2011. "Occupy SF Protestors Move to Justin Herman Plaza." *The San Francisco Examiner,* October 16. Available at http://www.sfexaminer.com/local/2011/10 /occupy-sf-protesters-move-justin-herman-plaza. Accessed May 31, 2012.

Crawford, Susan P. 2011. "The New Digital Divide." *The New York Times,* December 3. Available at http://www.nytimes.com/2011/12/04/opinion/sunday/internet-access -and-the-new-divide.html?pagewanted=all. Accessed June 5, 2012.

Dalton, Dennis. 2012. *Mahatma Gandhi: Nonviolent Power in Action.* New York: Columbia University Press.

Davis, Charles. 2012. "Supporters of Accused WikiLeaks Source Rally as Hearing Continues." *Truthout,* February 18. Available at http://www.truth-out.org/print/10482. Accessed June 5, 2012.

Dawkins, Richard. 1976. *The Selfish Gene.* Oxford: Oxford University Press.

Day, Paul, and Tomaj Cobos. 2012. "Spain Protestors Labor Reforms as Hundreds of Thousands Take to the Streets." *The Huffington Post,* February 19. Available at http:// www.huffingtonpost.com/2012/02/19/spain-protests-labor-reforms_n_1287491 .html. Accessed June 5, 2012.

De Freytas-Tamura, Kimiko. 2014. "For Muslims, Social Media Debate on Extremism Is Reflected in Dueling Hashtags." *The New York Times,* September 27. Available at http://www.nytimes.com/2014/09/28/world/for-muslims-social-media-debate-on -extremism-is-reflected-in-dueling-hashtags.html. Accessed September 28, 2014.

Deans, Jason. 2004. "Fox News Documentary Tops Amazon Sales Chart." *Guardian Unlimited News.* Available at http://www.film.guardian.co.uk/news/story/012589/html. Accessed August 1, 2004.

¡Democracia real YA! 2012. Available at http://www.democraciarealya.es/. Accessed May 31, 2012.

Denhart, Chris. 2013. How the $1.2 Trillion Debt Crisis Is Crippling Students." *Forbes,* August 2. Available at http://www.forbes.com/sites/specialfeatures/2013/08/07/how-the -college-debt-is-crippling-students-parents-and-the-economy/. Accessed November 13, 2013.

Denning, Dorothy. 2010. "Activism, Hacktivism, and Cyberterrorism: The Internet as a Tool for Influencing Foreign Policy." In *Networks and Netwars: The Future of Terror,* edited by Hohn Arquilla and David Ronfeldt, 239–288. Santa Monica, CA: Rand Corporation. Available at http://www.rand.org/content/dam/rand/pubs/monograph_reports/MR1382/MR1382 .ch8.pdf. Accessed August 4, 2013.

Diani, Mario. 1995. *Green Networks.* Edinburgh: Edinburgh University Press.

_____. 2000a. "The Concept of Social Movements." *Sociological Review* 40(1): 1–25.

_____. 2000b. "Social Movement Networks Virtual and Real." *Information, Communication and Society* 3(3): 386–401.

Dias, Elizabeth. 2011. "The 22-Year-Old Who Led the Charge Against Bank of America." *Time,* November 7. Available at http://www.time/com/time/nation/article /0,8599,2098715,00.html. Accessed July 4, 2012.

DiMaggio, Paul, Hargitta Eszter, Russell Neuman, and John Robinson. 2004. "Social Implications of the Internet." *American Sociological Review* 27: 307–32.

Dolphin, Myles. 2012. "Massive Montreal Rally Marks 100 Days of Student Protests." *The Globe and Mail,* May 22. Available at http://www.theglobeandmail.com/news/national /massive-montreal-rally-marks-100-days-of-student-protests/article4198301. Accessed January 15, 2013.

Donadio, Rachel. 2012. "Dear Friends: Pope Takes to Twitter, with an Assist." *The New York Times,* December 12. Available at http://www.nytimes.com/2012/12/12/world/europe /the-pope-now-on-twitter.html. Accessed August 1, 2013.

Drehle, David. 2008. "Obama's Youth Vote Triumph. *Time,* January 4, pp. 15–17.

Durac, Vincent. 2012. "Yemen's Arab Spring—Democratic Opening or Regime Maintenance?" *Mediterranean Politics* 17(22): 161–178.

Dutta-Bergman, M. J. 2006. "Community Participation and Internet Use After September 11: Complementarily in Channel Consumption." *Journal of Computer-Mediated Communication* 11(2): 469–484.

Earl, Jennifer. 2004. "The Cultural Consequences of Social Movements." In *The Blackwell Companion to Social Movements,* edited by David Snow, Sarah Soule, and Hanspeter Kriesi, 508–530. Malden, MA: Blackwell.

_____. 2010. "Protest Arrests and Future Protest Participation: The 2004 Republican National Convention Arrestees and the Effects of Repression." *Studies in Law, Politics, and Society* 45: 141–173.

Earl, Jennifer, Katrina Kimport, Greg Prieto, Carly Rush, and Kimberly Reynoso. 2010. "Changing the World One Webpage at a Time: Conceptualizing and Explaining 'Internet Activism.'" *Mobilization* 15(4): 425–446.

Ebright, Olsen, Antonio Castelan, and Beverly White. 2012. "When the Chalk Dust Settles Opinion of Occupy Los Angeles Latest Demonstration Varied." *NBC Los Angeles,* July 13. Available at http://www.nbclosangeles.com/news/local/Downtown-LA-Art-Walk -Protest-Arrest-DTLA-162338316.html. Accessed August 1, 2013.

EFE. 2011. "Spanish Police Break up Madrid Sit-In." May 17. Available at http://www. efeamerica.com/309_hispanic-world/1129105_spanish-police-break-up-madrid -sit-in.html. Accessed May 31, 2012.

Einhorn, Erin, and Corky Siemasko. 2011. "Mayor Bloomberg Predicts Riots in the Streets If the Economy Does Not Create More Jobs." *New York Daily News,* September 16. Available at http://www.infowars.com/mayor-bloomberg-predicts-riots-in-the-streets -if-economy-doesnt-create-more-jobs/. Accessed April 9, 2012.

El Mundo. 2011. "Acampadas en Cadena Hasta el Próximo 22-M." May 17. Available at http://www.elmundo.es/elmundo/2011/05/17/espana/1305649774.html. Accessed May 31, 2012.

Engler, Mark. 2012. "Quebec's Student Revolt Goes Viral." *Dissent,* May 29. Available at http://dissentmagazine.org/atw.php?id=769. Accessed May 26, 2012.

Escalona, Alejandro. 2011. "Young Dreamers Come Out of the Shadows." *Chicago Sun Times,* March 9. Available at http://www.suntimes.com/news/escalona/4220902–452/young-dreamers-come-out-of-shadows.html. Accessed September 25, 2014.

Escobar, Pepe. 2011. "Spain's Enormous, Inspiring Protests Are Rooted in Restoring Democracy and Decent Life in an Era of Turbocapitalism." *AlterNet,* May 24. Available at http://www.alternet.org/module/printversion/151065. Accessed June 5, 2012.

Estes, Adam. 2011. "LulzSec Document Release Targets Arizona Law Enforcement." *The Atlantic Wire,* June 23.

Fahim, Kareem. 2012. "Fierce Clashes Erupt in Egypt Ahead of Presidential Vote." *The New York Times,* May 2. Available at http://www.nytimes.com/2012/05/03/world/middleeast/deadly-clashes-erupt-in-egypt-ahead-of-vote.html?pagewanted=all. Accessed May 3, 2012.

Fahim, Kareem, and Mary El-Sheikh. 2013. "Crackdown in Egypt Kills Islamists as They Protest." *The New York Times,* July 27. Available at http://www.nytimes.com/2013/07/28/world/middleeast/egypt.html?pagewanted=all&_r=0. Accessed August 1, 2013.

Finamore, Carl. 2013. "Generals Still in Charge—Tough Days Ahead in Egypt." *Portside,* January 26.

Fisher, Daniel. 2012. "Inside the Koch Empire: How the Brothers Plan to Reshape America." *Forbes,* December 5. Available at http://www.forbes.com/sites/danielfisher/2012/12/05/inside-the-koch-empire-how-the-brothers-plan-to-reshape-america/2. Accessed July 8, 2012.

Foroohar, Rana. 2011. "What Ever Happened to Upward Mobility?" *Time,* November 14. Available at http://content.time.com/time/magazine/article/0,9171,2098584,00.html. Accessed August 1, 2013.

Fung, Brian. 2014. "Pope Francis Calls the Internet 'a Gift from God.'" *The Washington Post,* January 23. Available at http://www.washingtonpost.com/blogs/the-switch/wp/2014/01/23/the-pople-calls-the-interent-a-gift-from-God. Accessed April 25, 2014.

Gall, Carlotta. 2014. "Ukraine's Neglected and Battered Army Inspires Citizens to Pitch In." *The New York Times,* September 22. Available at http://www.nytimes.com/2014/09/23/world/europe/ukraine-soldiers-inspires-citizens-to-pitch-in.html. Accessed September 25, 2014.

Gamson, William. 1975. *The Strategy of Social Protest.* Homewood, IL: Dorsey Press.

———. 1990. *The Strategy of Social Protest.* Belmont, CA: Wadsworth.

———. 1992. *Talking Politics.* New York: Cambridge University Press.

Gamson, William, and Gadi Wolfsfeld. 1993. "Movements and Media as Interacting Systems." *Annals of the Academy of Political and Social Sciences* 528: 114–125.

Ganz, Marshall. 2004. "Organizing as Leadership." In *Encyclopedia of Leadership,* edited by George Goethals, Georgia J. Sorenson, James McGregor Burns, 1134–1144. Thousand Oaks, CA: Sage.

Garcia, Juan R. 2013. "Operation Wetback." *Encyclopedia of Race and Racism.* Volume 2. Detroit: Macmillan Reference USA, 2008.

Gardner, Harris. 2013. "For Rape Victims in India, the Police Are Often Part of the Problem." *The New York Times,* January 23. Available at http://www.nytimes.com/2013/01/23/world/asia/for-rape-victims-in-india-police-are-often-part-of-the-problem.html

?pagewanted=all&_r=0&gwh=EDA8F19813AF1529819DBC6356FA1497.   Accessed
August 3, 2013.

Gibson, Megan. 2013. "Will SlutWalks Change the Meaning of the Word Slut?" *Time*, August 12. Available at http://www.time.com/nation/article/0,8599,2088234,00.html.

Giddens, Anthony. 1991. *Modernity and Self-Identity. Self and Society in the Late Modern
Age.* Cambridge, MA: Polity.

Gilmore, Stephanie. 2011. "Marcha de las Putas: SlutWalking Crosses Global Divides." *On
the Issues Magazine,* Fall. Available at http://www.ontheissuesmagazine.com/2011fall
/2011fall_gilmore.php. Accessed March 17, 2013.

Ginger, Rough. 2010. "Brewer Has 'Concerns' About Immigration Bill; Won't Say If She'll
Sign or Veto." *The Arizona Republic,* April 19.

Giroux, Henry A. 2012. *The Twilight of the Social.* Boulder, CO: Paradigm Publishers.

Gitlin, Todd. 1980. *The Whole World Is Watching: Mass Media in the Making and Unmaking
of the New Left.* Berkeley, CA: University of California Press.

Giugni, Marco. 1998. "Was It Worth the Effort? The Outcomes and Consequences of Social
Movements." *Annual Review of Sociology* 98:371–393.

Giugni, Marco, Doug McAdam, and Charles Tilly. 1999. *How Social Movements Matter.*
Minneapolis: University of Minnesota Press.

Gladstone, Rick. 2014. "Russian Diplomat's Speech Depicts the West as Hypocritical." *The
New York Times,* September 27. Available at http://www.nytimes.com/2014/09/28
/world/russian-diplomats-speech-depicts-the-west-as-hypocritical.html. Accessed September 28, 2014.

Glantz, Gina. 2011. "The 'Occupy' Movement Lives." *The Washington Post,* December 30. Available at http://www.washingtonpost.com/opinions/the-occupy-move
ment-lives/2011/12/27/gIQAwCtNRP_story.html. Accessed May 31, 2012.

Gonzalez, Juan. 2011. *Harvest of Empire: A History of Latinos in America.* New York: Penguin Press.

Goodale, Gloria. 2012. "Student Loans: As Debts Hit $1 Trillion Mark Protesters Plan Oc-
cupy-Type Events." *The Christian Science Monitor,* April 25. Available at http://www
.csmonitor.com/USA/Education/2012/0425/Student-loans-As-debts-hit-1-trillion-
mark-protesters-plan-Occupy-type-events. Accessed August 1, 2013.

Goodman, Adam. 2012. "Undocumented and Unafraid." *Salon,* March 29. Available at
http://www.salon.com/2012/03/29/immigration_activists_announce_theyre_undoc
umented_and_unafraid/. Accessed May 31, 2012.

Goodman, Amy. 2012. "A Win for the Spanish Indignados." *SACSIS,* July 6. Available at
sacsis.org/za/site/article/1356. Accessed January 7, 2013.

Gordon, Larry, and Chris Megerian. 2012. "Pepper Spray Report Sharply Criticizes UC
Davis Leaders, Police." *Los Angeles Times,* April 12. Available at http://articles.latimes.
com/2012/apr/12/local/la-me-0412-uc-davis-20120412. Accessed April 13, 2012.

Gordon, Michael R. 2013. "U.S Steps Up Aid to Syrian Opposition Pledging $60 Million."
The New York Times, February 28. Available at http://www.nytimes.com/2013/03/01
/world/middleeast/us-pledges-60-million-to-syrian-opposition.html?_r=0. Accessed
March 1, 2013.

Gould, Roger V. 1993. "Collective Action and Network Structure." *American Sociological
Review* 58: 182–196.

Greenstone, Michael and Adam Looney. 2013. "Rising Student Debt Burdens: Factors Behind the Phenomenon." *Brookings Institution.* Available at http://www.brookings.edu

/research/papers/2014/05/student-loan-debt-rising-gale-harris. Accessed September 25, 2014.

Grieco, Lou, and Mary McCarty. 2013. "Social Media Under Fire in Steubenville Rape Case." *Dayton Daily News,* January 13. Available at http://www.daytondailynews.com /news/news/local-govt-politics/social-media-under-fire-in-steubenville-rape-case /nTsWg/. Accessed March 13, 2013.

Guardian. 2011. "To the Occupy movement – the occupiers of Tahrir Square are with you." *The Guardian,* October 25. Available at http://www.theguardian.com/commentis free/2011/oct/25/occupy-movement-tahrir-square-cairo. Accessed October 9, 2014.

Gusfield, Joseph. 1970. *Protest, Reform, and Revolt: A Reader in Social Movements.* New York: Wiley.

Gwynne, Kristen. 2012. "Following Arrests at an Occupy Oakland Candle Light Vigil, Protestors Shut Down City Hall." *AlterNet,* January 7. Available at http://www.alternet.org /module/printversion/newstandviews/759590. Accessed June 5, 2012.

_____. 2013. "Social Media Campaign Finally Forces Facebook to Be Less Pro-Rape." *AlterNet,* May 29. Available at http://www.alternet.org/social-media-campaign-finally -forces-facebook-be-less-pro-rape. Accessed July 5, 2013.

Habermas, Jürgen. 1989. *The Structural Transformation of the Public Sphere.* Cambridge, MA: MIT Press.

_____. 1993. *Justification and Application: Remarks on Discourse Ethics.* Cambridge, MA: Polity Press.

Habib, Toumi. 2011. "Al Jazeera Turning into Private Media Organization." *Gulf News,* July 13. Available at http://gulfnews.com/news/gulf/qatar/al-jazeera-turning-into-private -media-organization-1.837871. Accessed July 7, 2014.

Hauslohner, Abigail. 2011. "Harvesting the Arab Spring: Tunisia Goes to the Polls." *Time,* October 23. Available at http://content.time.com/time/world/article/0,8599,2097589,00 .html. Accessed December 29, 2012.

Heath, Terrance. 2012. "The Secret of Joy: Six Lessons from Quebec's 'Maple Spring.'" *Truthout,* June 8. Available at http://truth-out.org/opinion/item/9671-the-secret-of-joy -six-lessons-from-quebecs-maple-spring. Accessed June 8, 2012.

Hedges, Chris. 2013. "We Are Bradley Manning." *Portside,* March 13. Available at http:// www.portside.org/print/node/1938. Accessed March 5, 2013.

Heestand, Mela. 2012. "UC Davis Students and Faculty Face Prison Time for Peaceful Protest Against Bank." *AlterNet,* April 27. Available at http://www.alternet.org /story/155185/uc_davis_students_and_faculty_face_11_years_in_prison_for_peace ful_protest_against_bank_. Accessed April 29, 2012.

Herszenhorn, David, and Alexandra Odynova. 2014. "Soldiers' Graves Bear Witness to Russia's Role in Ukraine." *New York Times,* September 21. Available at http://www .nytimes.com/2014/09/22/world/europe/soldiers-graves-bear-witness-to-russias -role-in-ukraine.html?gwh=85955341389AB1797C74FE2E2B2AE9C8&gwt=pay &assetType=nyt. Accessed October 10, 2014.

Heuvel, Katrina vanden. 2012. "The Occupy Effect." *The Nation,* January 26. Available at http://www.thenation.com/blog/165883/occupy-effect. Accessed September 22, 2014.

Himmelein, Gerald. 2009. "Anonymous vs. Scientology: Tom Cruise Signs Mask." *Heise Online,* January 9. Available at http://www.heise.de/newsticker/meldung/Anonymous-vs -Scientology-Tom-Cruise-signiert-Maske-748264.html. Accessed May 31, 2012.

Hindman, Matthew. 2007. "Open-Source Politics Reconsidered: Emerging Patterns in On-line Political Participation." In *Governance and Information Technology: From Electronic Government to Information Government*, edited by Viktor Mayer-Schonberger and David Lazer, 143–170. Cambridge, MA: MIT Press.

Hing, Juliane. 2012. "Arizona's Suite of New Anti-Immigrant Bills Moves to Senate." *Colorlines*, February 23. Available at http://colorlines.com/archives/2011/02/arizona_clears_suite_of_anti-immigrant_bills.html. Accessed November 20, 2012.

Holliday, Joseph. 2011. "The Struggle in Syria in 2011: An Operational and Regional Analysis." The Institute of the Study of War. Available at http://www.understandingwar.org. Accessed May 2, 2012.

Honan, Edith. 2012. "College Students Protest Debt on 'Trillion Dollar Day.'" *Reuters*, April 25. Available at http://www.reuters.com/article/2012/04/26/us-usa-colleges-debt-idUSBRE83O1JL20120426. Accessed May 31, 2012.

Hoveyda, Fereydoun. 2003. *The Shah and the Ayatollah: The Iranian Mythology and Islamic Revolution*. Westport, CN: Greenwood Press.

Howard, Phillip, and Muzammil Hussain. 2013. *Democracy's Fourth Wave?* New York: Oxford University Press.

Huang, Carol. 2012. "Facebook and Twitter Key to Arab Spring Uprisings: Report." *The National*, June 6. Available at http://www.thenational.ae/news/uae-news/facebook-and-twitter-key-to-arab-spring-uprisings-report. Accessed August 30, 2014.

Hubbard, Ben. 2014. "New Islamic State Video Features British Hostage as Group Spokesperson." *The New York Times*, September 19, p. A8.

Hubbard, Peter. 2013. "Cracks Emerge as Egyptians Seek Premier." *The New York Times*, July 6. Available at http://www.nytimes.com/2013/07/07/world/middleeast.html. Accessed July 27, 2013.

Hunt, Scott, Robert Benford, and David Snow. 1994. "Identity Fields: Framing Processes and the Social Construction of Movement Identities." In *New Social Movements: From Ideology to Identity*, edited by Enrique Larana, Hank Johnston, and Joseph Gusfield, 185–208. Philadelphia: Temple University Press.

Isango, Eddy. 2013. "Arab Spring: A Reflection of its Birthplace, Tunisia." *The Guardian Express*, August 5. Available at http://guardianlv.com/2013/08/arab-spring-crisis-a-reflection-of-its-birthplace-tunisia/.

Jacobs, Deborah L. 2011. "Occupy Wall Street and the Rhetoric of Equality." *Forbes*, November 1. Available at http://www.forbes.com/sites/deborahjacobs/2011/11/01/occupy-wall-street-and-the-rhetoric-of-equality/. Accessed May 31, 2012.

James, Miles. 2009. "Tiananmen Killing: Were the Media Right?" *BBC News*, June 2. Available at http://news/bcc.co.uk/2/hi/8057762.stm. Accessed August 2, 2013.

Jasper, James. 1997. *The Art of Moral Protest: Culture, Biography, and Creativity in Social Movements*. Chicago: University of Chicago Press.

Jasper, James, and Francesca Polletta. 2001. "Collective Identity and Social Movements." *Review of Sociology* 27: 283–305.

Jenkins, Craig, and William Form. 2006. "Social Movements and Social Change." In *Handbook of Political Sociology: States, Civil Society and Globalization*, edited by Thomas Janoski, Robert Alford, Alexander Hicks and Mildred Schwartz, 331–349. Cambridge, MA: Cambridge University Press.

Jenkins, Craig, and Charles Perrow. 1977. "Insurgency of the Powerless: Farm Worker Movements (1946–1972)." *American Sociological Review* 42: 249–296.

Jenkins, Henry. 2006. *Convergence Culture*. New York: New York University Press.

Johnson, Tim. 2012. "Growing Mexican Student Protests Target Televisa, TV Azteca over Coverage of Presidential Campaign." *Truthout,* May 25. Available at http://truth-out.org/news/item/9366-growing-mexican-student-protests-target-televisa-tv-azteca-over-coverage-of-presidential-campaign. Accessed May 25, 2012.

Johnston, Hank. 1994. "New Social Movements and Old Regional Nationalisms. In *New Social Movements: From Ideology to Identity,* edited by Enrique Larana, Hank Johnston, and Joseph Gusfield, 267–286. Philadelphia, PA: Temple University Press.

Jordan, Tim. 2001. "Measuring the Net: Host Counts Versus Business Plans." *Information, Communication and Society* 4(1): 34–53.

Kahn, Richard, and Douglas Kellner. 2003. "Internet Subcultures and Oppositional Politics." In *The Post-subcultures Reader,* edited by D. Muggleton, 299–314. London: Berg.

Kane, Alex. 2013. "Shameless: The NYP Lied Under Oath to Lock Up Occupy Activist." *AlterNet,* March 4. Available at http://www.alternet.org/news-amp-politics/shameless-nypd-lied-under-oath-lock-occupy-activist. Accessed March 4, 2013.

Kang, Cecilia. 2011. "Number of Cellphones Exceeds US Population." *The Washington Post,* October 11. Available at http://www.washingtonpost.com/blogs/post-tech/post/number-of-cell-phones-exceeds-us-population-ctia-trade-group/2011/10/11/gIQARNcEcL_blog.html. Accessed July 3, 2012.

Kansaku-Sarmiento, Alana. 2011. "Borders Bookstores Close Final Chapter." *The Times,* July 21. Available at http://www.tigardtimes.com/news/print_story.php?story_id=131120238899080900. Accessed June 5, 2012.

Kantrowitz, Alex. 2013. "A Successful Media Push for Immigration Reform? Don't Forget Email and SMS." *Media Shift,* February 1. Available at http://www.pbs.org/mediashift/2013/02/a-social-media-push-for-immigration-reform-dont-forget-email-and-sms032/. Accessed October 14, 2014.

Karr, Timothy, and Clothilde Le Coz. 2011. "How Western Corporations Have Been Helping Tyrants Suppress Rebellions in the Arab World." *AlterNet,* March 28. Available at http://www.alternet.org/story/150408. Accessed June 5, 2012.

Kaye, Harvey J. 2011. "Thomas Paine's 'Common Sense' Is the Cure for Cynical Citizens." *The Next New Deal: The Blog of the Roosevelt Institute.* Available at http://www.nextnewdeal.net/thomas-paines-common-sense-cure-cynical-citizens. Accessed October 10, 2014.

Keller, Jared. 2010. "Evaluating Iran's Twitter Revolution." *The Atlantic,* June 18. http://www.theatlantic.com/technology/archive/2010/06/evaluating-irans-twitter-revolution/58337/. Accessed August 1, 2013.

Kelley, Lauren. 2011. "Occupy Updates: NYPD Takes Generators as Temps Drop, Threatens to Sue OWS, Oakland Mayor Says No Camping Overnight." *AlterNet,* October 28. Available at http://www.alternet.org/newsandviews/article/686499/occupy_updates%3A_nypd_takes_generators_as_temps_drop,_threatens_to_sue_ows%3B_oakland_mayor_says_no_camping_overnight/. Accessed June 5, 2012.

Kelly, John, and Bruce Etling. 2008. "Mapping Iran's Online Public: Politics and Culture in the Persian Blogosphere." *Berkman Center Research Publication,* number 2008–01.

Kennis, Andrew. 2012. "Mexico's Youth Uprising: How a Social Media-Powered Student Movement Upended the Presidential Election." *AlterNet,* July 1. Available at http://www.alternet.org/world/156107/mexico's_youth_uprising%3A_how_a_social_media-powered_student_movement_upended_the_presidential_election. Accessed July 2, 2012.

Kim, Susana. 2011. "Verizon Cancels $2 Fee." *ABC News,* December 30. Available at http://abcnews.go.com/blogs/business/2011/12/verizon-cancels-2-fee/. Accessed August 1, 2013.

Kingsley, Patrick. 2014. "Who Is Behind ISIS's Terrifying Online Propaganda Operation?" *The Guardian,* June 23. Available at http://www.theguardian.com/world/2014/jun/23/who-behind-isis-propaganda-operation-iraq. Accessed September 25, 2014.

Kirkpatrick, David D. 2012. "Egyptian Court Sentences Mubarak to Life in Prison." *Truthout,* June 2. Available at http://truth-out.org/news/item/9548-egyptian-court-sentences-mubarak-to-life-in-prison. Accessed June 2, 2012.

Kirkpatrick, David D. and Ben Hubbard. 2013. "Morsi Defies Egypt Army's Ultimatum to Bend to Protest." *The New York Times,* July 2. http://www.nytimes.com/2013/07/03/world/middleeast/egypt-protests.html?pagewanted=all&_r=0

Kirkpatrick, David D. and Kareem Fahim, 2013. "Morsi Faces Ultimatum as Allies Speak of Military 'Coup.'" *The New York Times,* July 3. http://www.nytimes.com/2013/07/02/world/middleeast/egypt-protests.html?pagewanted=all

Kirkpatrick, David D., and Liam Stack. 2012. "Violence in Cairo Pits Thousands Against Police." *The New York Times,* November 20, p. A1.

Klandermans, Bert, Hans Peter Kriesi, and Sidney Tarrow (eds.). 1988. *From Structure to Action: Comparing Movement Participation Across Cultures.* Greenwich, CT: JAI-Press.

Klein, Naomi. 2000. *No Logo.* New York: Picador Press.

Knowlton, Brian. 2014. "Digital War Takes Shape on Website over ISIS." *New York Times,* September 9. Available at http://www.nytimes.com/2014/09/27/world/middleeast/us-vividly-rebuts-isis-propaganda-on-arab-social-media.html/. Accessed October 10, 2014.

Kornhauser, William. 1959. *The Politics of Mass Society.* Glencoe, IL: Free Press.

Kraut, Robert, Michael Paterson, Sara Kiesler, Vicki Lundmark, Ridas Ukopadtyah, and William Scheller. 1998. "Internet Paradox: A Social Technology that Reduces Social Involvement and Psychological Well-Being?" *American Psychologist* 53(9): 1017–1031.

Kristof, Nicholas D. 2012. "After Recess: Change the World." *The New York Times,* February 4. Available at http://www.nytimes.com/2012/02/05/opinion/sunday/kristof-after-recess-change-the-world.html. Accessed June 5, 2012.

Kroll, Andy. 2012. "The Tea Party Plan to Save Scott Walker." *Mother Jones,* February 1. Available at http://motherjones.com/politics/2012/01/scott-walker-recall-tea-party. Accessed June 5, 2012.

Kuebler, Johanne. 2011. "Overcoming the Digital Divide: The Internet and Political Mobilization in Egypt and Tunisia." *CyberOrient* 5(1). Available at www.cyberorient.net/article/do?articleID=6212. Accessed December 12, 2011.

Kumar, Radha. 1993. *The History of Doing: An Illustrated Account of Movements for Women's Rights and Feminism in India 1800–1990.* New Delhi: Zubaan.

Kurzman, Charles. 2004. *The Unthinkable Revolution in Iran.* Cambridge, MA: Harvard University Press.

Lackey, Katharine. 2014. "ISIL Releases Propaganda Video with British Hostage." *USA Today,* September 19, p. 11A.

Laghmari, Jihen, and Mahmoud Kassem. 2011. "Tunisia President Hands Power to Prime Minister Before Leaving Country." *Bloomberg,* January 14. Available at http://www.bloomberg.com/news/2011-01-13/tunisia-president-to-stand-down-in-2014-slash-prices-amid-riots.html. Accessed September 28, 2014.

Lakshmi, Rama. 2013. "India Struggles with Social Media Following Rape Uproar." *The Washington Post*, January 4. Available at http://www.washingtonpost.com/world/asia_pacific/india-struggles-with-social-media-following-rape-uproar/2013/01/04/7896933e-559a-11e2-89de-76c1c54b1418_story.html. Accessed March 13, 2013.

Landers, Chris. 2008. "The Internets Are Going to War." *Baltimore City Paper*, January 25. Available at http://blogs.citypaper.com/index.php/2008/01/the-internets-are-going-to-war/. Accessed May 31, 2012.

Lasn, Kalle. 1999. *The Culture Jam: The Uncooling of America*. New York: William Morrow.

Lawrence, William. 2013. "Against the Odds: The Black Swans of Libya's Arab Spring." *World Politics Review*, July 23. Available at http://www.worldpoliticsreview.com/articles/13112/against-the-odds-the-black-swans-of-libya-s-arab-spring. Accessed August 1, 2013.

Lee, Brianna. 2011. "Half of California 'Dream Act' Becomes Law." *Need to Know on PBS*, July 28. Available at http://www.pbs.org/wnet/need-to-know/the-daily-need/half-of-california-dream-act-becomes-law/10745/. Accessed June 23, 2012.

Leier, Elizabeth. 2012. "Québec's Student Strike Turning into a Citizens' Revolt." *Truthout*, May 25. Available at http://truth-out.org/news/item/9372-quebecs-student-strike-turning-into-a-citizens-revolt. Accessed May 25, 2012.

LeVine, Mark. 2011. "Tunisia: How the US Got It Wrong." *Al Jazeera*, January 16. Available at http://www.aljazeera.com/indepth/opinion/2011/01/20111167156465567.html. Accessed June 5, 2012.

Levinson, Charles. 2013. "Egypt Turns a Blow to Muslim Brotherhood." *The Wall Street Journal*, July 3. Available at http://online.wsj.com/article/SB10001424127887324260204578583740992967694.html. Accessed August 1, 2013.

Leyden, John. 2008. "Scientologists Fight Back Against Anonymous but Fails to Get Injunction." *The Register*, March 17. Available at http://www.theregister.co.uk/2008/03/17/scientology_anonymous_round_three/. Accessed May 31, 2012.

Lindsay, Michael. 2013. "Quebec's Student Tuition Protest: Who Really Won the Dispute?" *CBC*, September 15. Available at http://www.cbc.ca/news/canada/quebec-s-student-tuition-protest-who-really-won-the-dispute-1.1327562. Accessed September 28, 2014.

Lovett, Ian. 2011. "U.C.L.A. Student's Video Rant Against Asians Fuels Firestorm." *The New York Times*, March 15. Available at http://www.nytimes.com/2011/03/16/us/16ucla.html. Accessed May 31, 2012.

Macey, Jennifer. 2013. "Online Protests Prompt Facebook to Crack Down on Pages Promoting Violence Against Women." *ABC News*, May 29. Available at http://www.abc.net/au/news/2013-05-29. Accessed July 20, 2013.

MacFarquhar, Neil. 2012. "Syrian's Defection Signals Eroding Support for Assad." *The New York Times*, July 6. Available at http://www.nytimes.com/2012/07/07/world/middleeast/opponents-of-syrias-president-gather-in-paris.html?pagewanted=all. Accessed July 7, 2012.

_____. 2013. "Yemen Making Strides in Transition to Democracy After Arab Spring." *The New York Times*, May 25. Available at http://www.nytimes.com/2013/05/26/world/asia/yemen-makes-strides. Accessed July 20, 2013.

Mahanta, Siddhartha. 2011. "Saudi Women to Clinton: Help Us Win the Right to Drive." *Mother Jones*, June 3. Available at http://www.motherjones.com/mojo/2011/06/women-drivers-saudi-arabia-hillary-clinton-arab-spring. Accessed June 5, 2012.

Maharawal, Manissa M. 2012. "What Has Occupy Been Up To? 6 Great Actions You Can't Miss This Spring." *AlterNet,* March 14. Available at http://www.alternet.org /story/154411/what_has_occupy_been_up_to_6_great_actions_you_can't_miss _this_spring/?page=entire. Accessed June 5, 2012.

Maharawal, Marissa, and Zoltan Gluck. 2012. "How Students Are Painting Montreal Red." *Truthout,* May 27. Available at http://truth-out.org/news/item/9415-how-students -are-painting-montreal-red. Accessed August 30, 2014.

Mahindra, Anand. 2012. "Delhi Gang Rape Case: Social Media Fuels Rally at India Gate." *The Economic Times,* December 24. Available at http://articles.economictimes.india times.com/2012-12-24/news/35991878_1_delhi-gang-adhvith-dhuddu-social -media. Accessed March 13, 2013.

Malcolm, Hadley, and Sean McMinn. 2013. "Sagging State Tuition Jacks up College Tuition." *USA Today,* September 3. Available at http://www.usatoday.com/story/money /personalfinance/2013/09/02/state-funding-declines-raise-tuition/2707837. Accessed September 4, 2013.

Mann, Michael. 2000. "Has Globalization Ended the Rise of the Nation-State?" In *The Global Transformations Reader: An Introduction to the Globalization Debate,* edited by David Held and Andrew McGrew, 136–147. Cambridge, MA: Polity Press.

Markels, Alex. 2003. "Virtual Peacenik." *Mother Jones,* May 5. Available at http://www .MotherJones.com/news/hellriiser/2003/05/ma_379_01.htm. Accessed April 7, 2006.

Marshall, Andrew G. 2012. "From the Chilean Winter to the Maple Spring Solidarity: The Student Movements in Chile and Quebec." *Truthout,* May 26. Available at http://truth -out.org/news/item/9402-from-the-chilean-winter-to-the-maple-spring-solidarity -and-the-student-movements-in-chile-and-quebec. Accessed May 26, 2012.

Marszal, Andrew. 2014. "How Isis used Twitter and the World Cup to spread its terror." *The Telegraph,* June 24. Available at http://www.telegraph.co.uk/news/worldnews/middle east/iraq/10923046/How-Isis-used-Twitter-and-the-World-Cup-to-spread-its-terror .html. Accessed October 9, 2014.

Marullo, Sam, and David Meyer. 2007. "Anti-War and Peace Movements," in *The Blackwell Companion to Social Movements,* edited by David A. Snow, Sarah A. Soule, and Hanspeter Kriesi. London: Blackwell, 2004.

Mashayekki, Mehrdad. 2001. "The Revival of the Student Movement in Post-Revolutionary Iran." *International Journal of Politics, Culture and Society* 15(2): 283–306.

Massey, Daniel. 2012. "'Occupy' Movement Regroups, Targets BofA." *Crain's New York Business,* March 14. Available at http://www.crainsnewyork.com/article/20120314 /FINANCE/120319948. Accessed May 31, 2012.

Mather, Katie. 2013. "Audrie Pott Tormented Before Suicide over Alleged Sex Assault." *Los Angeles Times,* April 12. Available at http://articles.latimes.com/2013/local.html. Accessed August 2, 2013.

McAdam, Doug. 1982. *Political Process and the Development of Black Insurgency 1930–1970.* Chicago: University of Chicago Press.

McAdam, Doug, John McCarthy, and Meyer Zald. 1996. *Comparative Perspectives on Social Movements: Political Opportunities, Mobilizing Structures, and Cultural Framings.* New York: Cambridge University Press.

McAdam, Doug, and Ronnelle Paulsen. 1993. "Specifying the Relationship Between Social Ties and Activism." *American Journal of Sociology* 99(3): 640–667.

McCarthy, John, and Mayer Zald. 1973. *The Trend of Social Movements in America: Professionalization and Resource Mobilization*. Thousand Oaks, CA: General Learning Press.

———. 1977. "Resource Mobilization: A Partial Theory." *American Journal of Sociology* 82(6): 1212–1241.

McGreal, Chris. 2010. "Wikileaks Reveals Video Showing US Air Crew Shooting Down Iraqi Civilians." *The Guardian*, April 5. Available at http://www.theguardian.com /world/2010/apr/05/wikileaks-us-army-iraq-attack. Accessed October 10, 2014.

McKee, Yates. 2012. "As Occupy Wall Street Anniversary Approaches, Debt Emerges as Widespread Occupy Grievance." *Truthout*, July 15. Available at http://truth-out .org/news/item/10335-as-occupy-wall-street-anniversary-approaches-debt-emerges -as-widespread-occupy-grievance. Accessed July 15, 2012.

McLuhan, Marshall. 1964. *The Medium Is the Message*. London: Penguin Books.

McNally, Terrence. 2012. "Revolution 2.0: How the Internet Changed Wael Ghonim's Life and Helped Spark Egypt's Uprising." *AlterNet*, April 16. Available at http://www .alternet.org/world/154998/how_an_ordinary_egyptian_used_facebook_to_spark_ political_activism. Accessed April 22, 2012.

McVeigh, Karen. 2012. "Occupy the Courts Takes Aim at Citizens United and Super Pacs." *The Guardian*, January 20. Available at http://www.theguardian.com/law/2012/jan/20 /occupy-the-courts-citizens-united-election-ruling. Accessed September 28, 2014.

Medina, Jennifer. 2012. "Campus Task Force Criticizes Pepper Spraying of Protesters." *The New York Times*, April 11. Available at http://www.nytimes.com/2012/04/12/us /task-force-criticizes-pepper-spraying-of-protesters-at-uc-davis.html. Accessed April 13, 2012.

Melber, Ari. 2007. "The Virtual Primary." *The Nation*, July 7, p. 30.

Melucci, Alberto. 1980. "The New Social Movements: A Theoretical Approach." *Social Science Information* 19: 199–226.

———. 1989. *Nomads of the Present*. London: Hutchinson Radius.

———. 1996. *Challenging Codes of Collective Action in the Information Age*. Cambridge, MA: Cambridge University Press.

Meyer, David S. 2005. "Social Movements and Public Policy: Eggs, Chicken, and Theory." Introduction to *Routing the Opposition: Social Movements, Public Policy and Democracy*, edited by David S. Meyers, Valerie Jenness, and Helen Ingram, 1–26. Minneapolis: University of Minnesota Press.

Meyer, David S., and Debra Minkoff. 2004. "Conceptualizing Political Opportunity." *Social Force* 82(4): 1457–1492.

Middleton, Joel, and Donald Green. 2007. "Do Community-Based Voter Mobilization Campaigns Work Even in Battleground States? Evaluating the Effectiveness of MoveOn's 2004 Outreach Campaign." Yale University. Available at www.yale.edu/csap /seminars/middleton.pdf. Accessed January 19, 2009.

Milkman, Ruth, Penny Lewis, and Stephanie Luce. 2013. "The Genie's Out of the Bottle: Insiders Perspectives on Occupy Wall Street." *The Sociological Quarterly* 54(2): 194–198.

Mills, C. W. 1959. *The Sociological Imagination*. London: Oxford University Press.

Minnesota Prager Discussion Group. 2011. Available at mnprager.wordpress.com. Accessed July 4, 2012.

Mohney, Gillian. 2013 "Steubenville Rape Trial." *ABC News*, March 10. http://abcnews .go.com/US/steubenville-rape-trial-start-week/story?id=18693411#.UbDP2Xf4JHI. Accessed June 6, 2013.

Molina, Marta. 2012. "A Mexican Spring Begins to Blossom." *Waging Nonviolence*, May 29. Available at http://wagingnonviolence.org/2012/05/a-mexican-spring-begins-to-blossom/. Accessed June 2, 2012.

Monbiot, George. 2010. "The Tea Parties: Deluded and Propelled by Billionaires." *AlterNet*, October 25. Available at http://www.alternet.org/story/148619. Accessed June 5, 2012.

———. 2011. "Corporate-Funded Online 'Astroturfing' Is More Advanced and More Automated Than You Might Think." *AlterNet*, February 24. Available at http://www.alternet.org/story/150049/corporate-funded_online_'astroturfing'_is_more_advanced_and_more_automated_than_you_might_think?page=entire. Accessed June 5, 2012.

Montemurri, Patricia. 2014a. "Schoolkids Beckon Pope to Detroit." *USA Today*, September 12, p. 4A.

———. 2014b. "Students Create Video Inviting Pope to Detroit." *Detroit Free Press*, September 23. Available at http://www.freep.com/story/life/2014/09/23/loyola-high-video-papal-invite/16099799. Accessed September 25, 2014.

Morford, Mark. 2012. "Stephen Colbert Has Brass Cojones." *San Francisco Chronicle*, May 12. Available at http://sfgate.com/cgi-bin/blogs/sfgate/detail?blogid=3entry_id=4791. Accessed June 5, 2012.

Morozov, Evgeny. 2011. "Political Repression 2.0." *The New York Times*, September 1. Available at http://www.nytimes.com/2011/09/02/opinion/political-repression-2-0.html. Accessed June 5, 2012.

Morrison, Denton E. 1978. "Some Notes Toward Theory on Relative Deprivation, Social Movements, and Social Change." In *Collective Behavior and Social Movements*, edited by Louis E. Genevie, 202–209. Itasca, IL: Peacock.

MovedOn.org. Accessed various dates June 2003–2008.

Moynihan, Colin. 2011. "At May Day Demonstrations, Traffic Jams and Arrests." *The New York Times*, May 1. Available at http://www.nytimes.com/2012/05/02/nyregion/may-day-demonstrations-lead-to-clashes-and-arrests.html. Accessed October 7, 2014.

———. 2012. "Evicted from Park, Occupy Protesters Take to Sidewalks." *The New York Times*, April 12. Available at http://www.nytimes.com/2012/04/13/nyregion/evicted-from-park-occupy-protesters-take-to-the-sidewalks.html. Accessed April 13, 2012.

MSNBC. 2006. "The Rachel Maddow Show." Transcript. Available at http://www.nbcnews.com/id/36260269/ns/msnbc-rachel_maddow_show/. Accessed September 22, 2014.

Muawia, Amani. 2011. "Security Forces in Sudan Arrested the Opposition Leader and Head of the Popular Congress." *Press TV*, January 19. Available at www.edition.press.tv.ir.detail/160998.htm. Accessed August 1, 2013.

Mulvihill, Geoff. 2012. "Dharun Ravi Can Stay in United States After Jail. *The Huffington Post*, August 18. Available at http://www.huffingtonpost.com/2012/06/18/dharun-ravi-not-deported-ice_n_1606817.html. Accessed July 1, 2013.

Nagourey, Adam. 2011. "Dissention or Seeking Shelter? Homeless Stake a Claim in Protests." *The New York Times*, October 31. Available at http://www.nytimes.com/2011/11/01/us/dissenting-or-seeking-shelter-homeless-stake-a-claim-at-protests.html?pagewanted=all&_r=0. Accessed August 1, 2013.

Nie, Norman. 2001. "Sociability, Interpersonal Relations and the Internet." *American Behavioral Scientist* 45(3): 420–435.

Nie, Norman, and Lutz Erbring. 2000. "Internet and Society." *Stanford Institute for the Quantitative Study of Society*. Available at http://www.stanford.edu/group/siqss/Press_Release/Preliminary_Report.pdf. Accessed September 28, 2014.

Nir, Sarah, and Matt Flegenheimer. 2012. "Occupy Oakland Protests Leads to Hundreds of Arrests." *The New York Times,* January 29. Available at http://www.nytimes.com/2012/01/30/us/occupy-oakland-protest-leads-to-hundreds-of-arrests.html. Accessed August 1, 2013.

Nordland, Rod. 2012. "Latest Syrian Defectors Are from Higher Ranks." *The New York Times,* June 25. Available at http://www.nytimes.com/2012/06/26/world/middleeast/syrian-military-defections-reported.html?pagewanted=all. Accessed June 26, 2012.

Nowicki, Dan. 2010. "Arizona Immigration Law Ripples Through History, US Politics." *The Arizona Republic,* July 25. Available at http://www.azcentral.com/arizonarepublic/news/articles/2010/07/25/20100725immigration-law-history-politics.html. Accessed May 31, 2012.

Occupyarrests.com. Available at http://occupyarrests.moonfruit.com/. Accessed September 22, 2014.

Olson, Mancur. 1965. *The Logic of Collective Action: Public Goods and the Theory of Groups.* Cambridge, MA: Harvard University Press.

Oppel, Richard A., Jr. 2013. "Ohio Teenagers Guilty in Rape That Social Media Brought to Light." *The New York Times,* March 17. Available at http://www.nytimes.com/2013/03/18/us/teenagers-found-guilty-in-rape-in-steubenville-ohio.html?pagewanted=all. Accessed March 18, 2013.

Ottalini, David 2010. "Students Addicted to Social Media—New UM Study." April 21. University of Maryland press release. Available at http://www.newsdesk.umd/edu/sociss/release.cfm?AritcleD=2144. Accessed May 9, 2012.

Ouziel, Pablo. 2011. "Should Wealth Be Held by the Few or Everyone? That's the Central Focus of Protests from Spain to Greece." *AlterNet,* June 16. Available at http://www.alternet.org/module/printversion/151323. Accessed June 5, 2012.

Parr, Ben. 2010. "The Average Teenager Sends 3,339 Texts Per Month." October 14. Available at http://www.mashable.com/2010/10/14/nielsen-texting/stats. Accessed July 20, 2012.

Patesky, Mark. 2011. "Osama bin Laden Is Dead: News Explodes on Twitter." *Forbes,* May 1. Available at http://www.forbes.com/sites/markpatesky/2011/05/01/osama-bin-laden-is-dead-news-explodes-on-twitter/. Accessed May 1, 2012.

Peretti, Jonah. 2001. "My Nike Media Adventure." *The Nation,* April 9, pp. 22–24.

Pew Research Center. 2003. "Iraq and Vietnam: A Crucial Difference in Opinion." Available at http://pewresearch.org/pubs/432. Accessed July 3, 2005.

Pew Research Center. 2011. "Biggest Week Yet for Occupy Wall Street Coverage," *Journalism Project,* November 19. Available at http://www.journalism.org/2011/11/19/pej-news-coverage-index-november-1420–2011. Accessed September 22, 2014.

Pickerill, Jenny. 2003. *Cyberprotest: Environmental Activism.* New York: Manchester University Press.

Pilger, John. 2011. "The Revolt in Egypt Is Coming Home." *Truthout,* February 10. Available at http://www.truth-out.org/the-revolution-is-coming-home67624. Accessed January 10, 2014.

Pilkington, Ed. 2011. "Koch Brothers: Secretive Billionaires to Launch Vast Database with 2012 in Mind." *The Guardian,* November 7. Available at http://www.guardian.co.uk/world/2011/nov/07/koch-brothers-database-2012-election. Accessed June 6, 2012.

Piven, Frances, and Richard Cloward. 1977. *Poor People's Movements: Why They Succeed, Why They Fail.* New York: Pantheon Books.

Platt, Gerald M., and Stephen J. Lilley. 1994. "Multiple Images of a Leader: Constructing Martin Luther King Jr.'s Leadership." In *Self, Collective Behavior and Society: Essays Honoring the Contributions of Ralph H. Turner*, edited by Gerald Platt and Chad Gordon, 55–74. Greenwich, CT: JAI Press.

Polletta, Francesca. 2008. "Culture and Movements." *The Annals of the American Academy of Political and Social Science* 6(1): 78–96.

Polletta, Francesca, and James M. Jasper. 2001. "Collective Identity and Social Movements." *Annual Review of Sociology* 27: 283–305.

Pollock, John. 2013. "How Egypt and Tunisia Hacked the Arab Spring." *MIT Technology Review*, August 23. Available at www.technologyreview.com/featurestory/4251371/streetbook.

Potter, Trevor. 2003. "Internet Politics 2000: Over-hyped, then Under-hyped, the Revolution Begins." *Election Law Journal* 1(1): 25–33.

Power, Nina. 2011. "The Meaning of Time Magazine's Celebration of the Year of the Protester." *The Guardian*. December 16. Available at http://www.theguardian.com/comment isfree/2011/dec/16/meaning-time-magazine-celebration-protester. Accessed October 10, 2014.

Prasad, Akankstra, and Indu Nandakumar. 2012. "Delhi Gang Rape Case: Social Media Fuels Rally at Indian Gate." *The Economic Times*, December 24. Available at http://www.articles.economictimes.indiatimes.com/2012-12-24/news35991878. Accessed August 1, 2013.

Prashad, Vijay. 2012. *Arab Spring, Libyan Winter*. Oakland, CA: AK Press.

Preston, Jennifer. 2011a. "Movement Began with Outrage and a Facebook Page That Gave It an Outlet." *The New York Times*, February 5. Available at http://www.nytimes.com/2011/02/06/world/middleeast/06face.html?pagewanted=all. Accessed June 5, 2012.

———. 2011b. "Occupy Video Showcases Live Streaming." *The New York Times*, December 11. Available at http://www.nytimes.com/2011/12/12/business/media/occupy-movement-shows-potential-of-live-online-video.html. Accessed June 5, 2012.

Preston, Julia. 2012a. "Court Rulings Help Illegal Immigrants' College-Bound Children." *The New York Times*, September 5. Available at http://www.nytimes.com/2012/09/06/us/florida-and-new-jersey-courts-aid-illegal-immigrants-college-bound-children.html?gwh=B7BCF7EE44548E75FC61B0264625C290. Accessed September 6, 2012.

———. 2012b. "Record Number of Foreigners Were Deported in 2011, Officials Say." *The New York Times*, September 7. Available at http://www.nytimes.com/2012/09/08/us/us-deports-record-number-of-foreigners-in-2011.html?gwh=06F688AACAC F1279EE4F3E2D8D4F6200. Accessed September 8, 2012.

———. 2014. "Young Immigrants Turn Focus to President in Struggle over Deportations." *New York Times*. February 23. Available at http://www.nytimes.com/2014/02/24/us/politics/young-immigrants-turn-focus-to-president-in-struggle-over-deportations.html. Accessed October 10, 2014.

Preston, Julia, and John H. Cushman Jr. 2012. "Obama to Permit Young Migrants to Remain in the US" *The New York Times*, June 15. Available at http://www.nytimes.com/2012/06/16/us/us-to-stop-deporting-some-illegal-immigrants.html?pagewanted=all. Accessed June 16, 2012.

Preston, Julia, and Renando Santos. 2012. "A Record Latino Turnout, Solidly Backing Obama." *The New York Times*, November 7. Available at http://www.nytimes

.com/2012/11/08/us/politics/with-record-turnout-latinos-solidly-back-Obama.html. Accessed July 15, 2013.

Putnam, Robert. 2000. *Bowling Alone: The Collapse and Renewal of American Community.* New York: Simon and Schuster.

Quelly, Jon. 2013. "Blow the Whistle, Face Life in Jail, Progressives Slam Verdict in Manning Case." *Common Dreams,* July 30. Available at http://www.commondreams.org/headline /2013/07/30-9. Accessed August 2, 2013.

Radley, Whitney. 2013. "Houston Pastor's Protest Against Victoria's Secret 'Bright Young Things' Lingerie Ad Goes Viral." March 28. Available at http://www.houston.culture map.com/news/fashion/03-28-13-houston-pastors-protests-against-victim-assault. html. Accessed July 20, 2013.

Rainsford, Sarah. 2011. "Spain's 'Indignants' Lead International Protest Day." *BBC,* October 14. Available at http://www.bbc.co.uk/news/world-europe-15315270. Accessed May 31, 2012.

Rheingold, Howard. 2002. *Smart Mobs: The Next Social Revolution.* Cambridge, MA: Basic Books.

Romney, Lee. 2012. "Occupy Oakland Arrests Reach 400; City Hall Vandalized." *Los Angeles Times,* January 30. Available at http://www.latimes.com/news/local/la-me-occupy -oakland-20120130,0,7555243,print.story. Accessed June 5, 2012.

Rose, Lacey. 2010. "Glenn Beck Inc." *Forbes.com,* April 8. Available at http://socialtimes. com/gaza-flotilla-sparks-social-media-debate_b13926. Accessed June 6, 2012.

Rosenfeld, Adam. 2013. "AP Press to Drop the Word 'Illegal' in Immigration Coverage." *AlterNet,* April 2. Available at http://www.alternet.org/immigration/AP-to-drop-the -word-illegal. Accessed August 1, 2013.

Ryan, Charlotte, and William A. Gamson. 2006. "The Art of Reframing Political Debates." *Contexts* 5(1): 13–18.

Saba, Michael. 2011. "Twitter #occupywallstreet Movement Aims to Mimic Iran." *CNN,* September 16. Available at http://articles.cnn.com/2011-09-16/tech/tech_social -media_twitter occupy-wall-street_1_social-media-protest-campaign-financial -district?_s=PM:TECH. Accessed May 31, 2012.

Safranek, Rita. 2012. "The Emerging Role of Social Media in Political and Regime Change." *Discovery Guides,* March. Available at www.csa.com/discoveryguides/social_media /review.pdf. Accessed January 2, 2013.

Sandels, Alexandra. 2012. "SYRIA: Facebook Group Calls for Uprisings All over Syria on Saturday." *Los Angeles Times,* March 26. Available at http://latimesblogs.latimes.com /babylonbeyond/2011/03/syria-facebook group-calls-for-uprisings-all-over-the -country-on-saturday.html. Accessed June 5, 2012.

Sanger, David, and Anne Barnard. 2014. "U.S. Defending Kurds in Syria, Expands Airstrikes Against Islamic State Militants." *The New York Times,* September 27. Available at http://www.nytimes.com/2014/09/28/world/middleeast/us-strikes-isis-in-syria-to -defend-kurds.html. Accessed September 28 2014.

Saunders, Robert. 2008. "Five O'clock Shadow: 1960 Debates." February 13. Available at http://roger-saunders.suite101.com/five-oclock-shadow.a44454. Accessed June 5, 2012.

Savage, Charlie. 2013. "Cryptic Overtures and a Clandestine Meeting Gave Birth to a Blockbuster Story." *The New York Times,* June 10. Available at http://www.nytimes. com/2013/06/11/us/how-edward-j-snowden-orchestrated-a-blockbuster-story.html. Accessed August 30, 2014.

Schliebs, Mark. 2008. "Internet Groups War on Scientology." *news.com.au*, January 25. Available at http://www.news.com.au/technology/internet-groups-war-on-scientology /story-e6frfro0-1111115399994. Accessed July 2, 2010.

Seltzer, Mary 2011. "Occupy Oakland Raided by Police, Reports of Tear Gas, Rubber Bullets." *Alternet*, October 25. Available at http://www.alternet.org/newsandviews/article /685135/occupy_oakland_raided_by_police%2C_reports_of_tear_gas%2C_rubber _bullets. Accessed September 22, 2014.

Sengputa, Somni. 2012. "The Soul of the New Hacktivist." *The New York Times*, March 17. Available at http://www.nytimes.com/2012/03/18/sunday-review/the-soul-of-the -new-hacktivism.html. Accessed June 5, 2012.

Sengupta, Somini, and Nick Bilton. 2011. "Hackers Select a New Target: Other Hackers." *The New York Times*, July 4. Available at http://www.nytimes.com/2011/07/05/tech nology/05hack.html?pagewanted=all.

Sennitt, Andy. 2011. "Syria's Secret War Against the Cyber Dissidents." *Radio Netherlands Worldwide*, July 11. Available at http://blogs.rnw.nl/medianetwork/syrias-secret-war -against-the-cyber-dissidents.

Shane, Scott. 2011. "Spotlight Again Falls on Web Tools and Change." *The New York Times*, January 29. Available at http://www.nytimes.com/2011/01/30/weekinreview/30shane .html?_r=1. Accessed June 5, 2012.

Sharkey, Noel, and Sarah Knuckey. 2011. "Occupy Wall Street 'Occucopter'—Who's Watching Whom?" *The Guardian*, December 21. Available at http://www.theguardian.com /commentisfree/cifamerica/2011/dec/21/occupy-wall-street-occucopter-tim-pool. Accessed August 1, 2012.

Shear, Michael D. 2011. "Trailing G.O.P. with Cameras, Seeking Gaffes." *The New York Times*, July 8. Available at http://www.nytimes.com/2011/07/09/us/politics/09trackers .html?pagewanted=all. Accessed June 5, 2012.

———. 2013. "Seeing Citizenship Path Near, Activists Push Obama to Slow Deportations." *The New York Times*, February 22. Available at http://www.nytimes.com/2013/02/23/ us/advocates-push-obama-to-halt-aggressive-deportation-efforts.html?pagewanted =all. Accessed February 24, 2013.

Shepherd, Julianne E. 2011. "Egyptian Protesters March in Support of Occupy Oakland." *AlterNet*, October 29. Available at http://www.alternet.org/newsandviews/article /687291/egyptian_protesters_march_in_support_of_occupy_oakland/. Accessed June 5, 2012.

———. 2013. "Occupy New Year's Eve, 68 Arrested in Zuccotti Park Director Sam Levinson Captures Arrest Video near Union Square." *AlterNet*, January 2. Available at http:// www.alternet.org/module/printversion/newsandviews/757320.

Sherter, Alain. 2011. "Highest-Paid CEOs: Top Earner Takes Home $145 Million." *CBS News*, December 5. Available at http://www.cbsnews.com/8301-505123_162-57343611 /highest-paid-ceos-top-earner-takes-home-$145-million/. Accessed May 31, 2012.

Shirky, Clay. 2008. *Here Comes Everybody*. New York: Penguin Press.

Shiva, Vandana. 2013. "The Connection Between Global Economic Policy and Violence Against Women." *onebillionrising.org*, January 3. Available at http://onebillionrising .org/blog/entry/introducing-the-obr-article-series-dr.-vandana-shiva-1.   Accessed November 17, 2014.

Silva, Daniel. 2012. "One Year On, Spain's 'Indignants' Take to Streets." *Yahoo*, May 12. Available at http://news.yahoo.com/spains-indignants-over-streets-042623383.html. Accessed May 12, 2012.

Smelser, Neil J. 1962. *Theory of Collective Behavior.* New York: Free Press.

Snider, Erin, and David Faris. 2011. "The Arab Spring Versus Democracy Promotion in Egypt." *Middle East Policy* 18(3): 49–69.

Snow, David A., Burke Rochford, Steven K. Worden, and Robert D. Benford. 1986. "Frame Alignment Processes, Micromobilization, and Movement Participation." *American Sociological Review* 51: 464–481.

Solnit, Rebecca. 2012. "Occupy Your Heart." *Tom Dispatch,* December 22. Available at http://www.tomdispatch.com/archive/175483/.

Sonakski, Babbar. 2011. "Revealing the Face Behind the Delhi Slutwalks." *Hindustantimes,* June 20. Available at http://www.hindustantimes.com/News-Feed/Entertainment /Revealing-the-face-of-the-delhi-slutwalksArticle-7111.html. Accessed April 20, 2012.

Sorcher, Sara. 2011. "After Days in Captivity Four *New York Times* Journalists Are Released" *National Journal,* March 21. Available at http://www.nationaljournal.com/national security/after-days-in-captivity-four-new-york-times-journalists-released-20110321. Accessed August 1, 2013.

Souaiaia, Ahmed. 2011. "Qatar, Al Jazeera and the Arab Spring." *Mrzine,* June 12. Available at http://www.mrzine.monthlyreview.org/2011/souaiaia17111.html. Accessed April 20, 2012.

Soule, Sarah, and Brayden King. 2006. "The Stages of the Policy Process and the Equal Rights Amendment, 1972–1982." *American Journal of Sociology* 111(6): 1871–1909.

Staggenborg, Suzanne. 1988. "The Consequences of Professionalization and Formalization in the Pro-Choice Movement." *American Sociological Review* 53: 585–605.

Stauber, John. 2010. "Tea Party Money-Bomb Elects Scott Brown, Blows-Up Obamacare." *PRWatch,* January 19. Available at http://www.prwatch.org/node/8841. Accessed March 2, 2010.

Stelter, Brian. 2011. "Upending Anonymity, These Days the Web Unmasks Everyone." *The New York Times,* June 20. Available at http://www.nytimes.com/2011/06/21/us/21 anonymity.html. Accessed June 5, 2012.

Stepanova, Ekaterina. 2011. "The Role of ICTs in the Arab Spring: Implications Beyond the Region." *Ponars Eurasia: New Applications to Research and Security in Eurasia,* May, no. 159. Available at www.gov.edu/iercrgwi/assetts/docs/Ponars/pepm_159.pdf. Accessed January 5, 2012.

Stevenson, Seth. 2004. "Not-So-Amateur Night." *Slate Magazine,* January 13, p. 27.

Stewart, Ian. 2003. "Anti-War Group Revives 'Daisy' Ad Campaign." *Common Dreams.* Available at http://www.commondreams.org/headlines03/0116–06.htm. Accessed September 4, 2004.

Sudarsan, Raghavan. 2011. "Inspired by Tunisia and Egypt, Yemenis Join in Anti-government Protests." *The Washington Post,* January 29. Available at http://www .washingtonpost.com/wp-dyn/content/article/2011/01/27/AR2011012702081.html . Accessed September 28, 2014.

Swerdlow, Joel. 1992. *The Healing of a Nation: The Vietnam Vets Memorial/10th Anniversary.* New York: Perennial Press.

Tanenhaus, Sam. 2012. "History vs. the Tea Party." *The New York Times,* January 15. Available at http://www.nytimes.com/2012/01/15/sunday-review/gop-history-vs-the-tea-party .html?pagewanted=all. Accessed June 5, 2012.

Tarrow, Sidney. 1996. "States and Opportunities: The Political Structuring of Social Movements." In *Comparative Perspectives in Social Movements,* edited by Doug McAdam, John D. McCarthy, and Mayer N. Zald, 41–47. New York: Cambridge University Press.

_____. 1998. *Power in Movement. Social Movements, Collective Action and Politics.* Cambridge, MA: Cambridge University Press.

_____. 2001. "Transnational Politics." *Annual Review of Political Science* 4(1): 1–20.

Tarrow, Sidney, and Charles Tilly. 2006. *Contentious Politics.* Boulder, CO: Paradigm.

Tilly, Charles. 1978. *From Mobilization to Revolution.* Reading, MA: Addison-Wesley.

_____. 2004. *Social Movements.* Boulder, CO: Paradigm.

_____. 2006. *Regimes and Repertoires.* Chicago: University of Chicago Press.

Tomlinson, John. 1999. *Globalization and Culture.* Chicago: University of Chicago Press.

Toor, Amar. 2011. "Syrian Youth Create Facebook Group Calling for Peaceful Revolution." *Switched,* February 2. Available at http://www.switched.com/2011/02/02/syrian-youth-create-facebook-group-calling-for-peaceful-revoluti/. Accessed May 31, 2012.

Troup-Leasure, Karyl, and Howard Snyder. 2005. "Statutory Rape Known to Law Enforcement." *Juvenile Justice Bulletin,* August. US Department of Justice. Available at https://www.ncjrs.gov/pdffiles1/ojjdp/208803.pdf. Accessed September 22, 2014.

Urban, Mark. 2011. "From Arab Spring to European Autumn." *BBC,* November 11. Available at http://www.bbc.co.uk/news/world-1569177. Accessed May 5, 2012.

Utne, Leif. 2003. "MoveOn.org Holds Virtual Primary." *Utne,* June 23. Available at http://www.utne.com/community/moveonorgholdsvirtualprimary.aspx#axzz3FTg6jkX1.

Van Aelst, Peter, and Stephan Walgrave. 2003. "Open and Closed Mobilization Contexts and the Normalization of the Protester." In *Cyberprotest: New Media, and Citizen Social Movements,* edited by Wim Van De Donk, Brian Loader, Paul Nixon, and Dieter Rucht, 123–146. London: Routledge.

Verba, Sidney, Kay L. Scholzman, and Henry Brady. 1995. *Voice and Equality: Civic Voluntarism in American Politics.* Cambridge, MA: Harvard University Press.

Walsh, Michael. 2012. "Feminist Group Leaves Consent-Themed Panties in Victoria's Secret Stores to Protest 'Culture of Rape' and Company Themes It Finds Problematic." *New York Daily News,* December 18. Available at http://www.nydailynews.com/news/national/feminists-leave-consent-themed-panties-victoria-secret-stores-article-1.1221597. Accessed March 28, 2013.

Warner, Dan. 2008. "'Anonymous' Threatens to 'Dismantle' Church of Scientology via Internet." *APC Magazine,* January 24. Available at http://apcmag.com/anonymous_threatens_to_dismantle_church_of_scientology_via_internet.htm. Accessed May 31, 2012.

Welsh-Huggins, Andrew. 2013. "Online Threats Complicate Ohio School Rape Case." *USA Today,* January 12. Available at http://www.livingstondaily.com/usatoday/article/1820111. Accessed August 2, 2013.

Westcott, Lucy. 2014. "Modi: India's Shame at Rape and Violence Against Women." *Newsweek,* August 15. Available at http://www.newsweek.com/modi-indias-shame-rape-and-violence-against-women-264930. Accessed September 22, 2014.

Whitaker, Brian. 2003. "Battle Station." *The Guardian,* February 6. Available at http://www.theguardian.com/media/2003/feb/07/iraqandthemedia.afghanistan. Accessed July 11, 2014.

Whitlock, Craig. 2011. "Libyan Rebels Renew Hopes of Arab Spring." *The Washington Post,* August 22. Available at http://aritlces.washingtonpost.com/2011-08-22/world/3526947?libyan-rebels-arab-syria.html. Accessed May 12, 2012.

Whittaker, Zack. 2012. "Apple Patent Could Remotely Disable Protesters' Phone Cameras." *Zero Day,* September 4. Available at http://www.zdnet.com/apple-patent-could-remotely-disable-protesters-phone-cameras-7000003640/. Accessed April 25, 2014.

Wickham, Carrie. 2013. "Egypt's Missed Opportunity." *The New York Times,* July 27. Available at http://www.nytimes.com/2013/07/28/opinion/sunday/egypts-missed-opportunity.html?pagewanted=all&_r=0. Accessed August 1, 2013.

Williamson, Vanessa, Theda Skocpol, and John Coggin. 2011. "The Tea Party and the Remaking of Republican Conservatism." *Perspectives on Politics* 9(1): 25–43. Available at http://scholar.harvard.edu/files/williamson/files/tea_party_pop.pdf. Accessed January 2, 2013.

Wilson, Simone. 2011. "City Council Unanimously Passes Occupy L.A. Resolution —Protesters Struggle to Distance Themselves from Democrats, Unions." *LA Weekly,* October 12. Available at http://blogs.laweekly.com/informer/2011/10/city_council_passes_occupy_la_resolution_democrats_unions.php. Accessed May 31, 2012.

Wollenberg, E., M. Colchester, G. Mbugua, and T. Griffiths. 2006. "Linking Social Movements: How International Networks Can Better Support Community Action About Forests." *International Forestry Review* 8(2): 265–272.

Yardley, Jim. 2012. "Leaders' Response Magnifies Outrage in India Rape Case." *The New York Times,* December 29. Available at http://www.nytimes.com/2012/12/30/world/asia/weak-response-of-india-government-in-rape-case-stokes-rage.html?pagewanted=all. Accessed March 13, 2013.

Young, Patrick. 2010. "Tea Party Wants Your Illegal Immigration Horror Stories." Long IslandWins.com, August 4. Available at http://www.longislandwins.com/news/detail/tea_party_wants_your_illegal_immigration_horror_stories. Accessed November 17, 2014.

Zafar, Aylin. 2011. "Occupy Wall Street Inspires 'I'm Getting Arrested' Android App." *Time,* October 17. Available at http://newsfeed.time.com/2011/10/17/occupy-wall-street-inspires-im-getting-arrested-android-app/. Accessed June 5, 2012.

Zakarin, Jordan. 2013. "How Hollywood Fought Against the Iraq War." *Hollywood Reporter,* March 19. Available at http://www.hollywoodreporter.com/news/iraq-war-anniversary-hollywoods-anti-429697. Accessed September 25, 2014.

Zald, Mayer. 1996. "Culture Ideology and Strategic Framing." In *Comparative Perspectives in Social Movements,* edited by Doug McAdam, John McCarthy, and Mayer Zald, 260–274. Cambridge, MA: Cambridge University Press.

Zirin, David. 2013. "Why Did Steubenville Renew the Football Coaches Contract?" *The Nation,* April 29. Available at http://www.thenation.com/blog/1741000/dave-zirin-why-did-steubenville-renew-coaches-contract/. Accessed July 4, 2013.

CPSIA information can be obtained at www.ICGtesting.com
Printed in the USA
LVOW10s0517140115

422527LV00002B/2/P

9 780813 345864